# Chicken Soup for the Soul

for the Soul®

# Grand and Great

Our **101** BEST STORIES

## A Gift For:

_____

## From:

_____

# Chicken Soup for the Soul®

## Grand and Great

**Our 101 BEST STORIES**

### Grandparents and Grandchildren Share Their Stories of Love and Wisdom

Jack Canfield
Mark Victor Hansen
Amy Newmark

CSS

Chicken Soup for the Soul Publishing, LLC
Cos Cob, CT

Chicken Soup for the Soul

# Contents

**❹**

## ~No Obstacle for a Grandparent~

**❺**

## ~Legacies through the Generations~

**❻**

## ~Love Across the Generations~

## ❼
## ~Sharing Wisdom~

## ❽
## ~What a Child Can Teach Us~

## ❾
## ~Special Connections~

## ❿
## ~There Is No Place I'd Rather Be~

## ⓫
## ~Gifts and Gratitude~

**⑫**

## ~Treasured Moments~

Chicken Soup
for the Soul

# A Special Foreword

## by Jack and Mark

For us, 101 has always been a magical number. It was the number of stories in the first *Chicken Soup for the Soul* book, and it is the number of stories and poems we have always aimed for in our books. We love the number 101 because it signifies a beginning, not an end. After 100, we start anew with 101.

We hope that when you finish reading one of our books, it is only a beginning for you too—a new outlook on life, a renewed sense of purpose, a strengthened resolve to deal with an issue that has been bothering you. Perhaps you will pick up the phone and share one of the stories with a friend or a loved one. Perhaps you will turn to your keyboard and express yourself by writing a Chicken Soup story of your own, to share with other readers who are just like you.

This volume contains our 101 best stories and poems about being a grandparent and a grandchild. We share this with you at a very special time for us. When we published our first book in 1993, we never dreamed that we had started what became a publishing phenomenon, one of the best-selling series of books in history.

We did not set out to sell more than one hundred million books, or to publish more than 150 titles. We set out to touch the heart of one person at a time, hoping that person would in turn touch another person, and so on down the line. Fifteen years later, we know that it has worked.

Your letters and stories have poured in by the hundreds of thousands, affirming our life's work, and inspiring us to continue to make a difference in your lives.

On our fifteenth anniversary, we have new energy, new resolve, and new dreams. We have recommitted to our goal of 101 stories or poems per book, we have refreshed our cover designs and our interior layout, and we have grown the Chicken Soup for the Soul team, with new friends and partners across the country in New England.

Everyone has experienced the special ties between grandparents and grandchildren — the unlimited love, the mutual admiration and unqualified acceptance. In this new volume, we have selected our 101 best stories and poems about grandparents and grandchildren from our rich fifteen year history. The stories that we have chosen were written lovingly by grandparents about their grandchildren and by grateful grandchildren about their grandparents.

We hope that you will enjoy reading these stories as much as we enjoyed selecting them for you, and that you will share them with your families and friends. We have identified the 34 *Chicken Soup for the Soul* books in which the stories originally appeared, in case you would like to continue reading about families and senior life among our other books. We hope you will also enjoy the additional books about families, seniors, pets, and sports in "Our 101 Best Stories" series.

With our love, our thanks, and our respect,
*~Jack Canfield and Mark Victor Hansen*

# Chapter 1

# Grand and Great

## Becoming a Grandparent

*Few things are more delightful than grandchildren
fighting over your lap.*
*~Doug Larson*

# A Grandmother Is Born

*When a child is born, so are grandmothers.*
*~Judith Levy*

It's the phone call I've been awaiting for nine long months, yet when it comes, it's still a shock.

"This is it," our son-in-law says with a certain catch in his voice. "Jill's in labor."

And so the adventure begins. On the ride to the hospital, my husband and I cannot speak. For a man and woman who are about to become grandparents for the first time, it's all been said. All the fervent prayers for a healthy, whole baby already have been issued up to a higher power.

So we ride in silence, the silence of apprehension, excitement and joy waiting to explode.

At the birthing suite, all is surreal. While the rest of the inhabitants of planet Earth go about their business and pleasure on this brilliantly sunny afternoon, the entire world, for me, is enclosed within the walls of this waiting area.

My husband tries to read.

I pace in an unlikely caricature of those fathers-in-waiting from the Neanderthal days when mothers labored alone. Suddenly, I understand how those fathers must have felt.

Every now and then the midwife appears with a "bulletin." Those bulletins take on the breathless significance of a pronouncement about the future of world peace.

An hour passes. Two. Three. "Soon," our son-in-law tells us breathlessly in his one and only break from being on-site labor coach.

And at 3:42 on an ordinary afternoon, standing at the door of a modern birthing suite, I hear a cry. A baby's cry.

My heart stops.

Nothing in the world could have prepared me for this moment. Nothing will ever be the same for me in this glorious universe.

Today, I am somebody's grandmother!

Hannah—all seven pounds, thirteen ounces of her—has burst into the world.

I meet her moments later and fall madly, desperately, hopelessly in love. Nestled in my daughter's arm is this child of my child, a perfect pink and white miniature. I weep and laugh and thank God for allowing us this moment, this gift, this day.

Time is suspended. It is the deepest, most profound privilege to watch these new parents as they cuddle their baby daughter and explore her incredibly sweet face, her silky skin, her downy head.

Our son-in-law's parents are as speechless as we are. Hannah is the "we" of their son and our daughter, made tangible. In this room, on this day, we all know that this infant is our link to immortality. And this gritty, urban hospital suddenly feels holy.

It is another spectacular moment when I watch Hannah's great-grandmother—my own mother—meet her. I bear joyous witness to the awesome, incredible continuity of life's longing for itself.

Later, her new aunts and uncles greet Hannah, laugh joyously at her perfection, and touch her tiny, tiny hand.

We are dumbstruck, overwhelmed subjects of this tiny empress, and she seems to revel in the attention on this first day of her life.

This being, after all, the age of technology, the moments are dutifully recorded on video camera. Someday, we will watch—and laugh at our foolishness.

But for this day, it is totally acceptable to worship at the bedside of Hannah and to marvel at the new life that begins with the love of a man and a woman.

Despite all we enlightened moderns know of the biology of life—despite all the excesses of this Information Age—the wonder is the same. The awe remains undiminished.

A baby is born. The universal family of man—and our family—grows once again.

It is as old as time and as new as tomorrow's dawn.

The dance of life goes on. The circle grows.

And a dazed, overwhelmed new grandmother tiptoes out of a room where a miracle has happened, wondering how she ever got to be so lucky.

~Sally Friedman
*Chicken Soup for the Grandma's Soul*

# Thoughts on Being a Grandmother

*Grandmothers are special gifts to children.*
*~G.W. Curtis*

Ilie on the sofa and cuddle with the baby. My first grand-child! My daughter has gone on a quick outing alone and I have the honor of being the first babysitter. I watch his big brown eyes study my face and his tiny hands reach out in an effort to coordinate and touch what he sees. "Soon," I tell him. "Soon you'll be reaching and grasping everything in sight."

But I am in no hurry. I remember how I was constantly awaiting and anticipating the next new experience with my daughter. Her first smile, her first clumsy effort to sit up alone, that exciting first step, first word, first day of school. And then, suddenly, before I really had time to enjoy each of those special times, they were gone. I will not make that mistake again. With the wisdom of age and the experience, I will enjoy each precious moment.

His eyes become heavy and begin to close. I ease myself into a more comfortable position and he stirs and looks up at me for just a moment. With that glance, I recall another time, so many years ago, in another room on another sofa. I was cuddling with another child, my eighteen-month-old daughter. As she drifted off to sleep, she looked up at me and, in that one unique moment, I was able to envision for just an instant the woman my child would become. I recall the shivers that ran up my spine and the tears that appeared in my eyes and slid unchecked down my cheeks.

I recall saying a silent prayer for my little girl's future. I didn't think in grandiose terms of fame and fortune. I just prayed that someday a worthy (such an old-fashioned word, and yet so appropriate!) young man would look beneath her outer beauty and see the loyalty, the kindness, the determination that I had glimpsed so briefly and would cherish for so long.

Once again, I feel tears slide gently down my cheeks as I watch the sleeping baby boy. He is the representation of the fulfillment of all those prayers and dreams I carried in my heart for my daughter over the years. This tiny child, who fills me with such overwhelming love I can barely believe it, is my daughter's child.

I am thrilled for my daughter and all that awaits her as she watches this child grow and learn and become his own little person. Like me, she will experience great joys and survive major disappointments. She will rejoice in successes and regret more than a few mistakes. There will always be some guilt. But it isn't the important part. Love is the important part.

You can't love too much. Perhaps there are psychologists and sociologists who would disagree with me. But as I watch my sleeping grandson and think of that little one who is now his mother, I know deep down inside that the one thing I will never be guilty of is not loving enough. Love is the drive for every feeling I've ever had, every action I've ever taken and every decision I've ever made with regard to my child. The results have not always been perfect because the situations were not in line with my motivation. But the end results have been worthwhile; the mistakes more than justified. I will continue to love my daughter with this unconditional love for as long as I live.

And now I am a grandmother. I feel the same emotions toward him, but there is a subtle difference. I can't quite put my finger on it. I draw him nearer to me and feel the warmth of his tiny body as he nestles contentedly in my arms. He feels safe and loved right where he is, but in a few minutes his mother will appear and I'll see in her face that, though she was gone less than an hour, she missed him. She can't wait to pick him up, to hold him, to take him home.

And then I realize. That's the difference. She will take him home. As I stand by always with arms open as the ready caretaker, the willing supporter, the hopeful advisor, he will go home with my daughter. She will nourish him physically, emotionally and spiritually every day of his life in ways that I am not meant to do. I have a new role. I am his grandmother. I will watch his face light up in recognition when he sees me as he grows older. I will bake his favorite cookies and we'll sit together in a rocking chair sharing a favorite book. I'll listen lovingly as his mother shares the little stories that shape his growing-up years. I will be at his school plays or his softball games or his piano recitals. I will be a part of his life because I am his grandmother.

And I will never, ever be able to love him too much.

~Donna M. Hoffman
*Chicken Soup for the Mother & Daughter Soul*

# By Any Other Name

Contemplating my impending role as grandparent, I spent countless hours and multiple conversations debating what my new grandchild should call me. After all, this was a big decision: a sacred moniker—set in stone—to be used by countless future grandchildren.

I mused over the merits and disadvantages of various names, rolling them around my tongue, tasting them, savoring them—trying them on for size. Grandmother? Too formal. Grandma? Mundane. Nana? Nah.

From the quirky Punkin' to the colloquial Gran, the whimsical Oma to the formal Grandma-ma (with an elegant accent on the last syllable), I experimented with them all.

"Give it up," said my more experienced girlfriends. "That first grandbaby will call you what she will. And, anyway, the actual name won't matter. Why, you'll be so thrilled, it won't matter what she calls you. Trust us," they nodded in agreement. "You won't care."

Well, grandbaby Avery turned one and my daughter put her on the phone so I could hear her chatter across the two thousand miles separating us. I knew this verbose babe's burgeoning repertoire now included words like drink, ball, banana, hi and even the names of several animals. With any luck...

"Hello, sweet pea," I gushed. "Happy birthday!"

"Avery, say 'hi' to Grammy," my daughter coaxed at the other end. "Say 'hi.'"

And then it happened. It really happened. A precious, breathy little voice pulled together two words from her vocabulary and cooed into the phone, "Hi, dog."

My daughter giggled, then erupted into a full laugh—and baby Avery repeated her new achievement with enthusiasm, delighted that it appeared to make her mommy so happy.

"Hi dog, hi dog, hi dog."

Huh, I laughed, my girlfriends were wrong. I care. I care a lot.

~Carol McAdoo Rehme
*Chicken Soup for the Grandma's Soul*

# She'll Call Me "Ma"

*It is not the name that is important —*
*it is what it represents to you that is the key to its power.*
~Laura Spiess

"Guess what — I'm pregnant!" My stepdaughter phoned. Her joy was obvious. "That's wonderful," I said. "I'm going to be a grandmother!" We had always been close — bonded together by our mutual love for her father. I was sure that my love for this child was big enough to share with her child. What I wasn't sure of was my grandmothering ability.

I had often witnessed these women at church fellowships — huddled in a circle like football players planning their next play. They all had sweet names like "Mimi," "Nana," "Grammy" and "Grandma." Their purses bulged with photos that could be pulled out at a moment's notice. Their conversations revolved around sippy cups, Big Bird and onesies (which I had already mispronounced at a friend's baby shower as "o-nee-zees").

I, on the other hand, was young (only forty) and inexperienced and the stepgrandmother. I had lots of questions and all the fated answers. Would my stepdaughter pull away from me? It would only be natural that she grow closer to her real mother in the coming months. Would I suddenly feel like an outsider when my husband stepped into his role as grandfather? Blood is thicker than water. Would I ever get to be involved in this child's life? Never mind quality time... I would take any time. What would I be called by this child? "Stepgrandmother" would definitely not conjure up any warm, fuzzy feelings. And I knew that "Mimi," "Nana," "Grammy" and "Grandma" would quickly be claimed by the two grandmothers, two great-grandmothers and one great-great-grandmother who waited in the wings.

My relationship with my stepdaughter deepened as we talked our way through the months of waiting. "I just found out I'm having a girl," she cried. "You are coming to the baby shower, aren't you?"

"Of course I'll be there... if it's okay with your mom," I replied. Silence. Neither one of us needed to be reminded of our situation.

Two months later, it was finally time. "We're leaving for the hospital," her voice quivered. "We're on our way," I said. As my husband and I stepped off the elevator, we were greeted by our blended family. Time seemed to crawl as we all awaited the blessed arrival. Finally, she was here. "I'm a grandma!" I blurted out. All heads snapped to attention in my direction.

Had I said that out loud? I hadn't meant to. I suddenly imagined a sign over the hospital room door: "Only blood relatives admitted." I sheepishly smiled and stepped back as we all entered the room.

She was the most beautiful child (other than my own) that I had ever laid eyes on! I stood by as each one took his or her turn holding the tiny, red-faced stranger. Flashbulbs popped at every turn. She was so perfect. So tiny. And she possessed an unmistakable feature that drew me to her instantly... my husband's loving eyes. I knew I was falling in love with her and longed to cradle her in my arms like the others. Instead, I moved toward the door, trying to stay out of the way. All too soon, it was time to go and let Mama and baby rest. My eyes filled with tears. I hadn't gotten to hold her. With all the passing of the baby, I had gotten passed over. Just an oversight during all the confusion, I rationalized. Shouldn't get too attached, anyway.

That night, my prayers overflowed with pleas for a true relationship with this child. Opportunity for motherhood well behind me, all I had were memories buried under the difficulties of a bad first marriage. There had never been time for filling in baby books with first steps or first words. My daughter had basically raised herself, while my energy was spent just getting through it all. I desperately wanted a second chance.

The next day, I woke up anxious to get to the hospital and see my stepdaughter. I secretly hoped that no other relatives would be there so I could have her and the baby all to myself. When we arrived, all was well. Mama and baby rested as my husband and I exchanged labor and delivery stories with our son-in-law.

When it came time to go, I felt a lump rise in my throat. I still hadn't held the baby, and I felt silly being that emotional over what seemed like such a small incident. No one could have known how I longed to hold that child. I certainly didn't feel like a stepgrandmother. As far as I was concerned, that was my child and my grandchild in that bed. As I turned to leave, my son-in-law caught my eyes. He saw my emotion and somehow he knew what I had missed the day before. He walked over to the bed, reached in and picked up the baby and handed her directly to me.

More than two years have passed since that day. I now fit in quite nicely with the other grandmothers at church.

You see, we have so much in common. I, too, have earned one of these sweet names. Shortly after her first birthday, my granddaughter reached out to me as "Ma." It stuck. Sippy cups now crowd my tea glasses and "o-nee-zees" abide in my lingerie drawer. Big Bird makes a daily appearance in my living room, and a larger-than-life version of Tinky Winky has taken up residence under my bed. And I am always armed and ready for any photo contest that might break out at one of those church fellowships.

I have cradled my granddaughter often and have stored up enough laughs for a lifetime as I have replied to questions like, "Ma, can you come over every day and just paint my fingernails?" I receive more love in a day than I could give back in a lifetime. You see, we have always been close—bonded together by our mutual love for her mother.

As I write this, I am happily awaiting the birth of my second granddaughter and am sure that my love for my first grandchild is big enough to share with her sister. Gone are the doubts. Gone are the questions—she'll call me "Ma."

~Jackie Davis
*Chicken Soup for the Grandparent's Soul*

# Someone's Grandmother

*A garden of Love grows in a Grandmother's heart.*
*~Author Unknown*

I was a frustrated wannabe grandmother. Every time I saw a small baby, I'd hear the ticking of the biological clock. All right, I admit that it wasn't my clock. But our two adult daughters had healthy clocks that I could hear ticking, even if they couldn't. That the younger one had just reached adulthood and that neither daughter was married were beside the point. I wanted to be someone's grandmother.

One day Jennifer, our elder daughter, called with the news, "Mom, I'm getting married!" She followed this with more good news, "Chuck has custody of his two-year-old son. We plan to come home to Alaska for the wedding."

I was ecstatic to be an instant grandma. Then I had a moment's pause as I tried to figure out what to do with a grandson. We raised two daughters and I have a sister. It occurred to me that I had no idea how to entertain a small boy. Could I be his grandma? Would he accept me? Would Chuck let his son call me "Grandma?"

Jennifer, Chuck and Chase arrived in the spring, had a summer wedding and I officially became an instant grandmother. I tried to pace myself getting to know my young grandson. Over the summer we explored hiking trails along the Mendenhall Glacier and tide pools in Tee Harbor. We picked wild blueberries, watched tiny hummingbirds, baked cookies and had long talks in a child's language that I'd long forgotten. All the while I fretted over losing touch with him when Jennifer and Chuck moved south again. I knew I had only a few short months with Chase.

In late fall, fate stepped in. My carpenter-husband Bob took a fall. He had a double compound fracture of his right arm and would be off work for at least nine months. Winter loomed ahead. With the heavy snowfall would come snow shoveling, snow plowing, keeping the furnace running and other winter tasks around the house. Jennifer and Chuck decided to postpone their trip south until the next year so they could help us through the winter. I had another nine months to spend with my new grandson.

Over the winter, Chase and I watched Disney movies together, sang during baths about tiny frogs and bars of soap, danced the Hoochie-Koochie, read stories by Kipling and built snowmen. Spring was coming, and I knew that soon there would be talk of Jennifer, Chuck and Chase moving south again. They had been with us nearly a year, and I knew we weren't the Waltons. It hadn't been an easy winter and some days our big house felt small, yet I fought tears whenever I thought of them leaving.

Once again fate stepped in. An injury to my back required surgery and held me prisoner in our bedroom for nearly four months. Jennifer and Chuck delayed their departure again. Since Jennifer, Chuck and Bob were now working, Chase went to day care. I would wait in bed, listening for the sound of him coming through the back door and pounding his way upstairs to my bedroom. I delighted in listening to him as he sat on the end of the bed and told me about his busy day at "school." He shared garbled stories of coloring, cutting and pasting construction paper.

That summer we watched and rewatched *The Princess Bride, Zorro, Rikki-Tikki-Tavi* and countless other favorite movies with heroes and villains. Chase was as content to read books and watch movies with me that long summer as he had been to berry pick and hike the summer before. Yet I knew that autumn weather would once again bring talk of a move south.

The day did come when Chuck gathered their belongings into the truck and left on the ferry, and a few days later Bob and I took Jennifer and Chase to the airport to join him. I blinked back hot tears as we checked them in for a flight to Seattle. They might as well be moving to the moon. I knew that we would be lucky to see each other once a year. Chase would turn four soon. I doubted that he'd even remember me in a couple of months. I was certain everyone in the airport could hear my heart breaking.

Our house was horribly quiet those first weeks after they left for Oklahoma. I spent time building a small photo album for Chase, hoping that he'd remember his instant grandma in Alaska. I called Oklahoma often, though it was difficult to have a long telephone conversation with a three-year-old. My heart broke as he asked, "Grandma, come see me now. When am I coming home to Alaska? How is Papa?" And, "Grandma, do you know that in Oklahoma you can't even grow blueberries? Could you please send me blueberry bushes to grow?" I treasured each little chat we had.

The months passed and we got photos from Jennifer, a lot of e-mails and periodic phone calls from Chase. For his fourth birthday I sent him a video about a kangaroo in

Australia. Chase loved the movie and hurried to ask Jennifer if he could have a kangaroo. After all, they had some acreage and enough room for a kangaroo. Jennifer wisely told him, "It's okay with me, but go ask your dad." A very disappointed Chase returned to the kitchen to tell Jennifer that his dad said "no." Then his face lit with a great idea. In a small whisper he said to Jennifer, "Let's call Grandma in Alaska. She'll send us one!"

When Jennifer told me the kangaroo story, I knew that I'd made it. I was someone's grandmother, not for an instant, but forever.

~Valerie A. Horner
*Chicken Soup for the Grandma's Soul*

# The Bathroom Mirror

As I approach the bathroom mirror today, I cautiously scrutinize the reflection staring back at me. I have recently been given a new name. The name is "Grandma."

I brace myself against the counter while squinting my eyes at the face in the mirror. How could this woman possibly be a grandmother? She looks nothing at all like the grandmother who had been in my childhood. This woman doesn't have a speck of gray in her hair. And there is not a trace of wrinkles or age spots to be seen. Of course to be fair, my grandmother didn't have fifty different boxes of hair coloring conveniently awaiting her at the grocery store or the wonderful selection of anti-aging creams that stand lining my counter like good little soldiers. Still it is difficult to believe that I have earned this title of "Grandma."

Where have the years gone? My mind wanders back to my own childhood. I did have a very nice childhood I would dare say, nothing out of the ordinary. However, I do remember certain phrases that my mother used that I swore would never pass through my lips. I still gasp in horror when I remember uttering for the first time to my kids, "It's always fun and games until somebody gets hurt!" I swear, my head did a ninety-degree turn to see if my mother was standing anywhere near me. Had those words really come from my mouth? Those were my mother's words. Oh no, I was possessed! And the first time I heard my mother's laugh coming from my throat, well it was almost as if a full moon was turning me into a werewolf. I was downright quivering with fear.

Then there's the memory of when I was eight years old and I was storming down the hall, headed towards my bedroom in a real snit over one of my mom's judgment calls. I slammed the door behind me with all my strength, purging my rage. Mom appeared within seconds, demanding to know why I slammed the door. Being blessed with very large eyes that could widen to angelic heights, I softly whimper, "It was the wind, Mama. See, the window is open." It worked like a charm, and I am happy to report that it still worked when my kids used it on me.

There's something about the word "mama," when spoken by a child, that has the power to unleash a force so strong that it can turn a mother's heart into a puddle of quivering Jell-O. As I stand before the mirror this morning, I ponder what the word "Grandma" will do to me. I envision a huge bowl of mush with the words, "Help me. I'm drowning," written on top in brown sugar with two large eyes blinking through it.

How has my childhood blurred into my children's childhood and now into their children's childhood? Where has the time gone? I realize the answer is gazing back at me in the mirror. It is within me. It is in my spirit and within my heart. I have become my mother and, in turn, a grandmother. I no longer quake in fear over the transition.

I embrace it with a smile. This girl, this mother and now this grandmother is going to be just fine.

~Wanda Mitchell
*Chicken Soup for the Grandparent's Soul*

# 7

# She Looks Just Like...

*Family faces are magic mirrors. Looking at people who belong to us, we see the past, present, and future.*
*~Gail Lumet Buckley*

As I gazed in awe at my newborn granddaughter, all I could think about was the wonder of God's handiwork—until I heard the words, "She's all her mother, even her toes." Each word was spoken with emphasis, followed by an echo, "Yes, even her toes," as if that were the final word on the subject.

I stood outnumbered in a sea of in-laws. Gazing at the ten tiny pieces of evidence before the court of family opinion, I failed to see the referenced genetic code etched in such delicate pink appendages.

Can't my son claim even one little toe for our family? I silently cried out.

I had no idea what it would be like to be a first-time grandma. All my friends said it was the most wonderful experience in the world. So far my experience wasn't going too well.

Slowly, the in-laws' convictions got to me. I left the hospital with one prevailing thought: I guess I'm a grandma of another family's baby.

The personal grandma chamber in my heart closed up.

After waiting thirty years, it had flowed with grandma's blood for a brief thirty minutes only.

You need to pull yourself together, I thought as I climbed into the car. Suddenly, my first memories of the baby's mother flashed before my mind—how her smile illuminated the sanctuary when she was a high-flying angel at the Crystal Cathedral, how her fingers performed an Irish jig when she signed for the deaf, how her blond hair and flowered skirt blew in the wind of the spirit when she worship-danced. A rare beauty, within and without, she had stolen my heart.

Even if my son hadn't married her, she would have been my friend for life. Of course it's a privilege to have a grandchild who resembles her!

With excitement, I hung out at the baby's house the next day and the next. I watched and waited for my granddaughter to wake up so I could make early eye contact with that beautiful face. Days turned into weeks, but eventually the bluest eyes, rosiest cheeks, blondest hair and most radiant smile greeted me. I beamed back at her until my smiley muscles ached.

In another few months, her fingers, like precise pincers, held the tiniest of objects. I clapped my hands with amazement.

In a few more months, she toe-danced, twirled and reached for the sun. Overjoyed, I spun around and around with her.

She was just like her angel mother—her smile, her hair, her fingers and yes, even her toes.

The grandma chamber in my heart pumped with delight—until one startling day. I looked in her crib and saw a different child gazing back at me.

What is going on, God? You gave me a granddaughter

who looks like her beautiful mother. Now you steal her out of the crib one night and replace her with a child who looks like my son?

"Yes, she has her father's eyes and expressions," the court of family opinion confirmed.

I conceded. When she looked at me I saw her father's deep, contemplative eyes. When she said "uh-oh" as she picked up scraps from the floor, I realized she was a neatnik like her dad. When her legs grew off the doctor's charts, I knew they were her daddy's long legs. When she became strongly independent, I remembered, so was her dad.

My grandma's heart thrived with this fresh supply of past and present memories, until it suffered a second shock, six months later.

"Your granddaughter looks just like you," someone said to me. Family opinion voted affirmatively.

Oh, no, poor kid, I thought. I couldn't believe that in less than two years she had gone through three distinct metamorphoses, from a look-alike of her mother, a stamp imprint of her father, to a picture of me! What was she — a child or a butterfly?

Curious, I did some research. I learned that if I were to look into a cocoon in the early stages, I would find a puddle of glop that contains imago cells with DNA-coded instructions for turning cream of insect soup into a delicate, winged creature.

That's it! She's a child with the power of glop! She will change her identity many times, each time emerging like a beautiful butterfly. Yet I will be proud that this ever-changing display of beauty, in each stage of life, is my unique first granddaughter.

~Margaret Lang
*Chicken Soup for the Grandma's Soul*

# 8

# Good News, Bad News

*Babies are such a nice way to start people.*
*~Don Herrold*

"Hi Mom, get Dad on the phone, too." John seldom called from his temporary New Zealand home. "What's the matter?" I asked, then frantically motioned to Bob and mouthed, "It's John!" My breathing quickened.

John waited until his dad greeted him then asked, "Are you sitting down?" I slumped on the bed in our dark room. My mother's intuition kicked in. Something was wrong.

"I have some good news and some bad news," John said. I held my breath.

"I'll give you the good news first. You're going to be grandparents." A long moment of silence deafened our connection.

"Are you there?" he asked.

I voiced the bad news. "John, you're not married."

But John ignored my comment and continued, "Do we have any twins in our family? Cathy's family does. You're going to be grandparents of twins."

We'd learned about Cathy earlier in the year. From the

way John talked, we knew in our hearts that she was his true love.

I don't remember how Bob and I got through the conversation. After we hung up, I sensed John's worry of being forced into a situation he hadn't planned and couldn't control, much less afford on his teacher's salary. I didn't sleep much that night. Yet, my tears refused to flow.

In the morning, I attended a meeting in body, but not in mind. On the way home, the dam broke; tears blurred my vision. I struggled to see where I was going. As I passed our church my car seemed to turn into the parking lot on its own.

Once inside, I asked the secretary if I might speak to the parish priest.

"He takes Mondays off." She stared at my tear-stained face, then added, "You can call him at home."

"No, I won't bother him." Embarrassed, I rushed to my car. But at home, I recognized the need to talk to someone other than Bob, dialed the church and asked for Father's number.

"Don't push them into a marriage. Two wrongs don't make a right," my priest consoled calmly. "This doesn't have to be bad news. But let them make their own decision."

So Bob and I refrained from submitting advice. After Christmas, we received another call. "I gave Cathy a ring. We've decided since you're coming to New Zealand in March, we'll wait until you arrive to get married. The babies will be born in May."

Elated by the wedding news, we looked forward to meeting and getting to know Cathy, if only for a few days. When we arrived, we could see her Western Samoan heritage contributed to her outer as well as inner beauty. She proved to be all we'd hoped John might find in a partner.

Although disappointed we wouldn't be present for the birth of our first grandchildren, we returned to the United States. The knowledge that John, Cathy and the babies would follow within the year and call Colorado home appeased us.

At last we waited at Denver International. I stared through the large windows at the gate. Another plane filled the space where John, Cathy and our eight-month-old granddaughters would eventually arrive.

Departing passengers occupied all the seats in the gate area. I leaned against a pillar afraid to talk to Bob for fear of crying, not from sadness but joy. I'd never been so nervous. How long before the babies would accept us? Could we hold back and give them the space and time they needed? Out of necessity, their family would share our home. Could we make it work?

I wrung my hands and wiped them on my skirt.

"I can't do this. I'm shaking inside and out," I blurted. "Why are planes always late?"

Bob draped his arm around my shoulders and squeezed. "You can do it," he assured me.

I laid my head against his arm and fought the tears that stung my eyes. Had it only been a little over a year since we'd lamented about our having four granddogs and two grandhorses rather than grandchildren? How quickly things change.

A voice screeched from the speaker over our head "The flight from L.A. has landed and will wait for the gate to empty. It won't be long. Thank you for your patience."

I walked away from the gate and paced back and forth. My thoughts turned to the Christmas lights on the cul-de-sac still adorning our neighbors' homes. Usually, they take their decorations down the day after New Year's. But this time, they agreed to wait until January 5th so the lights might illuminate a warm welcome for our family.

At last one plane backed away and another took its place. Arriving passengers hurried through the doorway. We waited. My heart thumped in my ears. More people exited. We waited. Several times I gulped air and released it with a heavy sigh. We waited until no other passengers stepped through the doorway.

When a flight attendant appeared, I grabbed Bob's arm. My knees weakened. My stomach churned. I stammered, "Maybe they missed the connection in L.A."

Hand in hand we rushed to the attendant. "Is anyone else on the plane?" Bob's voice quaked. "A family with twin babies?"

I looked around. Passengers waiting to depart watched us, curiosity evident on their faces.

"Yes." The attendant smiled. "We misplaced their stroller. They'll be out in a minute."

Then John sauntered through the doorway with one baby in a large pack on his back. He stepped aside. Cathy shyly walked toward me cuddling the second baby. Tears gathered in my eyes.

Several flight attendants surrounded our family. "We wanted to see your reaction to these precious babies," one offered. "If you don't want them, we do!"

My hands quivered, and my legs felt like cement. I slowly moved toward Cathy and hugged her. I touched the dark hair of her baby. Black eyes questioned as they looked at me. I turned to John. From around one side of John's head and then the other, black eyes, a carbon copy of her sister's, peered at me. The beginning of a shy smile sparkled from her beautiful olive-skinned face. Her plump little hand stretched toward me.

I threw my arms around both John and baby and sobbed. Sobs so loud they echoed through the terminal. I stretched to include Cathy. I couldn't hold all of them close enough.

"I'm so sorry," I stuttered. "I'm sorry to embarrass you this way." Hiding my face in John's chest, my body shook uncontrollably.

After the embrace, John placed his hands on my shoulders and pushed me away enough to look into my eyes. He smiled. "Mom, you should see all the people behind you. They're crying, too."

I returned John's gaze and remembered when he'd called to share his "good news and bad news." As I hugged my son, my daughter-in-law and my grandbabies, I realized it was all good news.

~Linda Osmundson
*Chicken Soup for the Grandparent's Soul*

# Grand and Great

## From the Mouths of Babes

*They say genes skip generations.
Maybe that's why grandparents find their grandchildren
so likeable.*
~Joan McIntosh

# Amazon Woman Becomes a Princess

*What is in a name? That which we call a rose, by any other
name would smell as sweet.*

*~William Shakespeare*

Family members traveled to New Brunswick from all
over that summer: Winston-Salem, Colorado Springs,
Kalamazoo and Daytona Beach. Our youngest daughter
was about to marry a young man from Washington, D.C., and
all of us—uncle, aunt, two sisters, nieces, nephew, brother-
in-law and parents—were present to witness the event.

The groom had been married before. With the divorce
settlement, he gained custody of the two children—a boy,
five and a girl, three.

Not only were we gaining a new son-in-law, we would
become instant grandparents to two adorable children,
David and Stephanie.

On the afternoon before the wedding, family members
from both sides gathered in the groom's apartment to pass
the time and get acquainted. The two youngsters were a
part of this homogeneous group.

From previous conversations with my daughter, I knew

these children came fully endowed with six living grandparents. They had two grandmothers, two grandfathers and two great-grandmothers.

How would we fit into this galaxy of grands and great-grands? I wondered. How would the children designate which grand person they were talking about or talking to? And, by what names would they call me and my husband?

During a lull in the chit-chat, I became bold and expressed my thoughts out loud.

Young David looked at me with a shy grin on his face and spoke as if he had already figured this out.

"I'm going to call you 'Princess,'" he said.

The room grew very quiet. I suspect this announcement shocked them as much as it did me.

For some unknown reason, David had looked at me and decided I should be called "Princess."

All through school, I towered inches above my short girlfriends. I weighed more than I should, even with the added height. Consequently, I grew up thinking of myself as the Amazon Woman, never as a princess.

"What a lovely name," I gasped. "I'm honored and delighted that you want to call me by that name."

Then and there, I became "Princess." Soon after, they christened my husband "Pop-Pop."

Ten years have passed since then. Young David is fifteen, his sister Stephanie is thirteen, and they have a little sister named Rebecca. She is eight.

I often look back at that moment and consider it a turning point in my life. Yes, I had evolved from the tall, awkward young girl, into a more graceful woman with streaks of gray in my hair, and a calm, self-assuredness that only years of living can produce.

From time to time, someone might pay me a compliment, but no one, not even my husband, had ever called me "Princess." No one, that is, except David.

I'll always be grateful to him. He helped me replace the clumsy, gargantuan image I'd carried in my mind's eye, too long, with the image of a princess.

On some days I know I look more like a bag lady than a princess. But on a day ten years ago, a five-year-old thought I looked like a princess.

Perhaps it was the yellow summer dress I wore, or the jubilant smile on my face that said I approved of my daughter's choice of a life-mate. Whatever it was, the name thrilled me then as it does now.

Whenever I pick up the phone and a voice at the other end says, "Hi, Princess. Guess what happened at school today," a big smile spreads across my face and joy fills my heart.

And that's chicken soup for my soul!

~Adeline C. Erwin
*Chicken Soup for the Grandparent's Soul*

# Missing Pa

One day my four-year-old son, Sam, told me that he'd seen his babysitter crying because she'd broken up with her boyfriend. "She was sad," he explained to me. He sat back in his car seat and sighed. "I've never been sad," Sam added. "Not ever."

It was true. Sam's life was happy—in no small part because of his relationship with my father. Pa Hood was more than a grandfather to him. As Sam eagerly told everyone—they were best buddies.

Once Sam and I watched the movie *Anne of Green Gables*. In the scene when Anne wishes aloud for a bosom friend, Sam sat up and declared, "That's me and Pa—bosom friends forever and ever."

My father described their relationship the same way. When I went out of town one night a week to teach, it was Pa in his red pickup truck who'd meet Sam at school and take him back to his house. There they'd play pirates and knights and Robin Hood.

They even dressed alike: pocket t-shirts, baseball caps and jeans. They had special restaurants they frequented, playgrounds where they were regulars, and toy stores where Pa allowed Sam to race up and down the aisles on motorized cars.

Sam had even memorized my father's phone number and called him every morning and night. "Pa," he would ask, clutching the phone, "can I call you ten hundred more times?" Pa always said yes and answered the phone every time with equal delight.

Then my father became ill. In the months that he was in the hospital with lung cancer, I worried about how Sam would react to Pa's condition: the bruises from the needles, the oxygen tubes, his weakened body. When I explained to Sam that seeing Pa so sick might scare him, Sam was surprised. "He's my Pa," he said. "He could never scare me."

Later I watched adults approach my father's hospital bed with trepidation, unsure of what to say or do. But Sam, undaunted by the medical apparatus and the changes in Pa's appearance, knew exactly what was right: hugs and jokes, as always.

"Are you coming home soon?" he'd ask.

"I'm trying," Pa would tell him.

When my dad died, everything changed for Sam and me. Not wanting to confront the questions and feelings my father's death raised, I kept my overwhelming sadness at bay. When well-meaning people asked how I was doing, I'd give them a short answer and swiftly change the subject.

Sam was different, however. For him, wondering aloud was the best way to understand.

"So," he'd say, settling in his car seat, "Pa's in space, right?" Or, pointing at a stained-glass window in church, he'd ask, "Is one of those angels Pa?"

"Where's heaven?" Sam asked right after my father died.

"No one knows exactly," I said. "Lots of people think it's in the sky."

"No," Sam said, shaking his head, "it's very far away. Near Cambodia."

"When you die," he asked on another afternoon, "you disappear, right? And when you faint, you only disappear a little. Right?"

I thought his questions were good. The part I had trouble with was what he always did afterward: He'd look me right in the eye with more hope than I could stand and wait for my approval or correction or wisdom. But in this matter, my fear and ignorance were so large that I'd grow dumb in the face of his innocence.

Remembering Sam's approach to my father's illness, I began to watch his approach to grief. At night, he'd press his face against his bedroom window and cry, calling out into the darkness, "Pa, I love you! Sweet dreams!" Then, after his tears stopped, he'd climb into bed, somehow satisfied, and sleep. I, however, would wander the house all night, not knowing how to mourn.

One day in the supermarket parking lot, I caught sight of a red truck like my father's. For an instant I forgot he had died. My heart leapt as I thought Dad's here!

Then I remembered and succumbed to an onslaught of tears. Sam climbed onto my lap and jammed himself between me and the steering wheel.

"You miss Pa, don't you?" he asked.

I managed to nod.

"Me, too. But you have to believe he's with us, Mommy," he said. "You have to believe that, or what will we ever do?"

Too young to attach to a particular ideology, Sam was simply dealing with grief and loss by believing that death does not really separate us from those we love. I couldn't show him heaven on a map or explain the course a soul might travel. But he'd found his own way to cope.

Recently while I was cooking dinner, Sam sat by himself at the kitchen table, quietly coloring in his Spiderman coloring book.

"I love you, too," he said.

I laughed and turned to face him, saying, "You only say, 'I love you, too' after someone says 'I love you' first."

"I know," Sam said. "Pa just said, 'I love you, Sam,' and I said, 'I love you, too.'" He kept coloring.

"Pa just talked to you?" I asked.

"Oh, Mommy," Sam said, "he tells me he loves me every day. He tells you, too. You're just not listening."

Again, I have begun to take Sam's lead. I have begun to listen.

~Ann Hood
*Chicken Soup for the Mother's Soul 2*

# 11

# Twenty-Nine and Holding

*To me old age is always fifteen years older than I am.*
*~Bernard Baruch*

Our family had always been big on birthday celebrations and other special occasions. On each and every birthday, my entire family gathered together to share a meal, gifts and a song. My mother wasn't fond of her own birthdays. Like many women her age, when her birthday rolled around she only admitted to being twenty-nine, just as she was the year before.

At the ripe old age of twelve, my twin sons had figured out that Grandma was much older than she admitted, but didn't question her when she once again announced that she was twenty-nine and holding. My younger daughter, Becky, took her seriously, however. She believed every word that her grandmother told her. If Grandma said she was twenty-nine, as far as Becky was concerned, she was twenty-nine. There was no question about it.

A few months went by, and we joined together as a family to celebrate my thirtieth birthday. After everyone sang "Happy Birthday," we enjoyed heaping helpings of cake and ice cream. Finally, the time came for me to open my presents. Becky had been unusually quiet during the entire birthday celebration. She carried a worried look on her face.

After all of the guests left, she couldn't stand it any longer and sadly informed me, "Mamma, you're thirty, and Grandma is twenty-nine. I hate to have to tell you this, but you must've been adopted."

~Nancy B. Gibbs
*Chicken Soup for the Grandparent's Soul*

# 12

# Pennies from Heaven

"Nana! Help! I'm falling!" and suddenly the little girl with her new roller blades had fallen on the sidewalk for the one hundredth time.

"I can't do it!" the little girl cried as a tear rolled down her cheek.

"Don't worry. I'm here to catch you," whispered Nana as she wiped the tear away. "Remember, when it rains, it rains pennies from heaven!" Nana hugged the girl and started to hum the song.

From the time the girl was six weeks old, Nana took care of her in every way. She fed, rocked and played with the girl. She never seemed to mind when the little girl smelled dirty. She was always there with open arms when the little girl was wobbly or unsure of herself. She smiled and encouraged her when the little girl couldn't talk well and told her to keep practicing.

"You can do anything you want to do. Just put your mind to it," Nana would say to her.

Nana taught the little girl to play the piano. In Nana's shaky handwriting, she would write songs for the little girl to play on the piano. Every Christmas they saw *The Nutcracker* together. Nana would cheer and clap when the little girl would try to twirl and dance like the ballerinas.

"Remember, never give up. Just feel the music in here," and she would point to her heart. The little girl understood, because when she was with Nana she felt she could be and do almost anything.

During this time, the little girl didn't notice how Nana's hands and head shook for no reason at all. She didn't notice, and she didn't care. Nana loved her and was her very best friend.

Soon the little girl went off to school. She made new friends and became busy with all the things school brings. She had less and less time to spend with Nana. Nana's shaking got much worse, and soon the girl felt strange being with her. The little girl found out that Nana had a disease called Parkinson's, which is a disease that takes over a person's body. This disease forced Nana to move to a nursing home to be taken care of.

One day the girl went to visit Nana. Everything about the nursing home gave the girl a strange and uncomfortable feeling. She noticed the small, bare room. She noticed that Nana didn't smell as good as she used to. The girl heard Nana's teacup make a clinking noise against the plate as her Nana slowly took a sip. The girl could hardly watch as Nana got up and slowly, oh so slowly, tried to take a tiny step. The girl felt sad as she watched her Nana fall back on her bed. And then suddenly the girl saw a picture in her mind.

The girl remembered how Nana had gently encouraged her when she was learning how to try her new roller blades. She remembered how Nana would hug her and smile whenever the girl felt she couldn't do something. And then she realized something else Nana had given her. Nana had taught her what to do for someone who needed to feel safe, secure and loved.

The girl took her Nana by the hand and slowly helped her to her feet.

"Well, I can't walk as good as I used to. I don't feel so sure of myself," Nana slurred.

"Don't worry, Nana, you can do it. You know, when it rains, it rains pennies from heaven."

~Emily Erickson
*Chicken Soup for the Grandma's Soul*

# Everybody Knows Everybody

*Some things have to be believed to be seen.*
~Ralph Hodgson

Today was a special day, the type of day that restores a faith of sorts.

And in that faith I found a lesson, taught to me by my six-year-old son, Brandon.

I watched him at the kitchen table carefully packing his lunch bag. I was going to take him along with me to work. As he put it, "I'm going to be a worker-man."

Carefully laid out before him was an arrangement of everything he required to get him through the day—a small coloring book, crayons, a small box of Smarties, a blueberry muffin, an egg salad "samich" (as he called it) and three small Easter eggs.

To know Brandon is to understand that time has no meaning. I was running late and implored Brandon to "hurry up!" (I'm sure he feels the watch is a confidence trick, invented by the Swiss.)

Hurry he did. In fact, he forgot his well-packed lunch, a mistake I was painfully aware of on the forty-minute drive to town. He admonished me several times, saying, "Dad, you made me rush. Now I have no lunch." He changed the words over the duration of the scolding, but the meaning remained the same, "I need a lunch because you made me forget mine."

I purchased a sandwich and another muffin at a restaurant in town. Satisfied, he carried the bag to the van, and soon his mutinous thoughts of "no lunch, no work" vanished.

We arrived at a small bungalow in the suburbs of Kingston (Ontario, Canada). Our job: to install indoor-outdoor carpet on the porch and steps.

I rang the doorbell. I could hear the deadbolt being released, then the handle-lock and security chain. The door swung slowly open revealing an old, thin man. He looked ill. His white hair covered his head in patches. The powder-blue shirt hung from his shoulders as though on a hanger — his belt, several sizes too big.

I smiled, asking if he was Mr. Burch.

"Yes. Are you here to do the porch and steps?"

"Yes, Sir."

"Okay, I will leave this door open."

"Okay, I will get to work."

"Do you have a 'flidge?'" blurted Brandon. The old man looked down at Brandon, who extended his lunch.

"Yes, I do. Do you know where to find the fridge?"

"Yes, I do," said Brandon, walking past the man. "It's in the kitchen."

I was about to suggest to Brandon that he was being too bold by walking in, but before I could, the old man held his finger to his lips, gesturing it was okay.

"He'll be all right. He can't get into anything at all. Does he really help you?"

I nodded yes. Brandon returned, asking, in his most elf-like voice, "Do you have a coloring book?"

Again, I was about to suggest to Brandon that he was perhaps being bold. I extended my hand, beckoning him outside. The old man grasped my hand feebly. He looked at Brandon.

"Your father tells me you help him."

"Yes. I'm a worker-man," Brandon replied with pride.

I looked down, adding, "Apparently his job today is to keep the customer busy."

The old man looked at Brandon and released my hand, a faint smile appearing.

"Maybe you could do some work and show me how to color?"

With a most serious look, Brandon asked, "Dad, will you be okay?"

"Will Mr. Burch be okay?" I answered.

"We will be fine. We will be right here at the table. Come help me get out the book, worker-man."

I walked to the truck, returning with material and my notepad in time to hear Brandon comment, "You have already colored in this book. You are a good colorer."

"No, I didn't color these pictures. My grandchildren did."

"What are grandchildren?" Brandon asked curiously.

"They are my children's children. I am a grandfather."

"What's a grandfather?"

"Well, when you grow up and get married, then have children of your own, your dad will be a grandpa. Then your mother will be a grandma. They will be grandparents. Do you understand?"

Brandon paused. "Yes, Grandpa."

"Oh, I don't think I'm your grandpa," the old man suggested.

Brandon rubbed his hair from his eyes. Studying the crayons, he selected one and continued to color.

Brandon said, "Everybody knows everybody, you know?"

"Well, I'm not sure they do. Why do you say that?" The old man looked curiously at Brandon, who was diligently coloring.

"We all comed from God. He made us all. We are fambily."

"Yes, God made everything," the old man confirmed.

"I know," said Brandon in a lighthearted voice. "He told me."

I had never heard Brandon talk of such things before, other than one time when we had gone to church to watch a Christmas play. While waiting for the play to start, Brandon had asked which door God would be coming through and if he would be sitting with us.

"He told you?" The old man was clearly curious.

"Yes, he did. He lives up there." Brandon pointed to the ceiling, looking up with reverence. "I b-member being there and talking to him."

"What did he say to you?" The old man placed his crayon on the table, focusing on Brandon.

"He said we are all fambily." Brandon paused, then added logically, "So you're my grandpa."

The old man looked to me through the screen door. He smiled. I was embarrassed that he saw me watching them. He told Brandon to keep coloring; he was going to check on the job.

The old man made his way slowly to the door. Opening it, he stepped onto the porch.

"How's it going?" he asked.

"It's going okay," I said. "I won't be long." The old man smiled slightly.

"Does the boy have a grandfather?"

I paused. "No, he doesn't. They were gone when he was born. He has a nanny, you know, a grandmother, but she is frail and not well."

"I understand what you're saying. I have cancer. I'm not long for this Earth, either."

"I'm sorry to hear that, Mr. Burch. I lost my mother to cancer."

He looked at me with tired, smiling eyes. "Every boy needs a grandfather," he said softly.

I agreed, adding, "It's just not in the cards for Brandon."

The old man looked back to Brandon, who was coloring vigorously. Turning back to me, he asked, "How often do you come to town, Son?"

"Me?" I asked.

"Yes."

"I come in almost every day."

The old man looked back to me. "Perhaps you could bring Brandon by from time to time, when you're in the area that is, for thirty minutes or so. What do you think?"

I looked in at Brandon. He had stopped coloring and was listening to us. "Could we, Dad? We are fliends. We can have lunch together."

"Well, if it's okay with Mr. Burch."

The old man opened the door, returning to the table. Brandon slid from his chair and walked to the fridge. "It's lunch time, Grandpa. I got enough for both of us." Brandon returned to the table. He removed the contents from the paper bag. "Do you have a knife?" asked Brandon.

The old man started to get up.

"I can find it. Tell me where to look," instructed Brandon.

"The butter knives are next to the corner of the counter, in the drawer."

"Found it!"

Brandon returned to the table. He unwrapped his muffin. With the care of a diamond-cutter, he cleaved two perfect portions. Brandon placed one portion on the plastic the muffin was wrapped in. He pushed it toward Mr. Burch.

"This is yours." He carefully unwrapped the sandwich next and cut it in half. "This is yours, too. We have to eat the samich first. Mom says."

"Okay," replied Mr. Burch.

"Do you like juice, Brandon?"

"Yep, apple juice."

Mr. Burch walked slowly to the fridge. He removed a can of apple juice and poured two small glasses. He placed one in front of Brandon. "This is yours."

"Thank you, Grandpa." Brandon punctuated his eating with questions to Mr. Burch and fits of coloring.

"Do you play hockey, Brandon?"

"Yep," said Brandon, studying the end of his sandwich before biting into it. "Dad took me, Tyler and Adam in the wintertime."

"Years ago," Mr. Burch started, "I used to play for a Senior-A-team. I was almost ready to play for the NHL, but I was never called up. I did play once with a man who was called up, though. He was a fine player. Bill Moore. That was his name."

My heart leapt to my throat. "Tutter Moore?" I asked through the screen.

The old man was startled. He looked at me. "Yes, that's him... was called up to Boston a few times. You've heard of him?"

"Yes," I said, my voice cracking. "You're eating lunch with his grandson."

The old man looked back to Brandon. He stared for a few moments. Brandon looked innocently at Mr. Burch.

"Yes... I see now. He looks very much like Tutter. And the nanny is Lillian?"

"Yes," I replied.

The old man clasped Brandon's hand.

"Brandon, I owe you an apology. You were right, and I was wrong. Everybody does know everybody."

~Lea MacDonald
*Chicken Soup for the Grandparent's Soul*

# 14

# Papa's Gift to Kelsey

*If my heart can become pure and loving, like that of a child,*
*I think there probably can be no greater happiness than this.*
*~Kitaro Nishida*

My father was a very warm and caring man, quick to lend a hand to anyone who needed it. I always looked up to my father and deeply admired his way with people.

He was in a care center for years after suffering a series of strokes that impaired his ability to walk and caused his speech to be slow and slurred. It pained me very much to see him there, and we tried to visit him several times a month. My toddler daughter, Kelsey, read stories to him, and he lay listening as her imagination ran wild, pretending to read words from the books she held in her tiny hands. They loved each other dearly, and he was her "Papa."

Kelsey was only four years old when Dad died. I was distraught for weeks, and Kelsey tried to comfort me. Oftentimes she cried with me or tried in some way to make me feel better. Nothing helped. I needed my father on this Earth, and sometimes my heart ached so badly I thought it might burst from sadness.

While we were preparing to go to my in-laws' for Thanksgiving, I heard Kelsey talking to her daddy. They were chatting about Papa and how he had gone to heaven and was now watching over us. She said in the sweetest voice, "Daddy, since Mama doesn't have a daddy anymore, do you think you could just share yours with her?"

Laughing and crying, I thought my heart would burst.

From that day on, my grief eased. I knew my father had given Kelsey gifts of compassion, sympathy and concern for others.

He would live on forever, in her.

~Sonja Walder
*Chicken Soup for the Father & Daughter Soul*

# 15

# Raising My Sights

My six-year-old granddaughter, Caitlynd, and I stopped at a Tim Horton's donut shop for a blueberry muffin. As we were going out the door, a young teenage boy was coming in.

This young man had no hair on the sides of his head and a tuft of blue spiked hair on top of it. One of his nostrils was pierced, and attached to the hoop that ran through the hole was a chain that draped across his face and attached to a ring he was wearing in his ear. He held a skateboard under one arm and a basketball under the other.

Caitlynd, who was walking ahead of me, stopped in her tracks when she saw the teen. I thought he'd scared the dickens out of her, and she'd frozen on the spot.

I was wrong.

My Grandangel backed up against the door and opened it as wide as it would go. Now I was face to face with the young man. I stepped aside and let him pass. His response was a gracious, "Thank you very much."

On our way to the car, I commended Caitlynd for her manners in holding open the door for the young man. She didn't seem to be troubled by his appearance, but I wanted to make sure. If a grandmotherly talk about freedom of self-expression and allowing people their differences was in order, I wanted to be ready.

As it turned out, the person who needed the talk was me.

The only thing Caitlynd noticed about the teen was the fact that his arms were full. "He woulda had a hard time to open the door."

I saw the partially shaved head, the tuft of spiked hair, the piercings and the chain. She saw a person carrying something under each arm and heading toward a closed door.

In the future, I hope to get down on her level and raise my sights.

~Terri McPherson
*Chicken Soup for the Grandparent's Soul*

# Grand and Great

## Family Ties

*The love of my family is my estate.*
*~Horatio Nelson*

# 16

# Reflections of Hope

They didn't grow inside of me
Next to my heart,
But they have my genes
So they are my own.

Most of them hug me, giggle,
Clamor for attention,
Beg for stories, expect treats
Want to sing and sleep over.

In their world I build tradition;
I am Thanksgiving and Christmas,
A memory-maker serving cookies with praise
Encouraging their ambition.

To them I'm slow, old-fashioned
A helper of homework who speaks strange words
They tell me I sound "cool."
In their unstable world
I offer things that rarely change.

In them I see myself;
Two have my turned-up nose,
Another my moodiness, my laugh,

One has my passion for music
Still another, my fascination with words,
Some gather friends like flowers,
A mirror of me.

Each one is a reflection of hope
making rainbows
where their own light shines.

In this complicated world
I look to them with pride,
They look to me with trust.

This cherished brood is my treasure
I call them precious
They call me Gram.

~Yulene A. Rushton
*Chicken Soup for the Grandparent's Soul*

# 17

# Grandma's Necklace

I ran up the stairs to Grandma Flemming's porch as fast as my three-year-old legs would carry me. Slipping on the wet porch, I fell and cut my eyebrow on a glass milk bottle waiting to be picked up by the milkman. Loving arms enfolded me, "There, there, it will be alright. We'll make it all better." Those are the first memories I have of my mother's mother.

Not many years after that event my grandparents moved away from Ohio to Indiana, where my grandfather would pastor a succession of small churches until he retired. Grandma remained a very special person in my life in spite of the fact that I didn't see her as often as I would have liked. I have many happy, poignant memories of her funny, cackling laugh; her high nasal voice; spending several weeks with her one summer; the glass cabinet where she kept her collection of knick-knacks and novelty salt and pepper shakers; and her house near the railroad tracks. One Christmas, the rumbling of the train in the early-morning hours brought the nine-foot Christmas tree crashing to the floor!

Grandma died near the end of my senior year of high school after a long battle with cancer. As the oldest grandchild and granddaughter, I inherited two things from

Grandma: her wedding ring and a silver necklace given to her the year she was born.

When I got married only a few months after her death, my husband placed Grandma's wedding ring on my finger as Grandpa officiated. I wore the necklace rather reluctantly, only because it meant so much to my mother. The filigree daisy pattern had a diamond in the center. The chain was tarnished and tangled.

After our wedding I placed the necklace in a jewelry box and, quite honestly, I didn't think much about it for years. Then two things happened in rapid succession that made me reconsider the necklace: My older daughter, Susan, gave birth to her first child, Christine, and my marriage of twenty-four years ended.

Going through my things in the process of the divorce, I came across the necklace. For a minute I couldn't even remember where I had gotten it. Then I remembered Grandma. I bought a new chain to replace the tangled and tarnished one, and, had the pendant cleaned at the jewelers. I was amazed at the beauty of the little necklace. As I took off the wedding ring, I began wearing the necklace, and, I lovingly recalled my grandmother.

I saw my granddaughter often and babysat from the time I finished teaching until her mother came home from work at midnight, five days a week. She grew from an infant to a toddler to a little girl, and she loved the "flower necklace," as she called it. Since she is my oldest granddaughter, I let her know that, just as I had gotten the necklace from my grandmother, someday the "pretty flower" would be hers.

Christine is nearly twelve years old now, and growing into a young lady. I'm not going to wait until I die to pass this legacy on to her. The necklace will be one hundred years old the year Christine turns nineteen. I will pass her great-great-grandmother's necklace on to her, knowing she, too, will look back on happy, poignant memories.

~Carol Spahr
*Chicken Soup for the Grandma's Soul*

# Gift from Another Grandmother

*The measure of love is not how much that child loves me
but rather how much I dare to love that child.*
*~Lois Wyse*

Our son, Bob, placed a little stranger down in the middle of our living room. "Mom, Dad, this is my Bridget." Bridget, two and a half, stood there and just smiled, her hazel-brown eyes dancing from one of us to the other. She had been born in the northernmost part of Canada where the aurora borealis can be seen from her yard. This was her first trip to Washington State, and she took my breath away.

We hugged and laughed and greeted one another, then I asked if Bridget would like to help me in the yard. We gathered all the tools, and as I kneeled in the pansy beds beneath our birch trees, Bridget wiggled her plump body close. "Grandma, are you allowed to get dirty?"

"You bet. And so are you."

The next morning we threw our sleeping bags and groceries into the trucks and headed for the ocean. Bridget sat straight and tall between her grandfather and me. As we started off down the driveway, she smiled up at me and carefully took my arm, cradling it between both of her chubby hands, and just hung on for two hundred miles.

Bridget had learned the word, "Grandma," from our daughter-in-law's mother, who lived near their homestead. So we didn't need time to get acquainted. "Run, Grandma, run," Bridget called as we held hands, lifted our faces to the wind and ran toward the ocean waves. She giggled and splashed as the sun and surf painted rainbows across our toes at the water's edge.

That night, Bridget never left my side as we toasted marshmallows, our cheeks and fingers melding together with traces of white, sticky sweetness. At bedtime, she rolled out her bag and put it on the canvas floor beside my old army surplus cot in our nine- by nine-foot tent. Grandpa was already snoring and the other grandchildren chose to sleep under the stars with Uncle Brian. As Bridget and I talked about taking our pails to the beach in the morning, she lifted my hand to her lips, "Grandma 'Rean says you're nice." And we drifted off to dreams as the auspicious drone of waves and shifting sand washed across our world.

In the middle of the night, a noise awakened me. And in the faint, first light of morning through the tent screen flap, I saw Bridget sit up in her bag and lean onto my cot. She reached across my stomach and hugged me, then brushed her lips across my cheek. Very carefully she patted my arm. Then, she scooted back inside the Mickey Mouse bag, closing her dark lashes, and snuggling her ponytail into the pillow.

I caught my breath, and lay very still, allowing warm tears to wash the memory of Bridget's visit deep into my bones. I held a treasure, my grandchild's ready, open heart, the gift of Grandma Mearean, up north nearly two thousand miles away.

~Doris Hays Northstrom
*Chicken Soup for the Grandparent's Soul*

# 19

# The Rocker

*A grandmother is a mother who has a second chance.*
*~Author Unknown*

I stumbled with exhaustion, searching for the ringing telephone. Colicky three-month-old Max slept only two hours at a time, and my husband was away traveling again. My fatigued body ached. I found the phone under a receiving blanket and answered it.

My mother asked, "Is Max sleeping any better?"

"A little."

"You're not getting any sleep, are you?" She sounded worried.

My gritty eyes burned. "Not much."

"That must be so hard."

My throat closed. "Oh Mom, I'm exhausted! I can hardly think."

"I'm coming up."

Outside my window, a December blizzard moaned through the darkness. My mother would have to navigate icy canyon roads to reach my house. I said, "It's snowing hard here. Don't come. I'll be okay."

"I'm on my way." She hung up. Tears of exhaustion and relief blurred my vision. My mother has always been my rock.

The usual thirty-minute drive took her an hour. My mother arrived looking rosy-cheeked from the cold, snow frosting her reddish-brown hair. She took baby Max from my arms and ordered me to bed. I said, "But Max needs to eat in the night."

She shook her head. "I know how to warm up formula. Go to bed!" Her determined look told me not to argue.

My soft pillow beckoned to me, along with my cozy down comforter. I headed upstairs feeling relieved, but lying in bed I couldn't sleep. Guilt overwhelmed me. I should be able to take care of my baby. At least I could have offered to help. My mother wouldn't have let me, I realized. I heard her coo to Max as she climbed the stairs. Soon the rocking chair in baby Max's room creaked, back and forth, back and forth.

Suddenly I remembered my mother rocking me when I had the chicken pox. I was too big for rocking, but blisters invaded my throat, my ears, even the back of my eyelids. As we rocked my mother sang, "Rock-a-bye my big-big girl." The monotonous chant comforted me. I slept. When I woke in the night my mother offered sips of water and laid cold washrags across my burning forehead. I slept fitfully, but in the morning the blisters had crusted, and I felt better.

Now I could hear my mother chanting to Max, "Rock-a-bye my ba-by boy." Her monotone relaxed me, just as it had when I was a child. I slid toward sleep, knowing my baby was in capable hands. In the morning, I'd hug my mother, thank her, and tell her how her love had rocked both Max and me to sleep.

~Kendeyl Johansen
*Chicken Soup for the Mother & Daughter Soul*

# 20

# The Folks Next Door

Occasionally, I say something that's guaranteed to evoke a strong response. I tell people, "I live next door to my parents." Their reaction tells me a lot about the relationship they have with their own parents. I've heard everything from abject horror, to wistful sighs accompanied by, "That must be so nice."

In case you're wondering, I'm not some psychologically dependent cling-on. My parents and I haven't always been neighbors. For most of my adult life, I lived in a completely different (though, come to think of it, neighboring) community.

It was my last move, six years ago, that led us to share lot lines, garbage pick-up days and the same view of the night sky. My husband, three kids and I were looking for a larger home. At the same time, my parents wanted to downsize to a smaller, low-maintenance house. My husband, Greg, and I chose a subdivision and watched as our new house progressed from a hole in the ground to completion.

After looking at existing homes, my parents visited our builder to look at floor plans. They liked the area, but the visit was really a lark, or at least that's the story I was told. As it turned out, the house they loved was offered only on the lot next to ours. After they studied the room layout and toured a model, my mom asked, "Would you mind if we lived so close?" She assured me that they wouldn't be offended if we didn't like the idea. Greg and I thought it would work out fine, and luckily, it has.

I can't complain—the benefits have been enormous. Vacations are worry-free because we know that each of us will watch the other's house, pick up the mail and collect the newspapers. We're available for each other in the event that furniture needs moving (them) or kids need watching (us). My oldest son's first paying job was mowing their lawn. And when we say it's no trouble to bring back more takeout from the Chinese restaurant or pick up additional stamps at the post office, it really isn't.

I've found that my parents are the only neighbors I can be brutally honest with. When my dad bragged about his cost-effective, makeshift central air-conditioning cover, I took him over to my kitchen window. I showed him how aesthetically pleasing his plastic garbage bag secured with duct tape was from our viewpoint. Shortly thereafter, the bag was replaced with a less creative, traditional cover.

Our kitchen windows are the only direct view of each other's homes. Sometimes the timing of our kitchen duty will coincide, and I'll wave from my side. If they notice me, they'll wave back. Only once has this view posed a problem. On that occasion, I got up in the middle of the night to get a drink of water and noticed my mom awake in her kitchen. On a whim, I dialed her phone number. The frantic way she catapulted out of her chair made me realize there are times it's best not to call.

I've learned that respecting each other's time and space is the key to successfully living close to family members. Other relatives don't believe me when I tell them days go by when I don't even talk to my parents. My three sisters (they of the "better you than me" philosophy) will call asking, "Where are Mom and Dad? I've been trying to reach them all day."

I usually don't have an answer. Who can keep track of busy retired people? "You could do what I do when I can't get hold of them," I suggest.

"What?" they ask, waiting for the next-door neighbor secret.

"Leave a message on their machine. When they get home they'll call you back."

For some, life is a board game of cross-country moves to better job opportunities and bigger houses. Families keep in touch by phone, letter and e-mail and somehow they make it work. But I believe there's no substitute for being nearby. My children know my parents in a way I never knew my own grandparents. On a warm summer day, my kids will interrupt valuable playing time to dash over to my parents' yard for a hug from Grandma or to help Grandpa water his plants. It's good for a kid to have a haven close to home.

This parent next-door thing has been working out so well that I'm already thinking ahead to my own retirement. I try to imagine one of my three children as a future next-door neighbor. When asked about that possibility, thirteen-year-old Charlie said, "I probably will want to live as far away from you as possible."

The younger two are far more agreeable, in fact six-year-old Jack has said he wants to live with me forever. That may be a little too close — but if he wants to move in with Grandma and Grandpa, it's a deal.

~Karen McQuestion
*Chicken Soup to Inspire a Woman's Soul*

# 21

# I Love You Double

*To love is to receive a glimpse of heaven.*
*~Karen Sunde*

Taking a big bite of his pancake at our favorite breakfast haunt, out of the clear blue, with syrup dripping out of the corner of his mouth, my five-year-old grandson, Tyler, said, "How come I don't have a dad?"

The inevitable question had been asked, and I was the one left to answer it. Think! What do I say? In an important moment such as this one, when you need to think quickly and come up with the best possible response, it's amazing how much can run through your head in a flash.

Tyler's inquisitive face caused me to dredge up a lot of old memories—how challenging it had been raising my own three daughters alone. Countless times the girls would lament over not having a "normal" family, and I would go overboard trying to make up for their "lot in life" as children of a single parent. Adding to that, my relationship with the girls' father was always strained, we never had enough money, and we were four girls trying to grow up together at the same time (yes, me included). Just trying to survive wreaked havoc on the kind of home life I wanted to provide for my little family. All of it amounted to some pretty tough times—emotionally, mentally and physically.

Through the years, guilt was an emotion I often struggled with: from taking the initiative to leave the girls' father to not being able to provide for them financially in a single-parent home as well as they might have been provided for in a two-parent home. I ached for them daily, knowing none of us had it easy.

Snapping back to the present and looking at the beautiful child sitting across from me, I relished the gift of his being. Tyler was the best of all bonuses bequeathed me for all the years I struggled as a single mom. Knowing the legacy of single motherhood that had been passed on to my oldest child, I desperately wanted my daughter and grandson to have more stability and freedom from the challenges of being in a single-parent family than I had.

Tyler had posed a serious question, and I had to find the right answer for him, right then and there. Telling him that some children simply don't have a mom or dad just wasn't adequate, nor was it true in his case. Five-year-olds demand the truth. But should I tell him that his father is in prison? That Tyler's presence here on Earth goes back to a time when my daughter was having a tough time in her own life? Would that imply he was a mistake? No, no child is ever "a mistake," never, ever, regardless of the circumstances. But how do you explain any of this to a little boy? And what would his mother want me to say in this instance?

Then I realized what Tyler really was asking: Am I complete? Do I matter? Am I loved? And then the words came to me. "Tyler, you don't have a dad in your life right now, but you do have a mom who loves you double." I repeated and emphasized, "Double," adding, "and with Grandma loving you as much as I do, make that triple!"

Reflecting on my seemingly brilliant reply, it suddenly

hit me that the guilt I had immersed myself in for years and years had been useless. I realized I did the best I could given my circumstances, and that, in my case, the girls fared far better with just a mom than they ever would have in a two-parent family fraught with constant fighting, turmoil and unhappiness. I loved them double, too.

Responding to my answer, Tyler looked at me with a face full of satisfaction and replied, "Well, I guess that makes me pretty lucky then, doesn't it, Grandma?"

~Nancy Vogl
*Chicken Soup for the Single Parent's Soul*

# 22

# Grandpa's Gift

My grandfather was a dirt-under-the-fingernails blue-collar worker all of his life. He provided for his family and never complained but, in his heart, he fancied himself a writer.

Grandpa would sit for long winter evenings in his rocking chair in the kitchen—writing, laughing, erasing and rearranging until he was satisfied. He didn't want to be just any writer; specifically, he dreamed of being a joke writer for Bob Hope.

While growing up in his house, I thought that was the funniest joke of all—Grandpa, a writer for Bob Hope. But, whenever he brought out his boxes of jokes, I laughed with Grandma... assuming they were funny merely because Grandpa thought they were funny.

Every so often he rented a typewriter and, using the hunt-and-peck finger system, sat at the kitchen table diligently transferring his hand-written creations onto index cards. More than anything in the world, I wanted to be big enough to learn to type so I could type Grandpa's jokes for him.

Several years later, I elatedly interrupted Grandpa—who was still writing jokes—to show him the glistening engagement ring I'd received the night before. Slowly and somberly, he removed his glasses, folded his paper and carefully put away his pencil. There was no laughter in his voice and his only words were: "I hope you know what you're doing."

I knew Grandpa didn't dislike the man I was betrothed to; they got along quite well. What he could not accept was me marrying someone of a different religion.

After that day, Grandpa didn't write any more jokes. In fact, our once loving home was suddenly filled with angry words and tears, and now I couldn't wait to move out of the home I had grown up in.

Instead of anticipation, I despaired over thoughts of my wedding day. Of Grandpa not only refusing to walk me down the aisle, but refusing to set foot in my fiancé's church. The stubborn man made it quite clear that although he couldn't stop me, he didn't have to condone it, either. I was determined to marry even without my beloved grandfather at my side.

Preparations for our modest wedding were made out of Grandpa's sight and hearing. Grandma worked on my dress during the day while Grandpa was at work. We prepared invitations at my in-laws' home. At night, I stitched my dress behind the closed door of my bedroom to spare us all uncomfortable silences. Even though we didn't have a lot of money, I refused to let Grandma ask Grandpa to share in the expenses. I could be just as stubborn as he was and I was determined to let him know it.

The day before the ceremony, I set my pride aside and pleaded with Grandpa to be part of my wedding. He refused to attend. I had never known him to be so unbending. I always knew how he felt about this particular religion, but I never dreamed my final days at home would be so horrible.

That night, tears of frustration and pain soaked my pillow. My last night in this room, in this bed and in this house should have been filled with joy. Instead we were strangers on separate planets—a universe apart. How could he do this? How could I be married without Grandpa beside me?

My wedding morning dawned cloudy and dismal, a mirror image of my gloomy heart. I lay quietly looking around the room of my childhood, remembering the many times when Grandpa sat on my bed reading nighttime stories, soothing me after horrible nightmares and kneeling beside me for prayer.

I dreaded facing him at the breakfast table. Disheartened, I rolled over, sliding my hand up and under the pillow. Suddenly I felt something strange. An envelope? With a pounding heart, I carefully opened it and removed a letter written in Grandpa's familiar feathery script.

"My Dearest Child...."

Grandpa apologized, pouring out his heart in the most moving, heartfelt way he knew. He was sorry for spoiling my joy the past months, ashamed of his dreadful, selfish behavior. He explained his feelings and beliefs and said that, although they were his, he realized he had no right to impose them on me. He went on to ask forgiveness and—at long last—promised to welcome my new husband into his home and his heart. Just as he had welcomed me all those many years before.

As I continued to read, I saw a change in the handwriting and noticed blurred ink where a teardrop had fallen onto the paper in a splatter. Suddenly tears filled my own eyes. But I wept for joy, not sorrow, when I read his humble plea, begging the "honor" of walking me down the aisle.

Grandpa never did sell any jokes to Mr. Hope, but the greatest thing he ever wrote was that single cherished letter to a beloved, grateful granddaughter.

~Nicolle Woodward
*Chicken Soup for the Bride's Soul*

# Chapter 4

# Grand and Great

## No Obstacle for a Grandparent

*To be seventy years young is sometimes far more cheerful
and hopeful than to be forty years old.*
*~Oliver Wendell Holmes*

# Growing Old Disgracefully

I owe my life and liveliness to Grandma. If it hadn't been for her, I would have died of boredom... and I never would have learned the basic principles for growing old disgracefully.

My intensive training began at ten, the year I got some kind of weird skin disease on my feet. It was thought to be contagious and I couldn't go to school, so I spent all day, every day, at Grandma's house. The first time the doctor came there to look at my feet was a day I'll never forget. After carefully painting my toes with Mercurochrome, he wrapped each foot in miles and miles of gauze. He told me that I must sit very still all day so I wouldn't bump my feet, and that he'd be back the next day to take another look.

As soon as he left, Grandma turned to me, and, shaking her head, said, "That doctor may know medicine, but he sure don't know kids."

Patting my shoulder, she smiled down on me. "Don't you worry none," she said. "I know you can't sit still all day. We'll figure out a way for you to get around and still not bump those feet." And she did.

A little later, she slipped my feet into two shoeboxes

lined with a layer of fluffy cotton. She tied them in with strips of sheeting and drew on the boxes so they would look like cars in a choo-choo train. Because it hurt to pick up my feet, she taught me to shuffle along and say. "Choo-choo, choo-choo, comin' through," so I would laugh and forget the pain.

But that night when I went to bed, the pain was so bad I couldn't forget it. I cried and cried. Grandma heard me and came to me. Instead of telling me not to cry, she encouraged me to cry louder. It helped somewhat, but not enough.

Then she bent down over the bed and whispered in my ear.

"I know some magic words that always take away pain. I think you are old enough to hear them. But you mustn't ever let anyone know you know them, 'specially your mother."

Peering over her shoulder on one side and then the other, as if to make certain nobody was listening, she continued, "Remember these words are to be used only in an emergency, after you've tried everything else and nothing works. And once you've started saying the string of words, you must keep repeating them over and over until the pain goes away."

Then softly she said these words in a sing-songy chant, and we practiced saying them together: "Hell, damn, shitty, poop, farty, pee. Hell, damn, shitty, poop, farty, pee. Hell, damn, shitty, poop, farty, pee."

And what she said was true. It was magic. After saying the words over and over, the pain did go away, and I went to sleep.

The next day, when the doctor came, he found me sitting quietly in the place he had last seen me, and the shoebox choo-choo trains were hidden in the closet. Grandma warned me not to tell the doctor what we had done.

"Honey," she whispered, "there is just one way to treat the wise guys in your life who tell you what to do: Listen carefully to 'em, and then do what you think is best."

Grandma's sister lived next door to her. She was humorless and crotchety and so different from everyone else in our family, I used to wonder how she ever gained admission. While Grandma was round and soft and looked as though she ate sweet rolls every morning for breakfast, my great-aunt Lee was tall and bony and looked as if she sucked vinegar through a straw. At least once a day, every day, she would bemoan the fact that, "Growing old is no laughing matter."

If anyone seemed to be listening, she'd go on to complain about her rheumatism and how much it hurt to move and how she couldn't "see nor hear so good no more." Sitting at the kitchen table, dunking a doughnut into her coffee, she would recite a lecture I soon knew by heart.

"You'd better enjoy yourself while you're young because when you get to my age, you won't be able to any more. You had better obey your parents and make it easy for them because they are getting older too, and life is difficult for older people. Growing old is no laughing matter!"

One morning, after I'd heard her repeat that favorite phrase of hers for maybe the fifth time, I started to laugh. Pretending to have a fit of coughing, I ran from her house, for I knew she'd hit me if she thought I was laughing at her. And, of course, I was.

While watching her jerky movements and listening to her rasping voice and endless complaints, I suddenly had a fantasy of her on the stage, like a character in a play, a female Scrooge. I laughed because I realized she was a character in a play—one of her own making.

When I ran from my great-aunt's house, I sped next door to Grandma's. Still laughing out loud as I ran in, I let the screen door slam shut behind me. Grandma came out from her room to ask what was going on.

When I explained the situation, she started laughing too.

"You're quite right," she said. "That old lady is a character in a very dull play."

She took my hand and led me toward the kitchen, which smelled of freshly baked bread.

"Let's talk about it while we enjoy some hot bread. Remember, though, it's not good for your stomach to eat bread while it's hot like this. But a person has to do something now and then that's not good for them. Just do those things in moderation.

"You know, I think 'God's favorites' are those persons—children or adults—who are slightly wicked—not bad-bad, but just a little naughty now and then. You can tell they are God's favorites because he gives them better dispositions, and people like to be around them more than they like to be around the saintly ones!

"I think people who try 'not to rock the boat' and try to make everyone happy are to be pitied. Their brain gets damaged by a too-tight halo that prevents the circulation of interesting thoughts."

At Thanksgiving and Christmas, Grandma, Mama and Aunt Emma would work together for days getting ready for the big family gathering, preparing the house, the table and the feast. Then, on the big day, after everyone had stuffed themselves, Grandma would announce to her daughters and the other women present, "I know you'll do a good job clearing away the dishes and cleaning up the kitchen. You don't need me now. I've done my share. It's time for my reward."

Then, taking all the men with her, she'd go into the living room and wait. As soon as the table was cleared, the tablecloth removed and the women cloistered in the kitchen with the dining room door closed, Grandma and her entourage would return, re-cover the table with an army blanket and proceed to play poker or craps. Sometimes she'd even smoke a cigar.

I would sneak into the living room and curl up in one of her overstuffed chairs, my arms around my overstuffed stomach. Half dozing, I'd watch, listen and marvel at my grandmother—who didn't act at all like other kids' grandmothers. I knew that I wanted to grow up and be just like her—I wanted to grow old disgracefully!

I'm eighty-five now, older than Grandma was when she died. And I've caused more than a few raised eyebrows along the way. It's been a life full of heart and humor and irreverence—just the very kind of legacy I planned so long ago on Grandma's couch.

~Emily Coleman
*Chicken Soup to Inspire the Body & Soul*

# 24

# Grandma's Cake

*Attitude is a little thing that makes a big difference.*
*~Winston Churchill*

"Let's go on a walk," Grandma suggested cheerfully while twisting her wavy, snow-white hair into a bun. The rest of the family was busy in the fields harvesting hay, and it was my responsibility to watch Grandma.

"Oh, no," I cautioned. "Last time you stepped in a big mud puddle and Mom was very upset."

"Oh, posh," Grandma replied. "I'm not going to sit and rock all day. Idle hands are the devil's workshop. Let's make a cake."

"Grandma, we can't make a cake. You can't see," I reminded her anxiously.

She laughed. "You can do anything you want to if you just try," she said. "God gave us five senses and seeing is just one of them." She pulled herself up from the rocker, and I guided her to where her apron hung on the wall. "Now, get a kitchen chair, child," she directed.

I pushed the chair up to the counter in our big, sunny pantry. Following Grandma's directions, I carefully retrieved a teacup from the cupboard. Putting one chubby hand on Grandma's shoulder, I nestled the cup in her hand. Then I found a big bowl and placed it in front of her. Deftly, she measured two level cups of flour in a big bowl. In amazement, I watched as she blindly searched the containers in the cupboard.

"Now find me the baking powder," she commanded.

"But Grandma, I can't read," I stuttered.

"You can taste, can't you?" she replied tartly.

I found a can and handed it to her. She screwed the top off, licked her finger, dipped it in the powder and tasted it. "Oh, no, that's baking soda," she declared. "Now you try it." It tasted bitter and fizzy.

The next container I found was not quite so bitter, and Grandmother announced that it most certainly was baking powder. I found the sugar and flour, and Grandma said we could tell which was which by tasting or feeling.

We identified vanilla easily by its smell. Grandma made sure that the lids were replaced on every container and that the containers were put back where they belonged. Then she showed me how to crack an egg properly and let me help beat the cake. By now the pantry was showing the effects of our cake-making.

Grandma ran her hand over the countertop. "Lands, child," she laughed. "We have made a mess. Never mind, we will have it spic-and-span in a jiffy." I got a dishpan of sudsy water and wiped the counter vigorously with the dishcloth. I watched as Grandma carefully ran her hand over the counter, feeling to see if it was clean enough. She had me wipe the counter again and then again. Finally she declared it was thoroughly clean.

Just as I wondered how we would be able to fire up the cook stove, Mom walked into the kitchen. She added kindling to the coals and a little later carefully opened the oven door and stuck her hand inside. She announced that the temperature was just right. I proudly carried the cake to the wood stove, and Mom popped it into the oven.

Grandma eased herself back into the rocker and said with a smile, "Someday you will face difficulties. Don't be too blind to look around and see how you can overcome them. Use the materials and abilities that God gives you. Count what you have, not what you don't have."

I don't remember how the cake turned out, but I have never forgotten the making of it.

~Norma Favor
*Chicken Soup for the Grandma's Soul*

# 25

# Lisa

*Be ever gentle with the children God has given you.*
*Watch over them constantly;*
*reprove them earnestly, but not in anger.*
*~Elihu Burritt*

The steam rising from the sudsy dishwater clouds the window, blurring my view of the backyard. But I know she is out there. I can tell by the rhythmic squeak of the swing set. I can tell by the abandon in her high-pitched, singsong voice. I know she is there, all right.

I take a deep breath and turn my attention back to the dirty dishes. There will not be time enough to finish before she comes running through the yard, dogs in tow, consumed with high drama and frantic energy, needing and demanding all the energy I have left.

Nothing productive happens when Lisa is around; she fills a room to bursting with her presence. Every breath, every word, every shrugged shoulder captures her attention. "Why?" "How come?" "What does that mean?" "What did I do?" she demands constantly.

Lisa talks loudly and incessantly. She is constantly in motion. She walks into walls. She trips over her own feet. Once, midstream in endless dinnertime chatter, her entire chair tipped over. My husband and I exchanged glances. Lisa kept right on talking.

When Lisa first came to live with us, I thought I was a terrible grandmother. She was always getting hurt. She fell from gymnasium bleachers and broke her new front tooth. She backed into the iguana's heating lamp and scorched her backside. She peeked through the crack of an open door just as I shut it and got her lip and nose pinched. She got her finger stuck in a pop bottle. She reached for a ball in the swimming pool and nearly drowned herself. A somersault from her bed required four stitches to her scalp. Pretty soon, I figured out that I was not doing anything wrong with Lisa; Lisa is simply out of synch with her own body.

I'm nearly finished with the dishes when I hear Lisa let out an ear-splitting whoop. She comes running for the back door with the dogs, her beautiful long, woolly braids a tangled mess. "I'm bored," she exclaims loudly, her soft, full lips forming a perfect little pout. I take a long, calming breath that I wish I could somehow transfer to her. I pat her sweaty head and gently disentangle myself from her clutches. "How about watching a movie until dinner's ready?" I try hopefully.

Somehow, videos calm Lisa. Therefore, she owns dozens. She can recite them all, word for word, and act them all out perfectly—but not today. "Oh, pu-leeze!" She flaunts dramatically and rolls her eyes, behavior better suited to a sixteen-year-old than a six-year-old. She has practiced the look from her latest video. And then she is off again, already forgetting how "bored" she is.

I am the only one who loves Lisa; everyone else just yells at her. Even though she exhausts me, even though she can reduce me to a screaming, out-of-control maniac, even though my favorite pastime is fantasizing about a life without her, still, I am the only one who loves her. I am the only one who knows how unhappy she really is.

Lisa was expelled from two nursery schools, flunked preschool and could not pass the entrance exam at three different kindergartens. I enrolled her directly into first grade at a public school that could not turn her away. That year was a disaster. I fought her teacher daily. Susie wrote things like "violent and irrational behavior" instead of "high-strung" or "underdeveloped impulse control," which was, at least, equally true. Susie felt that Lisa should repeat first grade. I refused. I knew that Lisa would be the same diffi-cult, hard-to-love, hard-to-teach child a year later. Besides, I will be sixty-five when Lisa graduates high school. I can-not hang on for "extra" years.

Lisa wishes she had a mommy like all the other kids, a mommy young enough to still be afraid of teachers instead of a granny, who sees her teacher as a girl young enough to be her own daughter. Lisa wishes for a mommy who will call her teacher "Miss King" instead of Susie. Lisa wishes for a lot of things, but mostly, she wishes for her mommy.

Pots are boiling all over the stove, dogs are chasing Lisa around the kitchen table, and my husband is trying to engage me in conversation when the telephone rings. Her cousins are coming over to play. I see a flicker of panic in Lisa's eyes.

Lisa is extremely social; she needs to be around people, and she usually seeks them out the way a diabetic seeks out sugar. But she knows her medication has worn off. She knows she is out of control. I try to calm her, reassure her. "You'll have fun playing with them," I tell her. She knows different. I know she is right.

The medicine was a concession to Teacher; in return

she agreed not to recommend Lisa's dismissal from the school. Lisa knows the medication changes how she feels; it's scary that she has made the connection between drugs and behavior. I am not so sure that is a good thing for the child of a drug addict to know.

Lisa's mommy is my daughter. She is a street person, a drug addict and a crack-head; a casualty of the failed war on drugs. Lisa idolizes her "Santa Claus, Tooth-Fairy Mommy." Lisa has created an imaginary Bestest Mommy Ever, and she loves her fiercely. It is heartbreaking to see, totally impossible to stop. I don't even know if I should try.

The cousins are here, the dogs are out of control and so is Lisa. She cannot cope with the excitement. One tattle of "Lisa hit me!" is followed by "Lisa pushed me!" followed by a crash that no one can identify but everyone is sure is Lisa's fault. Lisa is wound tight, ready to explode. I brace for it, too exhausted to plan an intervention. Then the lamp falls, crashes into a potted plant, which falls to the floor and breaks into a million pieces. The shards of glass pierce Lisa's fingers. Not badly enough to require stitches this time, I decide, but there is enough blood to make her hysterical. My husband handles first aid this time; I concentrate on cleaning up the mess and keeping calm. I will not lose control this time. I will not start yelling this time.

People accuse me of spoiling Lisa. They say I let her get away with too much. But I know when she is speaking disrespectfully, she is really reciting dialogue from a movie, because she doesn't know how to express herself. I know her frequent accidents are her way of getting loving attention, so different from the attention she usually gets. I know that the children at school are cruel to her and will not play with her. They tease her because she cannot read and has to sit at the blue table all by herself. They tease her because she does not have a mommy. I can't counterbalance all the hurt she has to endure, but I try. I really am the only one who loves her.

The cousins have gone home, the dogs have been fed, and Lisa has had a good cry and a warm bath. The tension is released from her little body, and she is exhausted. So am I. We cuddle on the couch, too tired to walk into her bedroom. "I'm sorry, Granny," she whispers in a tiny voice. She begins to cry all over again, her skinny shoulders shaking. I hug her tightly and let my tears mix with hers.

Tomorrow, I will call her teacher "Miss King."

~Christina Miranda-Walker
*Chicken Soup for the Caregiver's Soul*

# 26

# Granny's Last Cartwheel

Being a family today is complicated, but it hasn't always been this way. When I was growing up in a small town in the fifties, life—and family—were simple. Like all my friends, I lived in a house with two parents, and Mom was there every day when I came home from school, filling our home with the cozy smells of something cooking. Dad worked long hours and came home exhausted, but not too weary to watch my tricks when I performed somersaults, handstands and my favorite of them all—the cartwheel.

He would sit on the porch in the evening trying (I now understand) to have a few moments of solitude, yet he would always have a cheer for me as I performed my one-woman, amazing circus act on the soft, green lawn of our front yard. A somersault got a nod. With handstands, he helped me count the seconds I could remain upside down, legs splayed, balanced on those skinny little arms. But it was my cartwheel—my amazing, back-arched, legs-perfectly-straight, toes-pointed-to-the-sky cartwheel—that won his applause.

My grandmother was a gray-haired, elderly woman who lived halfway across the world in another country called Minnesota. She wasn't fond of noise or noisy children. When she came on the train for a visit, I was reminded that children "should be seen and not heard." My grandmother never saw my cartwheel.

Yes, life was simple then. Everyone knew the rules, and everyone knew their roles in that choreography we called "family." But life changes, with twists and turns along the way. I grew into adulthood and created my own family. By midlife, I found that I was not only grandmother to my own children's children, but to the progeny of my new husband's children as well. Family was no longer simple.

Even the question of "What should they call me?" was complicated, because they already had the ideal number of two grandmothers. I dubbed myself "Granny Nanny" and hoped that it would take. It did.

I didn't want to be the granny who lived on the other side of the world and didn't like noise when she visited. I didn't want to be the granny whose visits they feared or dreaded. I wanted to be the granny who listened and laughed and loved and played with her grandchildren. In short, I wanted to be a "cool" granny.

On one trip to our granddaughters Alison and Melissa's home, we visited a beautiful park. It was the very same one I had often taken my own daughters to when they were children. It was here that my children and I had spent many weekends frolicking in the park. Just as I had performed for my father as a child, my children would also run, skip, jump and somersault with glee, shouting, "Watch me! Watch me, Mommy!" Then I would join in and amaze them with my perfect, back-arched, legs-straight, toes-pointed-to-the-sky cartwheel.

On this sunny summer day, Alison and Melissa were bursting with the joy of youth. They began to run and jump and amaze us all with the gymnastic feats they could accomplish. No mere somersaults or cartwheels for these two young gymnasts: they twisted and whirled with back flips, round-offs and amazing multiple cartwheels. I applauded in awe.

When they paused and walked back toward me, I couldn't resist. I knew better—or should have—but I was caught up in the excitement of the show. "I can do an amazing perfect cartwheel," I announced. Both girls grinned at each other as if to say, Granny—a cartwheel? "I don't think so," Melissa even snickered.

Of course, I accepted the challenge. The sun was bright, the sky was filled with puffy cumulus clouds and there was just a little breeze. In the distance, birds were warbling to each other. I inhaled deeply and with a drum roll playing in my head, began the running skip that introduced my cartwheel. Arms raised overhead, I catapulted heels over head, back arched, legs perfectly straight, toes pointed to the sky. I was flying! I was still amazing!

I was in pain! The centrifugal force of the circular spin of the cartwheel became too much for my middle-aged joints. With a loud Crack! my left leg, the trailing one, came out of its hip socket. As I ended my circular descent, however, with both arms raised overhead—the way you always end the show—my left leg slammed back into its socket with a dull thud. The pain! Oh the pain! But not wanting to frighten the children, I blinked back my tears.

"Wow! Granny, you really can do a cartwheel!" Alison exclaimed, and Melissa beamed at me with a newfound respect for her granny. I vaguely remember mumbling something about how we should always warm up before exercising, and that I had forgotten to do it that day.

The next morning, my husband had to help me get out

of bed. Every joint in my body ached with a vengeance. Warmed-up or not, I knew that yesterday had taught me something. That was Granny's last cartwheel.

Yes, family today is complicated, but I can still visit all my grandchildren, those related to me through blood or by marriage, and be called Granny Nanny. We can still listen and laugh and love and play together because, be it through shared DNA or shared history; that's what family is.

One day in the park the sun was bright, the sky was filled with puffy white clouds, and I heard the birds call to each other. A soft breeze blew just enough, and for a brief moment in time I soared, back arched, legs perfectly straight, toes pointed to the sky, performing Granny's last cartwheel for my granddaughters' pleasure. And they absolutely knew that their granny was cool.

~Nancy Harless
*Chicken Soup to Inspire the Body and Soul*

# Forgiveness
# Tastes Sweet

In the prewar Soviet Union, few Russians would openly call themselves Christians. People disappeared for lesser slips of the tongue.

In their crowded communal apartment in Leningrad, only my grandmother's children could occasionally hear her whispering prayers early in the morning behind closed doors. The state would take away her children and place them in an orphanage if her "religious influence" on them became known. It was in her best interests, and her children's, to keep her faith to herself.

That's why the prewar census worried my grandmother. Everybody was told to report to census centers organized at schools, hospitals and other public places. Many dressed up for such a festive occasion; few people knew that the state used the information collected to prosecute its own citizens.

Grandmother watched her neighbors standing in line, answering the census clerks' questions. Piles of completed questionnaires towered on the desk. Age, education, place of birth, native tongue—religion? "Atheist," people answered without fail. Few of them were truly atheists, and some even ventured to church, making sure no one saw them enter. But they all chose the safe answer.

Finally, my grandmother faced the census clerk. Breathless, she could feel her heart beating in her ears. His questions seemed to last for an hour. She prepared to lie, for her children's sake.

"Religion?"

She looked at the other people in the room. All the census officials needed from her was a statistic, a figure to add to others. God knew the truth—so she wasn't really telling a lie, was she?

"Atheist," she said.

After that, her life changed. Once a cheerful young mother of three, she grew depressed and quiet. In her disturbed mind, she kept asking herself whether she still had a right to pray to God, and whether she still belonged to Him.

World War II started. In September 1941, the Germans surrounded Leningrad and bombed the city's food stores. The 900-day siege of Leningrad had begun. By December, the townspeople's daily rations consisted of four ounces of smelly bread made of bran, starch and sawdust. The winter temperatures fell to a record 40 degrees below zero. City plumbing collapsed and frozen sewage covered apartment floors. There was no water, no food, no heat. People died by the thousands—daily. They passed away in their beds, on the street, in offices and factories. They all quietly shared one silent resolve: not to let the enemy enter their city.

One December evening, as her children fell asleep fully dressed under layers of quilts, my grandmother knew her time had run out, too. She was going to die before morning. By that time, all people had learned the signs of approaching death from starvation—a sudden bout of appetite, bloody diarrhea, lethargy. Grandmother wanted to spare her children the horror of waking up next to their mother's dead body. She desperately needed to survive until the morning. And she knew of only one power capable of stopping death. She prayed.

She didn't think she had a right to ask for God's help. But a mother will do anything to save her children, even face God's wrath. That night, my grandmother screamed her heart out, begging God to let her live until the morning. As she finished praying, she remembered one thing that was said to delay death from starvation: movement. She looked around the room. They had already burned most of the furniture for fuel, but a few pieces remained—a nineteenth-century carved oak bed and mahogany book-cases weighing hundreds of pounds. Now a dying, emaciated woman was going to push and pull them around in a desperate attempt to prolong her life with exercise.

Afraid of waking the kids, my grandmother started with the kitchen. She felt her way through the dark apartment and forced an oak table away from the kitchen window. She barely moved the buffet from the corner. Sacrificing a match, she investigated the floor behind the buffet. Not a crumb of bread. Not even a dead mouse—the towns-people had eaten the mouse population a long time ago.

As the flame was dying out, she noticed something in the corner by the wall. She squeezed her frail body into the crack to check it. She lit another match to see what it was. A brown bag sat in the corner, covered with cobwebs, lost and forgotten since the happy prewar days. She took it out and placed the heavy pack on the kitchen table.

Sugar.

In the morning, she woke her children and gave each

a see-through slice of heavy, moist bread sprinkled with strange white powder.

"What's that, Mom?"

"Eat it. It's cake."

The elder daughter doubted the answer as she remembered fancy cream cakes in the prewar shop windows. But this one tasted a hundred times better.

Their mother laughed with them now, as happy and beautiful as she was before the siege.

Two pounds of sugar can save quite a few people. My grandmother didn't die that winter, and neither did her children, nor most of her family and neighbors. Sometimes, she said, it seemed the brown bag had no bottom at all.

Yet, my grandmother forever grieved that, just like Peter, she'd had to answer the question about whether she knew Christ or not. And she'd answered, "I do not know him."

Grandmother never forgave herself—but she knew God did.

~Elaine Freeland Galaktionova
*Chicken Soup for the Christian Woman's Soul*

# 28

# For My Grandson

*When the world says, "Give up,"*
*Hope whispers, "Try it one more time."*
*~Author Unknown*

I heard a story in church one Sunday about a family of Eastern European refugees, driven from their home by invading soldiers, who decide their only chance of escaping the horrors of war is to make it through the mountains that surround their village. They are sure they will find safety in a neighboring neutral country, if only they can make it over the pass. The grandfather is not well, however, and the days of his mountain hiking are long past.

"Leave me behind," he pleads. "The soldiers won't bother with an old man like me."

"Yes, they will," warns the son. "It will mean your grave."

"We can't leave you behind, Grandpa," implores the daughter. "If you won't go, then we won't either."

The old man finally relents, and the family, which numbers some ten people of varying ages, including the daughter's year-old baby girl, sets off after dark toward the blue-black mountain range in the distance. As they walk along silently, each takes a turn carrying the baby, whose weight makes travel more difficult, as they wind their way up the steep mountain pass.

After several hours, the grandfather sits down on a rock and hangs his head. "Go on without me," he says in a low voice. "I can't make it."

"Yes, you can," his son implores. "You have to."

"No," says the old man. "Leave me here."

"Come on," says the son. "We need you—it's your turn to carry the baby."

The old man looks up and sees the tired faces of the others in the group. He looks at the baby wrapped in a blanket and being carried now in the arms of his thin, thirteen-year-old grandson.

"Yes, of course," says the old man. "It's my turn. Come, give her to me." He stands up and takes the baby in his arms and looks into her small, innocent face. Suddenly, he feels a renewed strength, and a powerful desire to see his family find safety in a land where war is a distant memory.

"Come on," he says with a note of determination in his voice. "Let's go. I'm fine now. I just needed to rest. Let's keep moving." They all headed up the hill again with the grandfather carrying the baby.

The family reached safety that night, and everyone who started the long journey through the mountains finished it, including the grandfather.

~Floyd Wickman and Terri Sjodin
*Chicken Soup for the Father's Soul*

# Chapter 5

# Grand and Great

## Legacies
## through the Generations

*If you want happiness for a lifetime —
help the next generation.
~ Chinese proverb*

# The Silver Sugar Bowl

*Soon I will be an old, white-haired lady, into whose lap some-*
*one places a baby, saying, "Smile, Grandma!" — I, who myself*
*so recently was photographed on my grandmother's lap.*
*~Liv Ullmann*

I was traveling home to New Hampshire after visiting with my grandma and grandpa.

While waiting to go through security at the airport, I noticed an older lady in front of me struggling to open her carry-on bag. Apparently, there was something in her bag that looked "strange" on the X-ray.

After emptying everything onto the table, she pulled out a silver sugar bowl. The security inspector checked it over and then waved her through. As she struggled to re-pack her things, I offered to assist her. We got everything back into her bag, but the unpacking and packing had made her rather upset. I tried to calm her down, and we headed towards the gate.

We looked at our boarding passes and realized that we were sitting next to each other on the plane.

We talked about many things during our three-hour flight, including our families. She told me that she was going to visit her great-grandson. His wife had just given birth to her first great-great-granddaughter, and she just had to get to Vermont to see her before it was "too late."

"You see, I have cancer," she explained, "and I'm not going to be around for much longer. I just want to be able to see my new grandchild and give her parents the silver sugar bowl. It's been in our family for many, many years. My great-great-grandmother gave it to my father more than eighty years ago."

She looked up toward the overhead bin where I had put her bag and the bowl.

"Yes," she continued, "that bowl may be well-worn from all of the loving hands that have polished it over the years, but it's part of our family and it has to be given in person."

As we were talking, I discovered that I actually knew her great-grandson. He was a vendor at the small store I was working in at the time.

Walking off the plane, I thanked her for the most enjoyable conversation.

With a twinkle in her eye, she agreed, "Yes, dear, the time seemed to fly right by."

I carried her bag for her and she held on to my arm as we approached the arrival area. She was met by her great-grandson and her new great-great-granddaughter who was honored with the same name as her great-great-grandmother, Marion.

The luster and shine of the silver sugar bowl seemed to return as the family embraced. Tears streamed down the old woman's cheeks when she saw little Marion's smiling face reflected in the small vessel.

I wished them a wonderful visit, and I didn't see her great-grandson until two or three weeks later. He told me how much his great-grandmother had enjoyed our "little talk." When I asked how she was doing, he told me that sadly she had passed away just one week after she arrived.

Apparently, only days before, she had written down the history of the silver sugar bowl for little Marion in the hope that one day she, too, would pass her family's precious heirloom on to the next generation like her great-great-grandmother Marion had done with her—in person.

~Karen Carr
*Chicken Soup for the Grandparent's Soul*

# 30

# The Seed Jar

Being the youngest of four girls, I usually saw to Grandma Lou's needs at family gatherings. Lucinda Mae Hamish—Grandma Lou for short—was a tall twig of a woman, with a long gray braid and sharp features. She was the undisputed Master Gardener in our family, for she had come of age in the Depression, where she learned to use every old thing twice. And when it was worn out, she'd use it again—in her garden.

When Grandma Lou visited, she brought packets of her own seeds, folded in scraps of envelopes and labeled with instructions. Her handwriting was precise and square. She gave each of us a particular plant; usually tomatoes and carrots and marigolds for my sisters—foolproof sorts of seeds, for my sisters were impatient and neglectful gardeners. But for me, she saved the more fragile varieties.

At the time of my next oldest sister's wedding, Grandma Lou was eighty-four and living alone, still weeding her large beds herself. And as she had for my older sisters' weddings, Grandma Lou gave Jenny a Mason jar layered with seeds from her garden.

Round and round the colorful spiral of seeds curled in the fat-mouthed jar. Heavy beans in rich, deep earth tones held the bottom steady. Next came corn kernels, polished in cheesecloth until they gleamed like gold. Flat seeds of cucumber, squash and watermelon filled the upper reaches, interspersed with the feathery dots of marigolds. At the very top, separated with cheesecloth, were the finer herb seeds of mint and basil. The jar was crowned with a gleaming brass lid and a cheerful ribbon. There was a lifetime supply of seeds pressed into the jar; a whole garden's worth of food for the new couple.

Two years later, Grandma Lou suffered a stroke, which forced her into an assisted-living apartment. And though she was unable to attend my own wedding that year, I was delighted to see a Mason jar among the brightly wrapped gifts at my reception.

But unlike its predecessors, my jar held no graceful pattern of seeds. Instead, it was a haphazard blend, as if all the seeds had been dumped into a pillowcase and then poured into the jar. Even the lid seemed like an afterthought, for it was rusty and well used. But considering Grandma Lou's state of health, I felt blessed that she remembered the gentle tradition at all.

My groom, Mark, found work in the city, and we moved into a small apartment. A garden was all but impossible, so I consoled myself by placing the seed jar in our living room. There it stood as a promise to return to the garden.

Grandma Lou died the year our twins were born. By the time our sons were toddlers, I had moved the seed jar to the top of the refrigerator, where their curious little hands couldn't tip over my treasure.

Eventually we moved to a house, but there still wasn't enough sun in our yard to plant a proper garden. Struggling yet courageous fescue grass vied for what little space there was between the dandelions, and it was all I could do to keep it mowed and occasionally watered.

The boys grew up overnight, much like the weeds I continuously pulled. Soon they were out on their own, and Mark was looking at retirement. We spent our quiet evenings planning for a little place in the country, where Mark could fish and I could have a proper garden.

A year later, Mark was hit by a drunk driver, paralyzing him from the neck down. Our savings went to physical therapy, and Mark gained some weak mobility in his arms and hands. But the simple day-to-day necessities still required a nurse.

Between the hospital visits and the financial worries, I was exhausted. Soon Mark would be released to my care, and at half his size, I knew I wouldn't even be able to lift him into our bed. I didn't know what I would do. We couldn't afford a day nurse, let alone full-time help, and assisted-care apartments were way out of our range.

Left to myself, I was so tired I wouldn't even bother to eat. But Jenny, my sister who lived nearby, visited me daily, forcing me to take a few bites of this or that. One night she arrived with a pan of lasagna, and she chatted cheerfully as we set our places. When she asked about Mark, I broke down in tears, explaining how he'd be home soon and how tight our money was running. She offered her own modest savings—even offered to move in and help take care of him—but I knew Mark's pride wouldn't allow it.

I stared down at my plate, my appetite all but gone. In the quiet that fell between us, despair settled down to dinner like an old friend. Finally I pulled myself together and asked her to help me with the dishes. Jenny nodded and rose to put the leftover lasagna away. As the refrigerator door flopped to a close, the seed jar on top rattled against the wall. Jenny turned at the sound. "What's this?" she asked, and reached for the jar.

Looking up from the sink, I said, "Oh, that's just Grandma Lou's seed jar. We each got one for a wedding present, remember?" Jenny looked at me, then studied the jar.

"You mean you never opened it?" she asked.

"Never had a patch of soil good enough for a garden, I guess."

Jenny tucked the jar in one arm and grabbed my sudsy hand in her other. "Come on!" she said excitedly.

Half dragging me, she went back to the dinner table. It took three tries, but she finally got the lid loose and overturned the jar upon the table. Seeds went bouncing everywhere! "What are you doing?!" I cried, scrambling to catch them. A pile of faded brown and tan seeds slid out around an old, yellow envelope. Jenny plucked it from the pile and handed it to me.

"Open it," she said, with a smile. Inside I found five stock certificates, each for one hundred shares. Reading the company names, our eyes widened in recognition. "Do you have any idea what these are worth by now?" she asked.

I gathered a handful of seeds to my lips and said a silent prayer of thanks to Grandma Lou. She had been tending a garden for me all these years and had pressed a lifetime supply of love into that old Mason jar.

~Dee Berry
*A 5th Portion of Chicken Soup for the Soul*

# 31

# A Journey on Cane River

Growing up, I knew for an absolute fact that no one on the planet was stronger than my mother. So when she told me stories of who she admired growing up, I paid attention. She was clearly in awe of her grandmother Emily. She described her grandmother as iron-willed and devilish, physically beautiful and demanding of beauty from others, determined to make her farmhouse in central Louisiana a fun place to be on Sundays when family gathered, and fanatical and unforgiving about the responsibilities generated from family ties.

My mother drew parallels between her grandmother Emily and Jacqueline Kennedy. "Emily was class," she would say, describing her physical attributes: her long, graceful neck, her tiny, tiny waist. "Emily was class, Emily was elegant, just like Jackie."

How my mother came by this first-name familiarity with the president's wife I couldn't begin to imagine, but as I grew older and listened carefully to other stories about my great-grandmother Emily, that was the least of my bafflement. The pieces wouldn't fit. On the one hand, Emily, refined, graceful, elegant, soft-spoken, classy. On the other,

Emily, a woman from the backwoods of Louisiana, possibly born a slave right before the Civil War, unapologetic about dipping snuff, buzzed on her homemade muscadine wine each and every day. Not exactly "just like Jackie."

Emily intrigued me and the puzzle of this woman simmered on the back burner of my conscious mind for decades, undoubtedly triggering questions about who I was as well. Not until 1995 did the search really start to heat up, for the simple reason that I was no longer gainfully employed and suddenly had massive quantities of time on my hands. I had been a corporate executive, vice president and general manager of Sun Microsystems in Silicon Valley, when I decided to change my life by stepping off into the great unknown. I quit my job. Not a sabbatical. No looking back or second-guessing. Just walked away.

"When does your new job start?" asked my mother. Actually, what I heard was, "How could you possibly walk away from a good job you got only because I sacrificed to put you through school, and by the way, I spent fourteen hours in labor to get you here in the first place." She didn't really say the last part, at least not out loud, but that is what it felt like she said.

"I refuse to take a job for at least a year," I replied, trying to sound confident. "I need to listen to the silence, find the inner me, re-engineer myself outside the confines of corporate America."

My mother had no patience with this drivel. "Who's going to pay you to do that?"

"I've saved enough for a year or two."

"Can you get your old job back?"

"I don't want my old job. It's gone. There's something else I'm supposed to be doing," I said. "I just don't know what it is yet."

"You're supposed to have a job."

I let the silence build. For some things, there is no response.

"So what are you going to do for the next year?" she pushed.

Here was the critical moment where a persuasive argument could win her to my side, put her mind to rest, reassure her of my ability to adapt.

"I don't know," I said, which unbeknownst to me would become my mantra of the next few years.

I couldn't explain it because I didn't understand it, but I felt compelled to leave my job and research my ancestry. Gradually, and then overwhelmingly, I slipped into the dark, shadowy, addictive parallel universe of genealogy. Entire days disappeared from my life when I entered the bowels of the National Archives to pore over census records. Secretive trips to Louisiana to chase down fragile leads in local courthouses, newspaper archives and libraries followed. I began to lie to my friends, telling them I was "just relaxing, taking it easy, enjoying my newfound free time."

Meanwhile, the relentless search for dead relatives consumed weeks and then months. I lost all sense of shame, carrying tape recorders into nursing homes to interview people who couldn't remember what they had for breakfast but could spin sharp tales of events from eighty years ago. I craved one more fact, one more connection, one more story, but one was never enough. I had to have more, to know more about the people in my family, dead for a hundred years. I was hooked.

So hooked, I traced my mother's line to a place in Louisiana called Cane River, a unique area that before the Civil War housed one of the largest and wealthiest collections of free people of color in the United States. I decided to hire a specialist on Cane River culture, a genealogist who could read the Creole French records that I could not. The task I assigned her was to find my great-grandmother Emily's grandmother.

"Let's get the facts we know on the table, starting with her name," the genealogist said.

"I don't know." (The mantra echoed.)

"No first name or last name?"

"No."

"Okay. Was she from Cane River?"

"Maybe," I said encouragingly. "Her daughter was."

"Okay. Was she slave or free?"

"I don't know. I can't find any trace of her in the free census records, but I'm not sure."

The genealogist seemed doubtful, but she took the job anyway. I was, after all, paying her by the hour just to look.

No job, no paycheck, so how long could this foolish obsession to find my unnamed great-great-great-great-grandmother last? Turns out, for eighteen months, by the hour, until the genealogist recovered a document that banished any doubt I would write a historical novel based on the characters revealed. In a collection of ten thousand unindexed local records written in badly preserved Creole French, she found the bill of sale for my great-great-great-great-grandmother Elisabeth, who was sold in 1850 in Cane River, Louisiana, for eight hundred dollars.

I wondered whether my great-great-great-great-grandmother spent as much time envisioning her descendants as I had spent envisioning her life. I held the bill of sale in my hands, awed and humbled, curious what any one of the women who came before me, born slaves, would think of one of their own having the opportunity to become an executive at a Fortune 500 company. Could any of them have even dreamed of that possibility in 1850 as they changed hands at auction from one property owner to another? I wondered what they would think of the world we live in today. What would Elisabeth have thought of my quitting my job and spending far more than her selling price to find any evidence she had existed?

At this point, I had no choice. I had to write their story and document their lives—my history. They were, after all, real flesh-and-blood people. I pieced their lives together the best I could from over a thousand documents uncovered in my years of research, re-creating what life must have been like for them during the 1800s and 1900s. The result was *Cane River*, a novelized account covering one hundred years in America's history and following four generations of Creole slave women in Cane River, Louisiana, as they struggled to keep their families intact through the dark days of slavery, the Civil War, Reconstruction, and the pre-civil rights era of the Jim Crow South.

The rest—the dog-work of writing the novel, finding an agent, finding a publisher and doing the book tour—was as grueling and exciting as discovering my ancestry. Within days of being sent to several publishers, Warner Books purchased the novel. Once again, my family was on the auction block but this time in a more satisfying way, honoring instead of dishonoring. Things had certainly changed over the last hundred and fifty years. I wished I could show my great-great-great-great-grandmother Elisabeth the price our family commanded this time.

Three months after the publication of *Cane River*, the phone rang as I was packing for yet another book-signing trip.

"Hello, this is Oprah."

"Yeah, right!" I said, wondering which of my friends was playing this cruel practical joke. I waited for laughter that never came.

"This is Oprah," the distinct and ever-so-familiar voice said again.

As recognition registered, I mustered my most professional corporate voice in the midst of my total embarrassment and surprise.

"Hello, Ms. Winfrey. What can I do for you today?" My heart pounded so hard I could hardly hear what followed.

She had called to tell me she selected my novel for her book club, which ultimately led to *Cane River* spending seventeen weeks on the New York Times bestseller list and a readership broader than I dared dream.

My mother has conceded once, and only once, that quitting my job wasn't as disastrous as she had feared. But she still thinks I should be out interviewing for a corporate position, as a backup. The women in my family are strong, and strength is a mother's legacy. Worry, on the other hand, now that's a mother's prerogative.

~Lalita Tademy
*Chicken Soup for the African American Soul*

# 32

# A Tradition in the Waiting

*The art of giving presents is to give something which others cannot buy for themselves.*
~A.A. Milne

Tucked snugly in Gram's bed, I watched Sunday morning dawn. I loved the way the light sidled in around her vinyl shades to dance with the weightless dust that floated in its path before falling, silently, upon Grandma's braided rug. I could smell fried bologna and eggs and knew Gram would soon collect me for breakfast.

I crawled out of the bed to explore.

Across the room stood her dresser whose drawers, I knew, were full of cosmetics and perfumes and a jar of cold cream all mingling into the fragrant scent of Gram. But my attention focused on the unassuming jewelry box perched on top. Standing on tiptoe, I lifted it to the floor and knelt before it.

As quietly as my clumsy young hands would allow, I slid the top off the box and worked my way through all the things I deemed less valuable: bangles and baubles; costume jewelry; an old photo of a much younger Pop on his Harley.... And then I found it—the small blue box that seemed to call to me on my Sunday morning visits.

Despite its lackluster plastic facade, it contained the most beautiful ring I had ever seen. Reverently, I took the delicate circle from its nest of blue velour and slid it on my finger. Turning my hand this way and that, I admired its sparkle and pretended I was a bride.

I counted the small, crudely cut diamonds surrounding the large solitaire. Eight little ones circled one big one. Nine diamonds that looked just like a crystal flower. My young eyes didn't recognize the handcrafted workmanship. They didn't appreciate the intricate filigree of the band. But I saw it was worn and very old, and I could almost hear it whisper romantic stories from the past.

Gram found me gazing dreamily into her large mirror.

To my surprise, she didn't scold. Instead, she gathered me back to her bed.

"Sweetheart," she explained, "your grandfather gave me this ring as an engagement gift."

My eyes grew big. I knew it had a story. Listening intently as Gram continued, I reveled in the rosy glow of yesteryear.

"It was a tradition in his family for generations. A father would pass this ring to his eldest son when he decided to marry. And he, in turn, would pass it to his firstborn son."

From son to eldest son. Wow. I knew the ring represented the past—our family's past. It connected me backward through time to my ancestry and heritage. It told me something of who I was and who we were.

But Gram wasn't finished.

"...However, your uncle seems quite content to remain a bachelor. So, I'll make a deal with you." She leaned closer and whispered, "If he's still single by the time you get married, the ring is yours."

Mine!

"Now if you don't mind," she slipped the ring off my finger and back into its soft nest, "the eggs are getting cold."

Thirteen years passed.

At last, and never having forgotten Gram's promise, I was ready to announce my own engagement. Although my uncle remained single, it felt strange to ask for the heirloom ring. But Gram saw that I didn't have to.

As she hugged me in congratulation, Gram pressed the well-remembered box into my hand and smiled.

"Now you don't have to make believe."

~Lorraine Cheeka
*Chicken Soup for the Bride's Soul*

# 33

# Your Legacy

*Each of us can make a difference in the life of another.*
*~George Bush*

I had a philosophy professor who was the quintessential eccentric philosopher. His disheveled appearance was highlighted by a well-worn tweed sport coat and poor-fitting thick glasses, which often rested on the tip of his nose. Every now and then, as most philosophy professors do, he would go off on one of those esoteric and existential "what's the meaning of life" discussions. Many of those discussions went nowhere, but there were a few that really hit home. This was one of them:

"Respond to the following questions by a show of hands," my professor instructed.

"How many of you can tell me something about your parents?" Everyone's hand went up.

"How many of you can tell me something about your grandparents?" About three-fourths of the class raised their hands.

"How many of you can tell me something about your great-grandparents?" Two out of sixty students raised their hands.

"Look around the room," he said. "In just two short generations hardly any of us even know who our own great-grandparents were. Oh sure, maybe we have an old, tattered photograph tucked away in a musty cigar box or know the classic family story about how one of them walked five miles to school barefoot. But how many of us really know who they were, what they thought, what they were proud of, what they were afraid of, or what they dreamed about? Think about that. Within three generations our ancestors are all but forgotten. Will this happen to you?

"Here's a better question. Look ahead three generations. You are long gone. Instead of you sitting in this room, now it's your great-grandchildren. What will they have to say about you? Will they know about you? Or will you be forgotten, too?

"Is your life going to be a warning or an example? What legacy will you leave? The choice is yours. Class dismissed."

Nobody rose from their seat for a good five minutes.

~Tony D'Angelo
*Chicken Soup for the College Soul*

# Grandma's Pearls

*When the heart grieves over what it has lost,*
*the spirit rejoices over what it has left.*
~Sufi Epigram

Two weeks after Grandpa died, Grandma came to live with us. Every day, she sat in a rocker in the living room, staring out the window and fingering a small red pouch that she kept with her always. I would try to joke with her and make her laugh like she used to, but she would just nod sadly and continue rocking.

One day, I noticed Grandma looking out the window. I stood up, stretched my cramped legs and walked over to her. "What are you watching, Grandma?" I asked.

Grandma's head jerked, like she was waking up from a nap. "Nothing, really. Just looking into the past."

I didn't really know what to say. Grandma stared at me, seeming to really see me for the first time in the weeks since she'd moved in. I pointed to her lap. "Why do you keep that red bag with you?"

Grandma's skinny, bent fingers moved lovingly along the bright velvet. "Everything I ever learned is in this bag," she said.

I pulled up a stool and sat by her knees. "What do you mean?"

"I'll show you." Grandma gently pulled the worn ribbons that held the bag closed, then reached in and removed a strand of large, silvery-white pearls.

"It's beautiful!" I said. Leaning closer, I realized the huge pearls were strung on a slender length of leather.

"Your great-great-grandmother gave this to my mother, who gave it to me." Her eyes glistened. "I remember it like it was yesterday. She gave me this piece of leather, with one pearl strung on it. She called it a pearl of wisdom. She gave it to me because I ignored the stories everyone was telling about a man who had moved into town with his two daughters. I made friends with the girls, even though I lost my old friends for awhile. And she gave me this one when I didn't ask Jim Redmond to the Sadie Hawkins dance, even though I was terribly in love with him, because my best friend Penny wanted to ask him.

"She gave me another pearl each time she felt I'd done something special, learned some kind of lesson, or had done something she felt was wise."

"So, every pearl is a pearl of wisdom," I whispered, running my hand over the cool spheres.

"That's right," she said, slipping the pearls back into their bag. She pulled the ribbons tightly and smiled at me. "Your grandfather gave me the last one, on our fiftieth wedding anniversary, because he said marrying him was the wisest thing I'd ever done." We both laughed.

Grandmother died that fall. After the funeral, my mother gave me a round jewelry box of polished dark wood, with cut glass set in the top. "Your grandmother wanted you to have this."

I lifted the lid. Inside the box rested the red velvet pouch with a note written in my grandmother's crooked scrawl. "I should have given these to your mother a long time ago, but I always felt like I still had things to learn. I hope you'll keep these pearls safe, and continue the tradition with your own child."

Angry and sad, I stuffed the box with its contents into the very back of my dresser's bottom drawer. All the wisdom in the world didn't keep you from dying, I thought.

Three years later, I was fourteen. The last thing I wanted was to start high school with glasses so thick you couldn't see my eyes. I wanted contacts, but my parents couldn't afford them.

I mowed every lawn in the neighborhood that summer. I pulled weeds, painted garage doors and washed cars. Two weeks before school started, I picked up the contacts I had been able to order with the money I had earned.

I took the hated glasses and stuffed them in the very back of my bottom dresser drawer, and there was the box. I took it out and opened the lid. Smiling, I untied the leather and let all but one of the pearls fall into the pouch. "I'm not going to continue the tradition with my own child," I whispered, "I'll continue with me."

I had worked hard for something I wanted instead of expecting someone else to hand it to me. I added one more pearl, retied the ends and put the box on my dresser, where it should have been all along.

In those few moments, I felt I had learned something important. In my memories, and in those pearls, my grandmother and her wisdom lived on.

~Catherine Adams
*Chicken Soup for the Preteen Soul 2*

# 35

# Grandma's Surprise Party

Aneon envelope glowed between magazine circulars. Hmm, a letter, I thought. Anything other than junk mail and bills in the mailbox was rare these days, since most of my communications came by telephone and e-mail.

I examined the square envelope. The writing was unmistakably Grandma Caryle's, but why would she send a card? My birthday wasn't for another two months.

What's she up to this time? I wondered.

I ripped open the envelope as I walked back to the house. Inside was an adolescent-looking party invitation with the words "Happy Birthday" on the front. Opening the card, I read:

*You're invited*
*To a surprise party*
*At Grandma Caryle's house*
*On August 9 from 2-4 P.M.*

Laughing out loud, I ran to the house. My eccentric grand-mother always liked celebrating. In fact, her birthdays usually lasted all month, with many lunches, dinners and visits with friends and family members.

I dialed her number.

"Hi, Grandma, I got your invitation in the mail just now," I said.

"Oh!" she exclaimed in an exaggerated tone. "Did you call to RSVP?"

I giggled at her mock coyness. "Of course I'll be there. But it's customary that someone other than yourself host a surprise party when you're the guest of honor," I teased. "After all, you won't be surprised if you plan the party."

Grandma paused. "Well, you know how I love parties. I'm sure we'll have lots of surprises," she replied. "And if we don't, I promise to act surprised."

We both laughed and hung up the phone. Grandma had never planned a birthday celebration for herself and certainly never a surprise party, but then she'd never turned seventy-five years old either.

During the next few weeks, I tried to think of ways I could make Grandma's birthday special.

"Let me bake a cake," I offered.

"I already ordered one," she answered.

"What about decorations? May I decorate your house?"

"I'm using potted chrysanthemums," Grandma said. "Less to clean up, and I can plant them in my flower beds afterward."

Since she was planning the entire event, I wanted to do something extra to add an element of surprise. I decided to write on her driveway with sidewalk chalk and bring helium balloons. That ought to surprise Grandma, I thought.

Finally, Grandma's birthday arrived. I called that morning and sang "Happy Birthday." After the song, I playfully asked, "Are you surprised?"

"Oh, yes," Grandma said with glee.

Thirty minutes before the party, I chalked "Happy Birthday, Caryle" on her driveway. I attached balloons to the front yard trees and mailbox. Gifts and more balloons were unloaded from my car, and I rang the doorbell.

"Surprise," I shouted as she opened the door.

Grandma laughed. I put her gifts on the hall table and started into the dining area with the balloons. We always celebrated birthdays around the dining room table.

"Don't go in there," shouted Grandma as she blocked the doorway.

"I thought I'd tie the balloons to the dining room chairs."

"Take them into the living room. I don't want you to see the cake just yet," she instructed. "After all, this is a surprise party!"

Perplexed, I obeyed.

Soon, Grandma's best friend, sister-in-law, niece, step-daughter, daughter-in-law and her other granddaughter, my sister Shelby, arrived. We sat in the living room, talked and snacked from party trays.

"Where's Dad?" I asked. My father, her only child, was conspicuously absent.

"Not invited," she replied. "It's a girls-only party."

We all laughed.

"Say, Caryle, I could see your yard decorations from down the block," remarked Aunt Gay.

Grandma looked confused.

"Come see," I said, gently taking her arm. We walked outside.

"Are you surprised?" I asked.

"Oh, yes!" answered Grandma.

Back inside, someone suggested opening gifts. Grandma

sat down, and Judy, her daughter-in-law, handed over a gift bag.

"Open this one first," she ordered.

Inside was a rhinestone tiara.

"You're the birthday queen," proclaimed Judy.

Grandma's eyes glowed with excitement as she unwrapped the packages. Inside, I felt regretful that I'd never thought to throw her a party and that this one wasn't really a surprise.

Once the gifts were opened, Grandma announced, "We have cake in the dining room." She got up and led the way.

"That was abrupt," remarked my sister. "She must be hungry."

We filed into the dining room. On the table was a quarter sheet cake with the word "Surprise" on it and seven small boxes of various sizes.

We took our seats and Grandma began. "As you know, today is my seventy-fifth birthday and I've invited you here to celebrate with me. For many years, you've been a part of my life. I love you and although I'm not planning to die anytime soon, I want you to have something to remember me by."

We sat speechless.

"This is not a surprise party for me, but for you."

Grandma gave each of us a box.

"Stacy, you go first," she instructed.

I removed the lid. Inside was a diamond ring that I'd seen on Grandma's finger.

"It belonged to your great-aunt Hazel," she said quietly. "I inherited it when she died twenty-five years ago. I want you to have it."

Tears pooled in my eyes.

"Are you surprised?" mimicked Grandma in an attempt to lighten the mood.

"I thought sidewalk chalking was a big surprise," I said, hugging her neck. "Thank you so much. You're amazing."

On that, her seventy-fifth birthday, Grandma gave away her wedding ring set, her mother's strand of pearls, and several heirloom rings and bracelets. As each box was opened, she quipped, "Are you surprised?"

And indeed, we all were. Not only was the party a surprise for us, but a reminder of her generosity and love. Every time I wear that diamond ring, I think of Grandma Caryle and the legacy of fun I inherited from her.

Surprise!

~Stephanie "Stacy" Thompson
*Chicken Soup for the Grandma's Soul*

# Chapter 6

# Grand and Great

## Love
## Across the Generations

*Nobody can do for little children what grandparents do.*
*Grandparents sort of sprinkle stardust over*
*the lives of little children.*
*~Alex Haley*

# A Dance with My Grandmother

*The capacity to care is the thing which gives life*
*its deepest meaning and significance.*
*~Pablo Casals*

When I married my wife, Martha, it was the most beautiful day of my life. We were young and healthy, tanned and handsome. Every picture taken that day shows us smiling, hugging and kissing. We were the perfect hosts, never cranky or tired, never rolling our eyes at pinched cheeks or embarrassing stories from friends and loved ones. We were as happy and carefree as the porcelain couple on our towering wedding cake.

Halfway through the reception, in between the pictures and the cake and the garter and the bouquet, my grandmother tapped me gently on the shoulder. I hugged her in a flurry of other well-wishers and barely heard her whisper, "Will you dance with me, sweetheart?"

"Sure, Nonny," I said, smiling and with the best of intentions, even as some out-of-town guests pulled me off in their direction. An hour later my grandmother tried again. And again I blew her off, smiling and reaching for her with an outstretched hand but letting some old college buddies place a fresh beer there instead, just before dragging me off for some last-minute wedding night advice!

Finally, my grandmother gave up.

There were kisses and hugs and rice and tin cans and then my wife and I were off on our honeymoon. A nagging concern grew in the back of my mind as we wined and dined our way down to Miami for a weeklong cruise and then back again when it was over.

When we finally returned to our new home, a phone message told us our pictures were waiting at the photographer's. We unpacked slowly and then moseyed on down to pick them up. Hours later, after we had examined every one with fond memories, I held one out to reflect upon in private.

It was a picture of two happy guests, sweaty and rowdy during the inevitable "chicken dance." But it wasn't the grinning couple I was focusing on. There, in the background, was my grandmother, Nonny.

I had spotted her blue dress right away. Her simple pearls. The brand-new hairdo I knew she'd gotten special for that day, even though she was on a fixed income. I saw her scuffed shoes and a run in her stocking and her tired hands clutching at a well-used handkerchief.

In the picture, my grandmother was crying. And I didn't think they were tears of joy. That nagging concern that had niggled at me the entire honeymoon finally solidified: I had never danced with my grandmother.

I kissed my wife on the cheek and drove to my grandmother's tiny apartment a few miles away. I knocked on the door and saw that her new perm was still fresh and tight, but her tidy blue dress had been replaced with her usual faded housedress.

A feeble smile greeted me, weak arms wrapped around

me and, naturally, Nonny wanted to know all about our honeymoon. Instead, all I could do was apologize.

"I'm sorry I never danced with you, Nonny," I said honestly, sitting next to her on the threadbare couch. "It was a very special day and that was the only thing missing from making it perfect."

Nonny looked me in the eye and said something I'll never forget: "Nonsense, dear. You've danced enough with this old broad in her lifetime. Remember all those Saturday nights you spent here when you were a little boy? I'd put *The Lawrence Welk Show* on and you'd dance on top of my fuzzy slippers and laugh the whole time. Why, I don't know any other grandmother who has memories like that. I'm a lucky woman.

"And while you were being the perfect host and making all of your guests feel so special, I sat back and watched you and felt nothing but pride. That's what a wedding is, honey. Something old, something new. Something borrowed, something blue.

"Well, this OLD woman, who was wearing BLUE, watched you dance with your beautiful NEW bride, and I knew I had to give you up, because I had you so many years to myself, but I could only BORROW you until you found the woman of your dreams—and now you have each other and I can rest easy in the knowledge that you're happy."

Both of our tears covered her couch that day—the day that Nonny taught me what it meant to be a grandson—as well as a husband.

And after my lesson, I asked Nonny for that wedding dance.

Unlike me, she didn't refuse....

~Rusty Fischer
*Chicken Soup for the Every Mom's Soul*

# 37

# A Grandpa's Love

*A grandfather is someone with silver in his hair
and gold in his heart.*
*~Author Unknown*

I stared from the deck of my hotel room, intrigued. An older gentleman was assisting a young girl as she struggled to walk down the beach. He must be her grandfather, I thought. Somehow, I was drawn to the drama of the twosome, and winced as she fell. The graying man helped her to her feet, and she continued painstakingly plodding through the sand.

That evening, I ate in the hotel restaurant, and watched as the same young girl proceeded to get up from the table and reach for her walker. She grasped it firmly with both hands, and, leaning heavily, she made her way out of the restaurant, smiling as she went.

As I sipped my coffee in the lobby the next morning, I noticed a sign tacked to the announcement board. "Special Olympics Relays." Ah, I thought, that must be what the walking lessons are about.

Over the next three days, I watched as the grandfather patiently worked with his student. "You can do it, Sweetheart. Let's get up and try again." And at this encouragement, she would struggle again to her feet.

On the morning of the Olympics, as I visited with friends in the lobby, a beautiful bouquet of roses was delivered to the front desk. The girl soon appeared for her delivery, her face brightening at the sight. She smiled as she read the card.

As she walked away, the card slipped from her fingers and she continued down the hallway. I stepped quickly to retrieve it, glancing at the handwritten words as I hurried after her,

> *To my sweet Elizabeth—you have been the greatest encouragement to my heart these last few days. I love you and am proud of you. Win or lose, you will always be my little miracle from God.*
>
> *Love, Grandpa.*

She had disappeared around the corner, so I put the card in my pocket to give to her later.

Now attached to the little girl and her grandpa, I felt compelled to watch her Olympic event—a quarter-mile. She definitely was a fighter. I cheered as she crossed the finish line—second place. She smiled as she stood on the awards platform, and a tear slipped down her cheek as the medal was placed around her neck. She told the crowd, "I especially want to thank my grandpa for believing in me when I had no one else."

I found her later, and returned her card. I said, "Congratulations!" As we talked, she revealed that she and her parents were hit by a drunk driver three years prior. She was the only survivor. Her grandfather shook my hand and said, "By the grace of God alone, this little girl is alive and able to accomplish what she did today."

Elizabeth smiled and hugged her grandpa. "Everyone gave up hope that I would ever walk again. My grandpa was the only one who didn't."

~Scot Thurman
*Chicken Soup for the Grandparent's Soul*

# 38

# Love Bugs

*Look around for a place to sow a few seeds.*
~Henry Van Dyke

My father-in-law leaned against his garden hoe and in his gentle voice warned, "If you don't do something with those bugs, you won't have any potatoes!" It was the summer of 1981, and we had just planted our first garden after moving to the farm from the big city of Toronto. Not having any gardening experience, I'd thought I could just plant and harvest. I didn't know there would be many long hours spent in the hot summer sun before we would reap what we had sown.

Standing at the edge of the garden, looking down those long rows of potatoes, I felt very inadequate beside my father-in-law who had been a farmer all of his life. I wondered, Should I tell him I know nothing about getting rid of potato bugs?

As if reading my thoughts, he said he would buy me a bag of potato bug poison when he went to town, and all I would have to do is dust the potato leaves with the powder. It wasn't long before I saw his truck coming back down our lane. Though I had seen him dusting in his own garden in his shirtsleeves, I read the instructions and precautions on the bag and donned long pants, a long-sleeved shirt, rubber boots, gloves, cap and mask. Up and down the rows I went on a hot summer afternoon dusting the rows with white powder. A week later the bugs were just as bad. We offered our two small sons a penny for each bug they could pick. After they filled a gallon ice-cream bucket, their interest dwindled. So again I went through the same dusting procedure over and over all summer, wondering, Why did God make potato bugs?

After we harvested our first crop of potatoes, I forgot all about the bugs. That is until planting time came around again. How I dreaded the idea of putting poison on our potatoes—organic gardening is what we had been dreaming about in the city. The second summer I decided it was time to tell Grandpa I would do away with dusting the potatoes forever. I took my gallon ice-cream bucket to the garden and began picking bugs.

I was surprised when one morning Grampie joined me there, with his own bucket and a shingle. "It will be easier this way," he told me. "Just tap the leaves gently and the bugs will fall into the bucket." Together we went up and down the rows. When I went back to the garden after supper, Grampie was there again. When we finished our garden we went to his garden. The next morning I looked out the kitchen window wondering if he would come again. Sure enough, I saw his truck coming down the lane. I met him at the garden, and with our buckets and shingles, we started down the rows. As we began our chore, Grampie began telling me a story.

"I remember when..." and with each row we walked, Grampie told me stories of the river, stories of how the Lawsons settled here, stories of his mother and father, stories of what it was like when he was a boy and how farming was in days gone by. Every now and then one of us would stop, wipe the sweat from our brows and say, "What good are these bugs anyway?" and then continue on.

Each gardening season, Grampie and I continued picking potato bugs. As his steps grew slower it took twice as long to finish a row but the, "I remember when..." stories became even more precious.

It wasn't long before my daughter Melanie joined us in our quest to rid the garden of potato bugs, and even at the age of eighty, there were not many days that Grampie didn't join us in the potato rows. One day Melanie asked, "Grampie, why did God make potato bugs?"

He replied, "I don't know, Melanie. They are nothing but a bother."

Then came the summer his cancer progressed. One evening as I went alone to his garden, he called from his lawn chair. I left my bucket in the rows and joined him at the front of the house. The river that he loved so much was calm and peaceful that evening and we sat for a long time as he told me still more river stories. We wondered where we would sell our beans tomorrow and discussed those useless potato bugs.

The next summer Melanie and I were alone in the garden.

Early mornings and late evenings found us there planning our days, wondering where she would spend her gardening money and daydreaming about the mountains. Every now and then one of us would say, "Remember when Grampie..." and more often than not, we would straighten our tired backs and scorn the potato bugs.

By the summer of 1999, Melanie was in Vancouver. I stood at the edge of the garden alone. With bucket and shingle in hand I started down the first row, and from days gone by I heard, "I remember when...." Only now I have my own memory stories. I remembered days spent with

Grampie as we formed a rare and wonderful friendship, and days spent with Melanie as she daydreamed about life and the mountains.

I've planted my first garden of the new century, and this morning I start on the potato rows with a small boy at my side. My four-year-old nephew Jordan is visiting from Sherbrooke, Quebec. He only speaks French and understands very little of what I say to him, but he understands that I love him very deeply. So when I hand him a bucket and a shingle, he anticipates that Auntie has something exciting in store for him. We start down the first row, Jordan on one side and me on the other. As he reaches across the row with wonder in his eyes, he tucks his small hand in mine. I spot a bug and drop it in his bucket. He looks up surprised and chatters away in French. I explain to him in English why we have to pick these bugs. I continue to find more bugs and drop them in his bucket. He is now intent on finding some for himself — his little head close to the plants, searching. We continue down the rows, delighting in his ability to find as many bugs as he can. He bursts with excitement over all those bugs in his bucket — and so do I.

I finally know why God made potato bugs.

~Darlene Lawson
*Chicken Soup for the Christian Woman's Soul*

# 39

# The Heart Remembers

*Accept the pain, cherish the joys, resolve the regrets;*
*then can come the best of benedictions —*
*"If I had my life to live over, I'd do it all the same."*
*~Joan McIntosh*

"The mother she remembers is the mother she will become."

These words filled my head on the morning I became a mother for the first time. And as they placed Kaley in my arms, a warm, wriggling bundle with wide eyes, I'd vowed to myself that I was going to be the very best mother, the kind of mother that I did remember: loving, patient, ever-calm and placid. My whole life had pulsed with love, and as I stroked my baby's tiny head, felt her turn her face to nuzzle my finger, I vowed to her, "You will know only love, little one. Only that."

I remembered the quote again two weeks later, at 3:00 A.M. as I paced in circles with my screaming, colicky newborn in my arms. At that moment, however, the words were hardly a comfort. After all, what baby would want to remember me as I was then — sleep deprived, anxious, patience worn as sharp and thin as a razor blade.

And despite my earlier vow, I sure wasn't feeling love. I wasn't feeling much of anything. I was numb, weak with fatigue, trying to do everything by myself even though my husband and mother were asleep just down the hall. I shushed Kaley and cradled her closer, but she just kicked and flailed and wailed even louder. Suddenly I couldn't stop the tears. I sank to the floor in the darkened living room, lay her in my lap and sobbed into my hands.

I don't know how long I stayed that way, but even though it seemed like hours, it couldn't have been more than a few minutes. Through a haze of tears, I saw the light go on in the hallway, silhouetting the figure of my mother as she shrugged into her housecoat. Soon I felt her hand on my shoulder.

"Give me that baby," she said.

I didn't argue. Defeated, I just handed the screaming bundle over and crawled to the sofa, where I curled into a tight ball.

My mother murmured into Kaley's ear, and with an ease borne of decades of practice, shifted her to her shoulder. Eventually the crying turned to sniffles, the sniffles to hiccups, and in half an hour, I heard only muffled baby snores.

I felt relief but no real peace. What kind of mother couldn't calm her own child? What kind of mother didn't even want to try? I watched Mama ease into the rocking chair, watched her start the slow rhythm that I knew had lulled me to sleep on countless nights, and all I felt was a sense of desperate, exhausted failure.

"I'm a terrible mother," I muttered.

"No, you're not."

"You don't understand." Fresh tears thickened at the corner of my eyes. "Right now, I don't even like her. My own baby."

My mom laughed softly. "Well, she hasn't been very

likable today, now has she? But you stayed with her through it all. You've bounced her, rocked her, walked her. And when none of that worked, you just held her and kept her close."

I sat up and wrapped my arms tightly around my knees. "But all I feel inside is frustration and anger and impatience. What kind of mother is that?"

My mom didn't reply immediately. She just looked down at the sleeping baby in her arms. But her face grew thoughtful, and when she spoke, her voice had a faraway, wistful quality. "I remember all those," she said softly. "Especially the last one. After you were born, I used to pray for patience. Cried and begged for it." She looked at me, a half-smile on her face. "Still haven't gotten it yet."

I couldn't believe what I was hearing. "But, Mama, that's the thing I remember most about you. No matter what, you never lost your cool. You somehow managed to keep everything going all at once."

She had. No matter how many brownies needed baking at the last minute, no matter how many science project posters needed coloring, my mother always came through. Always calm. Always serene. As a nurse, she worked irregular hours, but at every play and every recital I was in, even if she didn't make the opening curtain, I could always count on seeing a familiar figure in white slipping into the darkened auditorium.

This was the mother I remembered, the mother who made every moment matter. The mother who never behaved the way I felt right then.

"I could always count on you," I said. "Always."

But to my surprise, she rolled her eyes. "That may be the way you remember it, but all I remember is being pulled in seven directions at once. You and your brother, your father, the people at work. They all needed me, but I never had enough time to be there for everybody."

"But you were always there!"

She shook her head. "Not like I wanted to be, not as often or for as long. And so I prayed for patience, so that I could make the best of the time we did have. But you know what they say. God doesn't send you patience. He just sends you moments that make you practice being patient, over and over again."

She looked down at Kaley. "Moments like this one."

I watched the two of them, and then suddenly I understood: Memories don't rest in our brains, which are apt to record the details wrong anyway, but in our hearts. My mom and I didn't recall my childhood in exactly the same way, but we did share the one thing that did matter.

We both remembered the love.

I moved from the sofa and sat at the foot of the rocking chair. We stayed that way for a while—my mother, my daughter and I. And even though the crying started again at sunrise, for that golden, still moment, as I sat at my mother's feet and lay my hand on the soft hair of my daughter, I breathed a silent "thank you."

If Kaley somehow remembers that night, I hope she will recall only the instinctive love that kept me by her side through it all.

~Tina Whittle
*Chicken Soup for the Mother's Soul 2*

# 40

# Divine Order

*You cannot teach children to take care of themselves unless
you let them try. They will make mistakes;
and out of these mistakes comes wisdom.*
~Henry Ward Beecher

I answered the phone at my office. It was my oldest daughter, Heidi. "Mom, can you meet me at Barbara's this afternoon?"

Barbara was a counselor my girls and I had seen periodically over the years, often to deal with our individual issues over the conflicts between their father and me — we had divorced years earlier. So when Heidi requested a visit to Barbara's office, I didn't think anything of it.

When I arrived, Heidi was already seated on the couch. Barbara sat in her chair opposite Heidi, and I parked myself in a chair next to the couch.

Barbara delved right in and asked Heidi, "Why are we here today?"

I looked over at Heidi. Her face reddened, she choked up and a single tear glided down her cheek. "I have something to tell my mother, and I'm too afraid to do it alone."

In that instant, I knew. I was about to hear the one thing many parents fear when raising a teenage daughter. I slid next to her on the couch, and asked, "Are you pregnant?"

Heidi was born on New Year's Eve, the only baby girl in the nursery. She was a born performer and loved to sing, dance and act—anything that involved entertaining. A personable, beautiful girl, she had many friends growing up, excelled in her classes and had big dreams of becoming an actress.

As she approached her seventeenth year, Heidi started skipping school, abandoned the friends she had and began to hang around a crowd of kids I didn't approve of. My bright and charming little girl became distant, depressed and unmotivated. I became distraught over this sudden change, and found it increasingly difficult to deal with. As a single mother, it was hard enough raising three beautiful daughters, but this new phase of Heidi's life proved more than challenging. When a new boy showed up in her life, I sensed trouble. And when I sat in the counselor's office that afternoon, I knew I had milliseconds to say and do the right thing to get my daughter back.

Heidi burst into tears, nodding yes when I asked her if she was pregnant. Putting my arm around her, I looked her square in the eyes and pronounced, "I'll do whatever you need me to do... that's what I'm here for."

Since Heidi was only nineteen years old, we mutually agreed it might be best to put the baby up for adoption, so he could be raised by two loving parents. It was a tough decision, but it seemed right at the time.

A thousand miles away, a lovely couple wanted to adopt Heidi's unborn baby boy. In Heidi's seventh month, she moved to be near the adoptive family. My heart was torn apart over losing my first grandchild and my daughter being so far away.

Weeks later, after a doctor's appointment, Heidi called to say she could go into labor at any time and wanted me with her. I hopped on a plane, and the next day met the adoptive family. They seemed very nice, and their little girl was darling. Yet something seemed amiss. I couldn't put my finger on it, but an uneasiness washed over me after meeting them.

The next morning, the phone rang. Heidi answered it; suddenly, all the color drained from her face. She hung up and flung herself on the bed, uncontrollable sobs drenching the long strands of hair that covered her face.

In the final hour, the adoptive family had backed out. Perhaps they sensed my breaking heart, and felt I might interfere with their rights as parents. Perhaps they were overwhelmed with taking on another child. We will never know the reason.

Brushing the hair away from her face, I asked Heidi what she wanted to do. Through long, drawn-out tears, Heidi said, "Mom, I never really wanted to give up my baby. I love him. But I can't afford to keep him!"

Sometimes, life has an amazing way of restoring divine order. Suddenly, all the times I toiled to keep a roof over my little family's head, make sure the bills were paid and still provide things like camp, dance lessons and birthday parties... all the struggle of raising my girls alone seemed inconsequential to what really mattered: love. Simple as that. And I knew right then and there that this new turn of events was meant to be.

Putting my hands on my hips, I firmly stated, "Heidi, I raised you and your two sisters on practically nothing. We made it, and so will you. Get your butt off that bed! We're going out to buy some baby clothes!"

Heidi has proven to be a wonderful mother. She went back to school and is now pursuing an acting career. Tyler, the absolute light of my life, is adored by his aunts and loved by our many friends. He has brought more blessings to us than we ever could have imagined. He is bright, fun and funny—a born performer, just like his mother.

He is oh so wise, too. One day, when he was about four, I was having a particularly tough afternoon. Tyler walked into my office, glanced up at me and said, "What's wrong, Grandma?"

I replied, "Grandma is a little sad today, honey. I wish I were happier."

Just like the day I slid next to his mother in the counselor's office, trying to find the right words to say, Tyler put his arms around me, looked me square in the eyes and pronounced, "Well, that's what I'm here for!"

~Nancy Vogl
*Chicken Soup for the Single Parent's Soul*

# 41

# Grandma Fujikawa

*The person who has lived the most is not the one with
the most years, but the one with the richest experiences.*
~Jean-Jacques Rousseau

Every Sunday after church, Mama would have the car
loaded with a picnic meal. We'd all hop in the car and
drive off to the beach. But first, we'd stop by to get
Grandma at her home in Nu'uanu. I'd be the one to run round
the back and up the gray, wooden stairs two steps at a time.

"Grandma!!"

"Olight, olight. Hai, hai, I coming!" (All right, all right.
Yes, yes, I'm coming!)

"Hurry up, Grandma!"

"Olight, olight," she'd laugh excitedly.

Grandma looked forward to our weekly Sunday pic-
nics at Ala Moana Park. She came to Hawai'i from Japan
a long time ago, but still couldn't speak much English. I
only heard her say, "Dinda, you gudu girl ne?" (Linda, you
good girl, yes?), while she patted me on the head as if she
were petting a dog. When I'd call for her in her tiny, gray
room, she'd gather up her purse, slip on her shoes and roll
the tops of her knee-high stockings until they were just
above her ankles. I never thought they looked funny. I just
thought that was the way she normally dressed.

She'd laugh all the way down the stairs and shuffle as fast as she could, all the way to the car.

At the beach, the older folks played Hanafuda (Japanese flower cards), but Grandma just sat and watched. I don't recall anyone talking to her. She just sat all afternoon, watched the Hanafuda game, laughed and walked around the park. Come to think of it, every time Grandma was with us she sat, laughed and just watched what was going on. She always seemed so happy.

I never thought of talking to her except to say, "Hi, Grandma!" nor did I ever think of disclosing my private thoughts. I wouldn't have known what to say because I didn't speak much Japanese, and she spoke very little English.

When I went to my first prom, I never even thought of sharing my excitement with Grandma. And when I had my first boyfriend, I merely introduced him to her. She just laughed and said, "Ali su. You get nisu boyfiendo." (Nice. You get nice boyfriend.)

When I graduated from high school, I just remember her stroking my arm saying, "Dinda, you smato girl ne?" (Linda, you smart girl, yes?) Later, when I graduated from college, Grandma came to see me. Her voice and the words were the same, and when I got married, Grandma sat at our wedding table. I didn't really talk to her because I was so caught up in the festivities, but I still remember her voice, "Dinda, you guru girl, ne?" (Linda, you good girl, yes?)

Shortly after I had my first child, my husband and I moved to Japan. It was a strange feeling to be a literate, college graduate one day, and an illiterate henna gaijin (strange foreigner) the next. That's when I began to understand what it felt like to live in a foreign country.

At first, I frantically thumbed through my little red

dictionary to search for the right Japanese words to express myself, but thoughts came faster than my fingers could move so I put the book away. It was easier to just smile and laugh. I slowly began to understand how Grandma must have felt when she moved to Hawai'i from her home in Japan. Suddenly I knew why she laughed a lot.

The first time I went to the neighborhood market to shop, I couldn't read the labels on the canned goods. They were all written in Japanese, so I had to guess what was inside by looking at the pictures on the cans. I wondered if Grandma shopped by the pictures, too.

I remember the time I caught the bus with my three-month-old baby. I thought I had the directions down pat; however, when I got off the bus, the landmarks were different. I was lost and didn't have a clue where I was. My heart pounded in my chest as I thought, Did Grandma feel as frightened as I?

Then there was the time when my baby was hurt, and I ended up at a small clinic where I couldn't understand a word the doctor was saying. As he pulled out a huge hypodermic needle, I wondered if Grandma had ever felt as helpless as I did at that moment.

When I had a liver ailment and was referred to a Japanese specialist, I took a friend to translate. When I began asking the doctor questions, however, my translator refused to convey them. Later I was told it was disrespectful to question the doctors in Japan. I wondered, How did Grandma deal with a new culture that expected her to ask questions in order to get information, when the very core of her upbringing did not allow her to speak up?

One day I decided to find out. I wrote Grandma a letter: "Did you feel stupid, illiterate, lost and lonely, too, Grandma? You must have had feelings of humiliation, isolation and pain just so we could have a better life. You always laughed and seemed so happy. I didn't know."

My letter was translated and then sent. Four weeks later I received a reply and the translation read, "For the first time in my life, I am so happy, so much so that I cannot help but cry. You see, for the first time in my life, someone understands, someone in my family really understands me."

I still have that letter. Every night as I lay in bed, I say a prayer and then gently slip Grandma's tear-stained letter out from under my pillow and read it.

Her words have become my own. Someone finally understands.

~Linda Tagawa
*Chicken Soup from the Soul of Hawaii*

# 42

# Timeless Generosity

*Blessed be the hand that prepares a pleasure for a child,*
*for there is no saying when and where it may bloom forth.*
~Douglas Jerrold

My grandmother's Social Security check was the highlight of her life. Everything depended on the arrival of her check. To this day, I have no idea how much it was, but she performed miracles with it. No matter what I wanted, she'd promise it to me, "when I get my check."

Her visits to our house were timed with its arrival. She could never come empty-handed. No sir, she came with delightful treats purchased with the money from that check. My dad would drive to Pittsburgh to bring her to our house two hours north. She'd emerge from the car laden with red licorice, cookies, chipped ham, potato chips, pop and her small blue suitcase. There was a small present for each of us, including my parents. After distributing her gifts, she'd take out of her pocket a list of things yet to be purchased with the remaining money.

These items always were the same, but she made the list anyway. Pond's face cream, hairnets, Jergen's hand lotion, support hose, chocolate-covered raisins, writing paper and envelopes, and some "good cheese." My dad would drive us into our small town with my grandmother sitting happily in the front seat clutching her pocketbook and my brother and sister and me in the back. Our destination was the G. C. Murphy store where, instead of just looking at things, we would be leaving with treasures.

Grammie, as we called her, loved these trips. She took her time examining the support hose, the hairnets and the cold creams. We hung by her side as she made her decisions... always choosing the same items. Then we were free to pick out something. I always got a book, my brother a car of some sort and my sister usually got chocolate candy. Grammie would then pick out something for our other sister, too little yet to go on these magical shopping trips.

Next we'd go to the grocery store and she'd load the cart with anything we wanted... all the things my mother never bought. I can still hear her urging our dad to get something. "Go ahead, Buddy. I have enough to pay for it." We laughed at hearing him called by his childhood name.

I never saw my grandmother buy a new dress for herself, but she gave me money for my high school graduation dress. I never saw her buy new shoes or even a coat. She was always "making do" with her own things, but spending generously on those she loved. She lived with my dad's sister and her other grandchildren in Pittsburgh, and they experienced the same generosity.

The only month of the year she did not follow this ritual was December. She saved that check for Christmas presents. Each December she made yet another list... the list of what we wanted for Christmas. We had to give her three or four ideas so she could surprise us with one. Christmas was wonderful with the arrival of Grammie and all her mysterious, oddly wrapped packages.

Time moved on and I went off to college. By this time there were seven children in my family and some of my cousins now had children of their own. Grammie's check had to be stretched even further. The first letter she sent me at college read:

*Dear Patti Jo:*

*My check came yesterday and I wanted to send you something, but I guess you have all the books you need there at college. Here are a few dollars so you can go out and have something nice to eat with your new friends.*

Inside the folded sheets of the familiar writing paper I had watched her purchase time after time were three carefully folded dollar bills. This was the first of many such letters I received at college. Each letter during that first year contained folded dollar bills... my grandmother's love reaching across the miles... her check stretching very far.

And then I got the last one. She sent a five dollar bill, a list of what I should get with it and instructions to save some too. The list was long. I laughed, knowing that it would never cover all that Grammie wanted me to have.

Before the next letter arrived, the news came that she was in the hospital. By the time I got to Pittsburgh, she had slipped into a coma. Sitting by her intensive care bed, I was besieged with grief, realizing that I would never talk to her again... never again witness her generosity and appreciation for the smallest of things.

My grandmother had no will, no bequests, nothing to leave anyone... she gave it all away to those she loved while she lived.

Not too long ago, I was out to dinner with my parents and I offered to pay.

"You're just like my mother," Dad said.

I've never ever received a nicer compliment. Grammie left me more than I ever realized.

~Patti Lawson
*Chicken Soup for the Grandma's Soul*

# Gran

*Grandmas hold our tiny hands for just a little while,*
*but our hearts forever.*
*~Author Unknown*

When I was a young mother, my grandmother, who was lonely after my grandfather's death, visited me every month for a few days. We'd cook together and talk, and she'd always babysit, so I could have time to myself.

By the time she was ninety-five, practically deaf and very frail, I was working part-time, and two of my three children were in school. Gran would come to our home on days when I wasn't working. Once when she was visiting, my older children were in school, my eighteen-month-old was sleeping, and Gran and I were having coffee. I always felt protected and relaxed when we were together. Then I got a telephone call that there was a crisis in my office — would I please come in for an hour or two. Gran assured me that she and Jeff, the eighteen-month-old, would be fine, and I left.

As I drove to work, I panicked. I'd left my deaf, elderly grandmother with an eighteen-month-old she was not strong enough to pick up and could not hear if he cried. But Gran inspired so much confidence that I felt it would be all right. And perhaps, if I was lucky, my son would sleep the whole time I was gone.

I returned two hours later and heard happy sounds coming from Jeff's room. He'd awakened, she'd dragged a chair next to his crib, and she was reading him a story. He sat there, enchanted by her voice, unperturbed by the bars of the crib that separated them. And our German shepherd lay at her feet, also completely content.

The drama of that day did affect Gran, who later admitted that communicating with an eighteen-month-old presented some problems. Unlike adults, if he'd needed something and wanted her to know about it, of course he couldn't write it down. The next week she enrolled in a lip-reading course at a local college. The teacher was a young intern, and Gran was her only student. After the first session, the teacher made the trip to Gran's apartment each week, so Gran wouldn't have to travel to the college, changing buses twice. By the end of the semester, Gran's ability to lip-read had greatly improved, and she felt infinitely more comfortable with Jeff and with the rest of the world.

Gran continued to communicate with Jeff in this way until she died, a few days before her hundredth birthday—leaving an unbearable void in my life.

~Mary Ann Horenstein
*Chicken Soup for Every Mom's Soul*

# 44

# Oh What a Day!

Last year, exasperated with epicurean excess overshadowing the blessed event and fearful of maxing out my credit cards once again, I began planning a simpler Christmas, unaware that I was about to create an unforgettable moment and a pretty terrific day.

I decided that although I would buy gifts for our twelve grandchildren, I absolutely would not buy presents for our seven adult kids. Absolutely not. Well then, I thought, I'll just make up a nice basket of goodies for each couple.

In August, I traveled to the outlet mall and purchased seven big baskets. I went to yard sales and bought cookie tins and cute little containers. Really saved some money, too. Next, I chose a few crystal and porcelain dishes just to dress things up a bit (I'm into elegant). I also bought red, green, silver and gold spray paint.

I wanted to personalize the baskets somewhat (I detest "cookie-cutter" gifts). So I decided to decoupage tall cans to match the decor of each family's home. Good grief! I had no concept of how much cutting or how many pictures and scraps it takes to arrange one simple design. I cut from our albums, encyclopedias, history texts, magazines and flyers. My husband's toes curled when he saw the job I did on his *National Geographics*. Of course, then I had to buy all the glue, brushes and decoupage stuff. One entire bedroom was set aside, and locked, for this project.

Meanwhile, I pored over new recipes seeking something special for each person. The decisions took me weeks. Next, I was off to the farmer's market to purchase bushels of apples for chutney, pies and applesauce. I foraged for days to find special salt to make beef sticks for the guys.

I chopped, sliced and diced until my hands resembled crazy explorer's maps. Oh, the pain. Homemade candied fruit, madeleines, mustards, relish, special sauces, rolled candies, decorated petit fours, dried fruit slices, potpourri. I was driven, a madwoman on a quest for perfection. I was on a complete Martha Stewart binge.

Did I mention the fifteen-cubic-foot freezer I bought just for this endeavor? Oh, yeah. Real savings there.

Time was running out. The pace quickened: shopping, wrapping, tagging, decorating, cleaning, baking. Spare moments were spent creating tiny marzipan flowers and fruits. My husband (and the dog) had the audacity to expect dinner every night in the midst of this frenzy. An additional little chore nagged at the back of my mind: Christmas dinner for thirty-five people. Just another incidental.

Finally, after scouring boutiques for cute little gold cards, I meticulously arranged the baskets. Now, the final touch: bows. I bought yards and yards of gold and silver ribbon; gorgeous stuff. I won't bore you with the details. Suffice to say, I failed Ribbon Making 101. Checkbook in hand, I stormed out of the house and dashed to the craft store. People dispersed in every direction as I entered; they saw the crazed look of a woman "on a mission." No one in my path was safe. I exuded danger. Quickly, I placed my order for seven huge bows with streamers. They were lovely and only cost eighty-eight dollars. Plus tax.

Earlier in the year, I'd made cookbooks for each daughter and daughter-in-law. These contained recipes of family favorites and little cut-outs of my favorite hymns, quotes and prayers.

The crowning touch was a personal poem for each, emphasizing individual traits, with endearments to match. Oh, they were such fun to do!

The great day arrived, and I was anxious. Just to be sure the fellas wouldn't be too disappointed by the excess of feminine accoutrements, I'd gone out Christmas Eve and found seven Star Trek mugs. They were only twenty dollars each. Well, my dears, the baskets were a raging success. "Oohs" and "aahs," and "Oh, Mom, this must have taken you days." (Excuse me — days?)

Suddenly, like a gentle ocean wave, a hush overcame the room (Ever notice when we women stop talking, no matter how many fellas are around, there is a hush?). Pages turned as silent tears fell — then audible sniffles — then, as the poems were shared, uproarious laughter filled the moment. Surrounded by hugs and wet faces, I glanced across the room at my husband. He grinned back with happy eyes. Love personified the moment. What a day.

~Lynne Zielinski
*Chicken Soup for the Soul Christmas Treasury*

# 45

# Love on the Edge of the Grand Canyon

I was seven when Jane Chaddock Davenport reached ninety. She was my great grandmother, a beautiful woman with large violet eyes, exquisitely groomed white hair, and magnificent hands, veined and transparent, which she enhanced with antique rings. She gave me one, an oblong purple amethyst set in heavy gold, which I love more as I get older. She wore brocade dresses with lace petticoats. The shoes on her little feet always matched her satin hair bands.

She liked to talk to me. I loved to listen. She told me many things, once about a love affair she had years earlier "on the edge of the Grand Canyon." She explained that she was much younger then—only seventy-four.

"On the very edge," she repeated in her crystal-clear, yet moss-soft voice. "It was very romantic. I looked straight down the canyon walls—a thousand miles below. We were passionate then and unafraid, being young."

At the time, I had no idea what she was talking about. I only imagined my exquisite and delicate great-grandmother in passionate embrace with a mysterious stranger on the very rim of the Grand Canyon, while a sunset of glorious oranges and golds spread across a darkening vast-ness. Holding hands, they dangled their feet over the edge, rapt in beauty. Then, when there was only black and silver and silence all around, they made love.

Many years later, my husband Alex and I were on our honeymoon, driving across the West. Late one afternoon, we found ourselves at the entrance to Grand Canyon National Park, and we decided to stay the night.

We followed the signs to the central complex, where a new hotel blazed in the center of what seemed to be a parking lot. Newly arriving travelers, all with reservations, crowded the lobby. The harried man at the desk was sorry, but there were no more rooms.

"I know that hotels always have an extra room for an emergency," Alex insisted. "Say a VIP arrives unexpectedly. Give us that room and we'll pay for it." Alex was in no mood to drive any farther.

"Sir, we would give you a proper room if we had one. But we have only one room left, one we never rent any-more. It is in the Old Inn, and people don't like it, so we don't bother to show it."

"Sounds perfect," Alex said.

A bellboy called ahead and then, gathering our bags, led us to the Old Inn. We followed him through its lovely old lobby and then down the corridors to the back of the building. We finally arrived at our room, its dimensions worthy of the Grand Canyon. The bedroom was the size of a ballroom, and the bathroom was as big as your run-of-the-mill living room. The tub itself was about seven feet long and four deep.

Everything was ready for us by the time we got there: large towels in the bathroom, bed turned down, curtains pulled. A fire had been lit and was burning cheerfully. The room was large but had a cozy feel to it: natural wood, green-and-white chintz and an antique silver mirror over the dressing table.

"Nothing wrong with this," I said.

The bellboy silently accepted his tip, put another log on the fire and left us.

I decided to take a hot tub. It took some time to fill, but soon the heat was loosening the tensions of the day. After a while, I remembered the sunset.

The window was right beside the tub. I only had to pull back the curtain and look out: sky orange and gold, shot through with giant splashes of green and purple. A star. A half-moon, green in the golden air. I looked over to the far side of the Grandest Canyon of them all. The edge was still visible. My eyes climbed slowly down to a silver ribbon, running in the already black canyon bottom. I got up on my knees to see better and gasped.

Grabbing a thick towel, I tumbled out of the bath and ran into the bedroom. Our bed was set right against an enormous window. I jumped on it and threw open the curtains. Sure enough, the bed, too, was right over the canyon.

I knew immediately that this had been my great-grand-mother's room all those years ago.

Speechless, I beckoned Alex. The pull of the dreadful height got to us. We lay on our stomachs to look. There was no rim on this side — nothing between us and the bot-tom. Only an awesome down. "Down a thousand miles," as my great-grandmother had described.

Alex looked at me and I looked at him.

That evening, we left the curtain open, and looked out and then down, straight down, as Great-grandmother

Jane and her lover had done, on the very edge of the Grand Canyon.

~Jane Winslow Eliot
*Chicken Soul for the Traveler's Soul*

# Chapter 7

# Grand and Great

## Sharing Wisdom

*Grandchildren and Grandparents are joined at the heart.*
*~Source Unknown*

# A Canadian's Story

*If the only prayer you said in your whole life was,*
*"thank you," that would suffice.*
~Meister Eckhart

One day when I was seventeen my best friend, Shelley, invited me to her home after school to meet her grandmother. When we arrived, a slim, fragile-look-ing, elderly lady with white hair and many wrinkles greeted us warmly. In a thick accent she invited us to help ourselves to freshly baked chocolate chip cookies. While we ate she asked many questions about our personal lives and listened intently to our answers. We both felt her genuine interest, and in spite of her accent, we understood her clearly. Her piercing, deep blue eyes sparkled as we talked, and her smile radiated a lifetime of inner strength and integrity. She captivated me.

She noted how fortunate we were to have such beautiful clothes, nice furniture and time to spend with our friends. When she excused herself for a moment, Shelley and I stared at each other in astonishment at her grandmother's appreciation of all the little things that we took for granted. In a whisper, Shelley explained that her grandmother had grown up in the Ukraine, where life had been very difficult. When she returned to the room, Grandma expressed her great pleasure in seeing all her children and grandchildren able to go to school and learn. When the conversation turned to my approaching eighteenth birthday, Grandma was thrilled and exclaimed how excited I must be at the thought of voting for the first time. Frankly, I had thought of all sorts of good things I would be able to do when I was eighteen, but voting wasn't one of them. I told her so.

A little saddened by my cynicism, Shelley's grandmother asked in her broken English if I would like to hear the story of her journey to Canada. She said she had not shared the details with many people, including Shelley. When I agreed, she began to tell her tale.

"Grandpa, myself and our six children lived in extremely modest conditions in the Ukraine. Everyone in the family who was old enough had to work. Our two eldest children were eight and ten. They did odd jobs for people who paid them with food rather than money.

"The other four children were too young to work, so they helped me with the household chores. The government did not want the people to be independent and think for themselves, and to ensure this, they prevented us from attending any religious services and forced us to worship the government. They also banned reading and writing, closed all the schools and destroyed all the books that disagreed with their oppressive philosophy. Anyone caught not complying with the new, closed-minded edict was put in prison. In spite of these severe consequences, those who knew how to read and write secretly taught those who did not. Many people managed to hide some of their beloved classic books before they could be destroyed.

"Many villagers dreamed of emigrating to Canada where they believed people were allowed to make choices and work hard to make a life for themselves. Although we were prevented from leaving with threats of imprisonment, many people attempted to flee because we were starving in the homeland. Grandpa and I and our six children were among those who made plans to escape.

"Our village was twenty miles from the border. We would have to walk and sneak past the border guards. On the other side of the border, we would be met by people to whom we paid our life's savings to help us travel across the land to the ocean, and across the ocean to Canada.

"Crossing the border was extremely dangerous—the guards were ordered to shoot anyone caught trying to pass illegally. For this part of the journey, we were on our own.

"Late at night, taking only what we could carry, we left our home and quietly stole out of the village. Because three of our children were still quite small, it took us five days to reach the border. When we arrived, we hid in the trees on the edge of a mile-wide open area that ran along it. We planned to wait until dark before trying to cross.

"As the sun began to set, my husband and I carried the three smallest children while our other three joined hands. We could see the border and began to run across that mile-wide open area towards freedom. Just as we reached the borderline a bright spotlight flashed on and caught in its glare the two older boys running with their younger brother, who was literally suspended in midair between them. A loud voice boomed over a bullhorn—'Halt! Immediately!'—but my sons paid no attention and continued to run.

"Gunshots rang out and continued even after we had crossed into the neutral country on the other side. The light still followed us and suddenly found me as I ran carrying the baby. When our eldest son, John, saw this, he let go of his two brothers and yelled for them to run. Then

John began to draw the guards' attention by jumping, yelling and waving his hands. The bright light settled on him as the rest of us finally reached the protective barrier of the trees on the other side of the border. As we turned back to look, several shots rang out. John, my ten-year-old son, fell to the ground and lay still.

"Thankfully, the guards left my son there, because he lay outside their jurisdiction. Your grandpa crawled out and dragged John back to where we were huddled in the trees. My child had been hit by one of the bullets, and he died there in my arms. We wept in agony, but our hearts were filled with pride for his heroism. If not for John's selfless actions, the baby and I would have certainly been shot. He gave his life that night so the rest of us might live.

"After we buried John, with heavy hearts we continued on and eventually found our way to Canada, and so to freedom."

When Shelley's grandmother finished her story, I had tears in my eyes.

"Since arriving in Canada I have enjoyed my freedom immensely," she continued. "I take great pleasure in every single choice I have made—including the time I took an evening job scrubbing floors so that Shelley's father could go to university."

As she clutched at her heart, the dear lady then expressed great pride in her second oldest son, who was eight during the family's flight to freedom. Out of gratitude for their new life in Canada, and because of the horror of seeing his brother shot down so long ago, he had enlisted in the Canadian army to defend his new country with his life.

Grandma confided that she valued her right to vote as very dear to her heart and had never missed her chance to have "her say." She told me then that she viewed voting as not only a right and a privilege, but also a responsibility. By voting, she believed she could ensure that Canada would be run by good people and never by the kind of people who would shoot and kill someone making a choice.

My life changed profoundly that day, as I looked through the window that this special woman had opened into a different world. I made my own commitment on the spot to seize every opportunity I was ever given to vote. And I began to understand, in some small way, the passion that motivates our Canadian soldiers, who volunteer to defend our country.

When Grandma finished her story, Shelley, who had become very quiet, softly asked, "Who was the baby you were carrying when you ran across the border, Grandma?"

As Grandma caressed her cheek, she replied, "The baby was your father, my dear."

~Pat Fowler
*Chicken Soup for the Canadian Soul*

# Change of Heart

*Grandfathers are for loving and fixing things.*
*~Author Unknown*

When our little sister was born sixty years ago, my brother was six and I was eight. I had always been the "Big Sister" and he had always been "The Baby."

Our sister's arrival was a complete surprise to both of us. In those days no one worried much about sibling rivalry, and no "experts" told us how to deal with another child in the house. We had wise and loving grandparents, however.

I was thrilled about the baby and loved to hold her and help care for her. My brother's feelings were quite different! He looked at her briefly and left, preferring to spend the evening in his room. When I went to his room to talk to him and try to get him to play games with me, he just looked away.

"Why did they have to go and get that old baby?"

Later that night, Grandpa came over to see the new baby. As he held her, he said to my brother, "You know, she's a lot like that lamb I'm raising on the bottle. I have to take care of her and feed her often, just the way your Mama does with the baby."

My brother said, "I'd rather have the lamb" under his breath, but just loud enough for Grandpa to hear.

Even though Grandpa seemed pretty old to me (at least fifty, I figured), he could hear very well, and he heard my brother's muttered comment.

"Well," said Grandpa, "if you'd rather have a lamb, maybe we could trade. I'll give you a day to think it over, and if you still want to trade tomorrow, we'll do it."

I thought I saw him wink at Mama, but I knew I must have been mistaken because Grandpa never winked at anyone.

After Grandpa left, Mama asked my brother if he wanted her to read to him. He cuddled up beside her, and she read to him for a long while.

He kept looking at the baby, and Mama asked him to hold his little sister while she went to get a diaper. When Mama came back, my brother was gently touching the baby's smooth black hair, and as he held her hand, she grasped his finger.

"Mama, look! She's holding my hand!"

"Sure, she knows you're her big brother," Mama smiled. He held the baby for a few more minutes, and he seemed much happier at bedtime. Grandpa came back the next evening as he had promised and called my brother to talk to him.

"Well, are you ready to trade the baby for a lamb?"

My brother looked surprised that Grandpa had remembered the bargain.

"She's worth two lambs now."

Grandpa seemed to be taken aback at this breach of contract. He said that he'd have to think it over and would be back the next night to talk about it.

The next day was a Saturday, and my brother and I

spent much of the day indoors watching the baby have her bath, watching her sleep and holding her. My brother held her three more times that day. He looked worried when Grandpa came to see us that evening and called him over to talk.

"You know, I've thought about that baby-and-lamb trade all day, and you really do drive a hard bargain. I've decided, though, that the baby is probably worth two lambs. I think we can do business."

My brother hesitated very briefly before answering Grandpa. "She's a whole day older now, and I think she's worth five lambs."

Grandpa looked shocked, and he slowly shook his head.

"I don't know. I'll have to go home and give your offer some serious thought. Maybe I'll have to talk it over with my banker."

Grandpa left soon after, and my brother seemed worried. I tried to get him to play some games with me, but he went to Mama's room and held the baby for a long time.

The next day, Sunday, Grandpa came to visit us in the early afternoon. He told my brother he had come early because if he had to round up five lambs and get a room ready for the baby, he'd need an early start.

My brother took a deep breath, looked Grandpa squarely in the eye and made an announcement.

"The baby is worth fifty lambs now!"

Grandpa looked at him in disbelief and shook his head.

"I'm afraid the deal's off. I can't afford fifty lambs for one little baby. I guess you'll have to keep her and help your parents take care of her."

My brother turned away with a little smile he didn't

know I saw, and this time I really did see Grandpa wink at Mama.

~Muriel J. Bussman
*Chicken Soup for the Golden Soul*

# Grandma's Words

M y grandma's words were full of wisdom. "You know, dear," she was fond of saying, "you never stop learning." You don't? I wondered about this line a lot as a child. Never? Even when you are as old as she is?

Grandma was a great listener and wanted to hear all about my job as a kindergarten teacher. "You are a real teacher," she would tell me.

Regularly she asked, "Tell me, sweetheart, is there anyone special in your life?"

I would tell her about the man I was dating and somehow her words would make me question. "Trust your heart," she'd say. "Your heart knows." And sure enough, when I took Grandma's advice, no, he was not the one.

In her early nineties she moved into an assisted-living home. Her stories became the same story over and over, but just hearing her voice was soothing. It didn't matter that I'd heard it all before.

She told stories of leaving Russia as a child, alone, sent by her father to join his parents in America. "I got out," she said. "We had no idea what was about to happen. The rest of my family didn't make it, but for some reason, I did."

Her stories of those years were about eating her first orange on the boat, about her stern but kind grandparents in New York City, walks in the rain to the library. "I couldn't get enough of the books," she said.

The night Grandma had a stroke, at age ninety-seven, we thought that would be the end of her long life, but she lived another two years. The stroke left her unable to walk and talk. For the first time in her life my grandma was forced into silence. Visiting her was sad. I had never spent time with her in so much silence before.

"Hi, Grandma," I'd say.

"Uhnnnnn," was all she was capable of saying.

"My garden's doing well but something got the peonies. Maybe deer."

"Uhmmm, mmmmn, uhhh mmm," she would mumble.

I would nod and say, "Yes... yes... that's right," here and there. I knew she was giving me advice about the garden. She murmured and muttered. I nodded and talked. My heart broke from missing her words, her voice.

The next summer, I met Andy. He became a great friend, and I was nothing less than thrilled when we began to date in earnest. I told him about Grandma and suggested we visit her. On the way to her nursing home, I filled him in as much as possible about her condition and her wisdom.

"Andy, she was always filled with the most amazing words. She could stop me in my tracks and really make me think. You have to realize that the woman you meet is not really her. All she can do now is sit and murmur. But know that if she could talk, she would be saying something really wise."

"I understand," he said, but still I felt he was about to miss out.

We found Grandma sitting in her room.

"Grandma," I said, "I'd like you to meet Andy."

She looked up at us, first at me, then Andy. She studied him for quite some time. Sometimes she looked at me like that, only to close her eyes and drift into a long nap. But this time she lifted her gnarled hand, a great effort for her, and gave it to him. As he held her hand she continued to look deep into his eyes for quite a while. I felt embarrassed. Would she never let go of his hand? Would she ever look away? Would it be okay for Andy to drop her hand? I was trying to think of words to break this awkward silence, but the most unlikely person found them first. In a loud and clear voice my grandma said to Andy, "Welcome to the family."

Andy and I were married within the year.

~Laura Mueller
*Chicken Soup for the Grandma's Soul*

# Trying Times
# and Dirty Dishes

I cleared the table and stacked the breakfast dishes on top of the dinner dishes left in the sink from last night's feast of macaroni and cheese with carrot sticks. I braced myself for the cold, clumpy feeling of the dishwater then plunged my hand deep into the sink, searching for the plug.

"Yuk! Why didn't I do these last night?" I asked of who knows who. The only people around to hear me were my six, five, three and two-year-olds and my six-week-old baby.

It wasn't just the dishes. The dryer had gone out that morning and sheets were drying over every available chair and table, to the great delight of my sons who were playing fort-town all over the house. I would have hung the sheets outside but it was ten degrees below zero.

The living room had exploded with toys, and the way things were going, it would be lunchtime before any of us were even close to being dressed. The flu that had run through the family had finally caught me after six nights of little to no sleep caring for each of my children's needs and comfort. It caught me the same day my husband, recovered and healthy, flew out of town on a business trip.

The hot water bubbled up in the soap-filled dishpan, and it encouraged me a little. "I'll have these done in no time...." But before I could finish my pep talk, my newborn began to cry.

I changed the baby's diaper, stepped over the basket of clean clothes that had already sunk into wrinkled neglect, pulled the sheet off the couch along with the full collection of my sons' horses and corral, and settled in to nurse my baby.

Idyllic moment? Hardly. As soon as I sat, books were tumbled into my lap. If Mom was sitting, she might as well read to us, was the common thought. So balancing the four toddlers, protecting the baby from their commotion while trying to turn pages with no hands, I began to read.

I read over the phone ringing and over the TV set clicking on and off at full volume because one of them was sitting on the elusive remote control.

I read over my pounding headache, around the errant thought of what to make for dinner and the doorbell ringing. The doorbell ringing! Oh no! All but the baby and I were off the couch to the door before I could grasp a moment of hope that whoever it was would give up and go away, never to see me at my unkempt worse.

"Grandma!" The children chorused while doing the Grandma-is-here dance of anticipated hugs and candy.

Grandma coming was always good news for all of us, but it couldn't be my mother! It couldn't be today. She lived three hours away. She never just dropped by. What would she think? I scanned the room and sighed. There was no way to recover this, no way to quickly put things to right.

Cold, fresh air rushed in ahead of my mother making me realize how stuffy and sick my house smelled.

"Cindy?" My mother called my name, startling the baby

and making her cry. I could hear my mother's uneven steps as she navigated around and over the things on the floor.

"Cindy?" she said again before spotting me among the Spiderman sheets.

I was stricken. I was embarrassed. I had forgotten it was Thursday in the sameness of each day. I had forgotten that my mother had planned to stop in on her way back home from the city.

"My, oh my, have things gotten out of control around here," she surveyed the room and started laughing when she saw my gowns drying on the bouncing horse with my nursing bra forming a hat over its head, its ears sticking through the drop down flaps.

Her laughter filled the house with the first ray of sunshine to make it through the wintery gray of the last mucky week.

I started to giggle, then to laugh right out loud before I teared up in my fatigue.

My mother cleared a space for herself beside me. "Cindy, weren't you raised in my home?"

I nodded, because no words could get around the choking of my tears.

"Was my house always perfect, always clean?"

I shook my head no.

"Did you think I was a failure as a mother or as a homemaker?"

Again I shook my head no.

"And I don't think that of you. I have sat where you are sitting now," she grinned at me while she reached over and pulled a toy horse from under my hip.

We chuckled together.

"Cindy, I can tell you one thing, and you listen to me," her voice became solemn with the depth of what she wanted to say. "These are the days you will smile fondly on when the years have passed and your time becomes quiet enough to roam the memories of your heart."

I recognized the love and truth in her words. I wrote them on my heart and contemplated them when my mothering days were both calm and sunny and hectic and never ending.

Now, the years have passed and my time has become quiet enough to roam my memories.

And when my daughters and daughters-in-law are pressed in and overwhelmed with the making of their families and homes, I remember and I say to them, "These are the days you will smile fondly on."

~Cynthia Hamond
*Chicken Soup for the Every Mom's Soul*

# 50

# Confidence

*We're only young once, but with humor,
we can be immature forever.*
~Art Gliver

Grandmothers have a way of uniting families through traditions. Some pass down favorite recipes and others share their sewing techniques, but the tradition my grandmother gave us was very different. Her favorite T-shirt read, "This is No Ordinary Grandma You're Dealing With!" And that said it all. Grandma was known by everyone to be an outgoing, witty and feisty woman. So, as you might expect, the tradition she passed on to our family was equally unique.

The summer after my high school graduation was the first time she told me the advice she gave to all the girls in our family. She had taken me shopping in preparation for my first semester of college. As we started toward the department store register with the cart full of everything a dorm room would need, we walked past the lingerie section and she stopped.

"Do you have your red underwear yet?" she asked.

"What? No... why?" I stammered, puzzled and embarrassed.

"It's important for every woman to have at least one

pair of red underwear." She glanced at the appalled look on my face. "To wear on those days when you need that extra bit of confidence. When you have a test, a speech, a job interview or any time you need a self-assurance boost." Grandma went on to explain her philosophy, that when women have their own personal secrets about their "sassy" red underwear, they somehow feel more powerful and self-assured.

"Only you will know this tidbit of information about yourself, and it will give you a little extra edge of confidence," Grandma counseled.

Standing in the store discussing my underwear choices with my grandma was extremely embarrassing. I assured her I didn't need any underwear and convinced her we should leave.

Months later, after my roommate and I had been up all night studying for our first set of final exams, I stumbled into anthropology class and saved her a seat. She hurried in and sat down beside me with a package under her arm. "I picked up the mail on the way to class and we got another package from your grandma!" We were both excited because Grandma often sent us care packages with cookies and goodies, so I ripped open the parcel right there—and yanked out a pair of red underwear! Her note simply said, "Thought you could use these. Love, Gram."

Classmates snickered and whistled as I desperately tried to stuff the contents back in the package, my face as red as the panties.

Many times after that, when discussing an important upcoming event, one of the girls in our family repeated Grandma's advice without hesitation, "Don't forget your red underwear!"

Ten years later, Grandma's time on earth came to an

end. As we made plans for her funeral service we decided on a final farewell to honor such an inspiring lady. Her daughters, nieces, granddaughters (and even my college roommate) all shared a common secret that day. The music played softly as we gathered together, holding hands in prayer before entering the chapel. We winked at each other and giggled, then walked down the aisle—each with that "extra edge of confidence."

~Jody Walters
*Chicken Soup for the Grandma's Soul*

# A Hug and a Kiss

*There is as much greatness of mind in
acknowledging a good turn, as in doing it.*
~Seneca

Mary, a recent widow and devoted "fifty-something" grandmother, worked as a nursing attendant. Her triumph over a heart attack and bypass surgery was remarkable, undoubtedly because of the deep love she held for her grandchildren.

But this time, Mary's hospital stay was different. Afflicted with a non-contagious form of pneumonia, she was stunned to learn of her diagnosis—full-blown AIDS.

As part of a hospital volunteer visitation team, I call on each assigned AIDS patient at least once a day. In my role as patient-advocate, I let each person know that someone else cares about them—aside from their family and the medical staff. Once we become better acquainted, I greet most patients with a gentle hug and a kiss on the cheek. I can usually sense whether or not a patient is comfortable with this gesture.

After my third visit with Mary, I asked politely, "Would you like a hug and a kiss on the cheek?"

Mary smiled, holding out two waiting arms, and whispered a barely audible, "Yes, I'd love one."

As I drew back, I noticed a tear working its way down one cheek. "What's wrong?" I asked.

"That's the first time anyone has touched me, since I was diagnosed with AIDS. The medical staff touch me, but... Mary turned onto her side, placing both hands over her face. "My sons won't even allow me to see my grandchildren," she said between sobs. "When my family visits, they sit clear across the room, as far away from me as possible."

I simply sat by her bedside and listened in silence—handing her tissues and trying to understand.

A few days later, when I stopped to see Mary again, one of her sons and his wife were visiting. "Good evening, Mary. I see that you have guests, so I'll stop back later," I said, giving her a gentle hug and a kiss on the cheek.

Mary grabbed my right wrist as I turned to leave. "Wait a minute, Mack. I want you to meet my son, John, and daughter-in-law, Sarah." During the introductions, her anxious family sat clear across the room from Mary's bed.

Later, when I looked in on her, her visitors were still maintaining their safe distance. I respected Mary's time with her family and didn't intrude.

The following evening, John and Sarah were back again, and the scenario repeated itself like a familiar rerun on television. I went in, gave Mary a gentle hug and a kiss, promising to come back later.

When I returned, something had miraculously changed. John and Sarah were seated in chairs—one on each side of Mary's bed—and they were holding hands.

Obviously choked with emotion, John said, "I guess if some stranger can hug and kiss my mother, we have nothing to be afraid of."

Fortunately, Mary became well enough to return home and continue her loving relationship with her family, including her cherished grandchildren—in spite of her illness.

~Mack Emmert as told to Tom Lagana
*Chicken Soup for the Volunteer's Soul*

# Nona's Garden

When my grandparents emigrated from Italy to this country, they joined the rest of their clan who'd already settled in the small town of Oelwein, Iowa. Here the men had found jobs working for the railroad. Because most of Oelwein's population was of German descent, the newcomers had a hard time fitting in. So, to give them a sense of community and belonging until they "learned the ropes," the heads of each family pooled their money and bought a square city block of homes.

In Italy, my people had loved their gardens. So when they settled into their new homes, the backyard fences came down and all that open space became flower and vegetable gardens. Cobbled pathways connected each house, while grape arbors provided shade, fruit and wine.

"What's wrong?" Nona, my grandmother, asked me one day when she caught me sulking in my room.

"Nothing," I said, not wanting to tell. The truth was too painful. I was tired of being the brunt of jokes at the playground. Tired of being the "different" girl everybody picked on because of my dark coloring and simple, hand-made clothes.

"You got nothing to do?" she said. "Then you come with me. Maybe you learn something today."

There was no saying "no" to Nona. I knew she knew what was wrong, and it was lesson time. I set my stubborn jaw and followed her downstairs where she snatched up her basket and garden shears. "You come," she said again.

We headed toward the herb garden first, a sunny spot that butted up against Zia Amalia's zucchini patch.

"See here?" Nona said, pointing to a thick bush, its rangy stems lifted toward the sun. "This is oregano."

Snip went the shears, and a handful of stems and leaves went into the basket. "Look," she said. "See the leaves? Small. Hardly anything to them."

She waited for me to nod in agreement.

"Smell." She rubbed a few teardrop-like oregano leaves between her fingers and wafted them beneath my nose. "Remember the smell," Nona said.

"Huh?" I blurted, wondering what she meant. It wasn't like I didn't know what these plants were already. I'd helped her put the seedlings in the ground last spring.

She moved to the next row of bushes, like an ambitious bee in search of nectar. "This is rosemary," she informed me, stooping to clip a lush frond stiff with spiky leaves. Again she crushed a couple of leaves between her fingers and made me inhale the scent. "Remember," she said.

Next came the basil plants, light green and dew-kissed glossy, their familiar scent the sweetest of all. We repeated the procedure, me wondering if Nona would ever just get to the point and let me go back to my brooding.

"Very different from the other two, eh?" she pointed out, snipping and tossing a few more bunches of basil into her basket. This time she didn't wait for me to answer. Instead, with me still in reluctant tow, she left the herb plot to gather several ripe tomatoes, a fat-to-near-bursting head of garlic and three purple eggplants.

"We make Melanzani Parmiggiano for supper tonight," she announced. "Your favorite."

Back inside the house, Nona tossed me an apron and asked me to rinse off the vegetables. I groaned.

"You got nothing else to do," she said. "You help me make the supper."

When the cleaned herbs and produce sat drying on dish towels, Nona said, "We start with the tomatoes. We peel the skins and put them in a pot to simmer. Look," she said. "They're very different from the eggplants, no?"

No kidding, I thought. Any dummy can see that.

She peeled and sliced the eggplant in fat rounds, dipped them first in beaten egg and then in seasoned bread crumbs, then fried them till golden in olive oil flavored with the fresh garlic we'd picked. After laying them flat in a baking dish, she turned her attention back to the simmering tomatoes.

"Now we add the herbs," she said, showing me what to do and how to do it. We stripped the leaves from the stems of each different herb and put them into three separate piles.

"Take a palmful of basil leaves," Nona said, then watched carefully as I obeyed. "Rub them between your hands and toss them in the pot. Bene. Don't it make your hands smell good? Now the oregano. Rub those, too. See how tiny the leaves are? Che bellezza! Different smell, eh?"

Helplessly, I looked at her and shrugged my shoulders.

"Toss."

I did.

"And now the rosemary," she winked. "Just a little kiss from Signorina Rosemary. Smell how strong her breath is?"

Nona smiled at my groan. "Good. This dish gonna be perfect. Toss."

I helped her slice the cheeses and then we assembled the casserole in layers of eggplant, cheese and tomato sauce.

And somewhere along the line, much to my amazement, I realized I was enjoying myself.

That evening after the blessing, Nona served the dish we'd made. The casserole's aroma settled around the table like perfume from heaven. My family dug in.

"Well," Nona said, her bright brown eyes snagging mine as I chewed my first hefty mouthful. "What did you learn today, granddaughter?"

"I don't know, Nona. What did I learn?" I teased. Of course I'd learned a lesson today, and she knew me well enough to know I'd gotten her point long before we'd finished preparing supper.

"Okay, smart girl, I tell you. Every person in my garden different," she said.

I giggled. To Nona, plants had personalities, lives uniquely theirs, just like people.

"Nobody the same as nobody else, see? But when you and me put everybody together today, we got something special. Something delicious."

"Yeah, we did," I admitted, a rush of emotion pooling in my eyes.

And that was the shining moment in which I committed myself to taking joy in every one of the unique differences that made me, me.

"God is very wise," Nona said. "Remember."

~Paula L. Silici
*Chicken Soup for the Gardener's Soul*

# Grandma Lois

*Nothing is better than the unintended humor of reality.*
*~Steve Allen*

A few years ago my husband and I were riding in the car with our friends Denny and Laurie Montgomery and Grandma Lois, Denny's mother. Having known the family for years, we were always braced for whatever Lois would say. She was about seventy-five at that time... somewhat hard of hearing, but alert and spunky as anything. Driving through an older part of North Seattle, we passed some weathered brick buildings that had advertisements and pictures painted on the sides of them. Coming up on our right was an old-fashioned eye clinic or something... an optometrist's office, probably. On the side of the building was a graphic painting of a gigantic eye with very special details—the pupil, iris, eyelashes....

Lois barked out from the back seat: "DENNY, WHAT IS THAT!?"

"On that building, you mean? It's a picture of an eye, I think, Mom."

"WHAT is it? A picture of what?"

"It's an EYE, Mom... a picture of an eye."

This irritated Lois for some reason... a giant picture of

an eye evidently didn't sit right with her. She seemed to find it ridiculous and annoying.

"Well! (tsk!) An EYE?! Why on Earth would anybody paint an EYE like that on a building!?" She rolled her eyes and abruptly crossed her arms.

Denny loved Lois dearly, and he never seemed to tire of her cynical nature. He was patient no matter what was bothering her, and something usually was.

"Well, the guy's probably an eye doctor, Mom, and that's his advertisement. It's probably an optometrist's office, or something. Maybe he's an optician."

"Well for heaven's sake!" Lois sniffed, thoroughly disgusted. "Humph!" She was shaking her head. "Aren't ya' just glad he wasn't a gynecologist!!!?"

~Patricia S. Mays
*Chicken Soup for the Grandparent's Soul*

# 54

# A Change of Seasons

I've been so involved with motherhood for most of my life that I hardly noticed when it ended. Oh, there was the year when our first bird left the nest, going to college just an hour away. I thought I'd see her often—my mistake!

For the first few months after she left, each time I passed her bedroom I'd look at the stuffed animals scattered about her colorful bedspread, her band jacket hanging in the closet, little trinkets of memories on her dresser. By the time I'd get to the piano in the living room, the tears were really falling. Then I'd head for the phone and call our daughter, just to hear her voice.

We had two more at home, and we were still actively involved at school, church and in the community. I hardly noticed when our oldest son left, because he lived in the area and he came home for meals. We were still busy and the changes were slight.

Two years later when our youngest son left for college, I packed to go with him! His school was three hours away. On the weekends when my hubby and I could no longer stand it, we would take a drive and go to see him. We would spend a couple of hours visiting, always taking him out to dinner, where he could get a good meal. Then I'd hug him goodbye and cry all the way home.

He was my baby and it was so hard to let go.

During the week, I'd drive by the ball field where we spent so much time watching the boys play and working at the concession stand with our daughter; my heart ached for a rerun of those years. All around town I'd see other kids walking along, going to all the activities our kids had once done. Who said, "You can never go home again?" I'd welcome them all back in a minute.

But I knew that wasn't how things were to be. Another season passed and our daughter got engaged and was planning her wedding. There were things to do, places to go, bridal showers to plan and many details to attend to. The empty nest was full again as summer came, and then empty as college resumed. In February, a beautiful wedding took place, and I knew things would never be the same. It was a happy day, but hard to believe my firstborn was becoming a wife.

It hit me one afternoon when I went into my gynecologist's office for my usual checkup. I looked around the room where mothers-to-be were seated. Their world was just beginning. Mine, I felt, was taking another turn. Hadn't it just been me sitting in this office, awaiting the birth of our now-married daughter? Then the boys. Where had the years gone? I headed for the ladies' room, and turned on the water in the sink and started to sob!

I knew this was a mere interruption in the pattern of things, but this was the most important job I'd had in my life. Why did it hurt so much now? I had friends who were starting new careers and many had jobs they were still at. But my job had been my husband and children and home. What would my life be now?

I splashed some water on my face and wiped my eyes. Then I went to take my seat with the young mothers. Why couldn't they have a separate room for us menopausal women? Don't they know how hard it is to sit and look and be reminded of the days when our bellies were huge!

When I got in to see my doctor I made this suggestion openly to him. He prescribed hormone replacement, some brisk walking and instructed me to "Get a life." I told him I'd had one, and always would—my children. I got a lecture, a prescription for estrogen and a sample of Prozac tablets.

That was several years ago. Today, I'm doing the work I enjoyed before my children came along—the work I placed on hold during those wonderful years. I also have two darling rewards in our grand-gals. What a blessing they are to me, and what a blessing to watch as our children continue growing into happy, responsible adults.

Maybe the seasons change too quickly, but each one is a wonder of beauty. And God gives us the strength to make changes in our own lives when needed. Our children are priceless. But so are those memories we've made, and each one will last a lifetime. Wherever we go, our memories remain, movies replayed in slow motion, ours to watch whenever we desire and to treasure deep within our hearts.

~Diane White
*Chicken Soup to Inspire a Woman's Soul*

# 55

# One Finger

*Just about the time a woman thinks her work is done,*
*she becomes a grandmother.*
*~Edward H. Dreschnack*

"Mom, you should put some of your things away. Baby-proof this house," stated our oldest son Mark as he lumbered up the stairs followed by his wife, Kim, and fifteen-month-old Hannah.

Visiting for the Thanksgiving holiday, he finished unloading the luggage and took it to the guest room downstairs. After driving all day from Salt Lake to Ft. Collins, his temper showed.

"That one-finger rule may work with the twins, but it'll never work with Hannah," he insisted.

When my three granddaughters were born four months apart and the twins moved into our house at eight months, my close friend offered me her secret to entertaining grandchildren with few mishaps.

"Teach them the 'one-finger rule.'" All of her five grandchildren learned it at a young age. The success of the method surprised me.

I picked up my granddaughter and said, "Well, Mark, you just watch." I hugged her and walked all around the great room.

"Hannah, you may touch anything in this room you want. But, you can only use one finger."

I demonstrated the technique by touching my forefinger to the African sculpture on the mantel. Hannah followed my example.

"Good girl. Now what else would you like to touch?"

She stretched her finger toward another object on the mantel. I allowed her to touch everything in sight—plants, glass objects, TV, VCR, lamps, speakers, candles and artificial flowers. If she started to grab, I gently reminded her to use one finger. She always obeyed.

But, Hannah, an only child, possessed a more adventurous personality. Her father predicted it would prevent her from accepting the one-finger rule.

During their four-day stay, we aided Hannah in remembering the one-finger rule. She learned quickly. I only put away the things that might prove to be a danger to a child. Otherwise, we watched her closely, and nothing appeared to suffer any damage. Besides, "things" can be replaced.

A few fingerprints on glass doors, windows and tables remained after Hannah and her family returned home. I couldn't bring myself to clean them for days. Each one reminded me of some wonderful experience with Hannah.

Months later, my husband and I drove to Salt Lake, and I watched Mark and Kim continue to practice the one-finger rule. But I refrained from saying, "I told you so." Yet, I smiled inwardly each time they prodded Hannah to touch with "one finger."

Mark, a salesman, always gave a packet of gifts to his potential clients. The night before we returned home, Mark sat on the floor stuffing gifts into their packets.

Hannah helped.

Then she picked up one gift, held it in her hand as if

it were a fragile bird, and walked toward me. At my knee, her beautiful blue eyes looked into mine. She stretched her prize to me and said, "One finger, Nana!"

~Linda Osmundson
*Chicken Soup for the Grandparent's Soul*

# 56

# Buddies

*Grandparents are similar to a piece of string—*
*handy to have around and easily wrapped around*
*the fingers of their grandchildren.*
*~Author Unknown*

Grandfathers and three-year-old boys are natural buddies. On this particular day in May, the grandfather was pleased to have the company of his best little pal when planting the vegetable garden. For a while, the boy seemed to like it, too. His small fingers were just the right size to pick up tiny seeds and drop them into Granddad-made holes. They were a great team.

But before long, the boy became restless and directed his irritation at the seeds themselves.

"What's this one, Granddad?"

"Beets."

"Ugh, I hate beets."

"Well, then, let's do the zucchini instead."

"Yuck. I really hate zucchini."

"Okay, buddy. What would you like to plant?"

"How about... doughnuts?"

Just in time, the grandfather stopped himself from saying there was no such thing as a doughnut seed. Looking at the unhappy little face, he suddenly got an inspiration.

"Wait a sec. I have to go inside and get the right seeds."

Granddad returned with a handful of Cheerios. He and the small boy solemnly planted them in a special corner of the vegetable garden.

Weeks later, when the real seeds began to break through the soil, the boy became entranced with the tiny seedlings. He spent many afternoons helping Granddad water and hoe and watch them grow. And when the first baby vegetables were harvested, he liked them after all.

For weeks, he forgot all about the doughnuts. But then one day at lunch, he said, "Granddad, what happened to our doughnuts? How come they didn't grow?"

Granddad paused a moment. "Well, you know, doughnuts are tricky. Some years when you plant them, you get lots of doughnuts." He sighed. "But other years, all that comes up are the holes."

~Maggie Stuckey
*Chicken Soup for the Gardener's Soul*

# 57

# Same Agenda

We were sitting in the crowded auditorium waiting for the program to view the performance of our seven-year-old grandson, Tanner, in his school's annual Christmas pageant.

It was difficult to say who was more excited—the children or the audience. I looked around and spotted my son and his wife, with their four-month-old baby boy, and Tanner's maternal grandparents seated several rows behind us. We acknowledged each other with a smile and a wave.

Then I saw them—Tanner's "biological" paternal grandparents. My son and Tanner's mother had dated briefly as sixteen-year-olds, split up, then became reacquainted shortly after their high school graduation when Tanner was just six months old. Even though my daughter-in-law never married Tanner's father, his parents had fought for grandparents' rights and won. Tanner may call my son "Daddy," but Tanner is bound by court order to go every other weekend for visitation with the parents of his "biological" father.

We had taken Tanner into our hearts as our own, and we weren't very willing to share him.

This had always been a particular sore spot for me. We did not know them well, and I feared the worst when he went with them on their weekend. In retrospect, we should have viewed it as commendable that they were interested enough in Tanner to pay a lawyer and go through the complicated legal system.

So there we were, separated by a few rows of folding chairs. There were only a few instances where we had been thrown together, and each of these meetings had been uncomfortable. I saw the woman look at us, nudge her husband and whisper in his ear. He immediately looked back at us as well.

My ears were burning as if on fire. I attempted to remember why we were here—our common bond, a child that meant so much to us.

Shortly thereafter the program started, and for the next hour we were enthralled. Before we knew it, the lights were on, and we were gathering our things to leave. We followed the crowd into the hall and searched for our grandson.

We soon found him, and suddenly three sets of grandparents were thrown together, each waiting to take our turn in congratulating Tanner on a fine performance. We eyed each other and spoke a brief "hello."

Finally, it was our turn to hug Tanner and discuss his job well done. His eyes were shining brightly, and he was obviously proud to be the object of so much adoration.

I leaned down to hear what he was saying. "Grandma, I'm so lucky!" Tanner exclaimed, clapping his hands together.

"Because you did such a fine job?" I innocently asked.

"No, because all my favorite people are here! My mom, dad, little brother, and all my grandmas and grandpas are here together, just to see me!"

I looked up, stunned at his remark.

My eyes met those of the "other" grandma, and I could

see she was feeling the same shame as I was. I was horrified at my thoughts and feelings over all these years.

What had given only me the right to love this little boy? They obviously loved him as much as we did, and he obviously loved each of us. They also no doubt had their own fears about us. How could we have been so blind?

As I looked around, I could see we were all ashamed of our previous feelings on this subject. We visited briefly, said our goodbyes and went our separate ways.

I've thought a lot about our encounter since that night, and I admit I feel that a weight has been lifted from my shoulders. I don't fear Tanner's weekend visits like I used to.

I discovered that we all have the same agenda—to love a little boy who truly belongs to all of us.

~Patricia Pinney
*Chicken Soup for the Grandparent's Soul*

# 58

# Walking with Grandpa

Grandfather was a wise and honorable man. His house was not far from ours, and I would visit him often going home after school.

No matter how rotten I had been, I could tell Grandpa anything. My secrets were safe. He always understood. He loved me.

I remember a time when a bunch of us were playing baseball in the field behind Mrs. Ferguson's house. I hit one pitch just right and... slam! It was a home run that soared high and away, and ended up shattering Old Lady Ferguson's kitchen window! We all ran!

Walking home, my best friend, Tom, asked, "How will she ever know who did it? She's blinder than a bat!" He had a point.

I decided to stop by Grandpa's. He must have known something was up by the expression on my face. I felt ashamed. I wanted to hide. I wanted to bang my head against a tree a thousand times and make the world just go away — as if punishing myself could undo things. I told him about it.

He knew we had been warned many times about the dangers of playing where we shouldn't. But he just listened.

"I was wrong," I told him, with my head down. "I hate myself for what I did. I really blew it. Is there a way out? Will she call the police?"

"Well," he said, "she has a problem, just like you. I'll bet if she knew you cared, she would be sad to know that you're afraid of her. I'll bet she wishes you would give her a chance... a chance to be understanding. It's your decision," he said, shrugging his shoulders. "Just so I don't say the wrong thing, is the plan to pretend nothing happened? Just keep quiet and carry your little secret around... hide what you're not proud of?"

"I don't know," I sighed. "Things might get worse...."

"Let's think it through," he said finally. "If you were Mrs. Ferguson, what would you do?"

I had been afraid that Mrs. Ferguson would stay mad at me, so I ran. I didn't know what she might do. On the way home, I imagined that she was a mean witch chasing me, and the farther away I ran, the more gigantic she grew... until finally she towered over the whole town, seeing my every move with an evil eye.

"Well," I said, taking a deep breath, "One solution is to tell Mrs. Ferguson I'm sorry and offer to fix her window."

"If you call her," asked Grandpa, "what's the worst that can happen?" I had to think for a moment. I realized that even if she did not accept my apology, it could not be any worse than seeing the disappointment on Mom and Dad's faces.

Grandpa smiled when he knew I had figured it out.

"Doing what's right is not always easy," he said, handing me the phone. "I'm proud of you." Grandpa did not make me do it. It was always my choice. I knew I had found the best answer, just by thinking it through. That's how Grandpa did things. As it turned out, things were not anywhere near as bad as I had first imagined.

"Owning up to what you're not proud of is the hardest thing of all," said Grandpa. "Choosing to be honest, on your own—even when you don't have to be—makes others trust you and respect you."

Besides, it made me feel really good about myself. No one can ever take that away. Thank you, Grandpa.

Mrs. Ferguson and I eventually became really close friends. She was so kind and grew to take a real interest in me. I started doing all kinds of odd jobs around her house after school, which eventually helped me to save enough to buy my first car. She once told me, "Fear can make the smallest things look so much bigger than they really are."

Just before he passed away Grandpa asked me, "Who will you turn to when I'm gone?"

Holding his hand I told him, "Honor is its own reward, Grandpa. And a good teacher lives on through his student. Thank you."

After Grandpa died, everyone was sad. So many people loved him and would miss him.

I still talk to him, in my thoughts. I imagine how he would approach things, what questions he would ask... what advice he might give... whenever there is a problem. His soothing voice is clear and simple.

Grandpa gave me the tools to fix many problems... and cut them down to size.

And most of all he showed me I was brave.

~Uncle Greg
*Chicken Soup for the Preteen Soul*

# Grand and Great

## What a Child Can Teach Us

*If my heart can become pure and loving,
like that of a child, I think there probably can be
no greater happiness than this.*
*~Kitaro Nishida*

# 59

# Just As I Imagined It

*Every day may not be good,*
*but there's something good in every day.*
*~Author Unknown*

I often walk at Kailua Beach, a two-mile crescent of white sand lined with palm trees on the windward side of O'ahu. I find walking there a good way to exercise and to shake off the "blues." One December morning I set out to rid myself of a weeklong depression. With the holidays coming, I was facing Christmas without my daughters, who lived in Massachusetts. This year, none of us could afford the expensive plane fare to or from the islands.

When I reached the beach, I tucked my rubber slippers under a naupaka bush. In Hawaiian mythology, its white flowers symbolize love's longing. How appropriate, I thought wistfully. As water lapped at my bare feet and waves curled over and collapsed with small explosions, all my senses conspired to conjure up memories of my girls romping in the waves and dribbling sand spires at the water's edge. Maybe a beach walk was not a good idea after all. I looked down at my hands. Yesterday I'd noticed how the blue veins knotted their way under the papery skin. I thrust them into my pockets. Just then, I saw that the sand ahead was littered with shells, an uncommon sight here.

Usually, the waves battered shells to bits on the offshore reefs. Some of the shells weren't even native to Hawaiian waters. Yet, here lay glossy cowries, curly whelks, spotted cones and abalones glistening like polished teal and silver bowls.

Amazed, I wondered where they'd come from. You could buy them in hotel shops or at the International Market Place on Kalakaua Avenue, but why were they here? More than curious, I wandered among them and picked up a whelk with a pale peach lip curling outward.

Suddenly, a voice rang out, "Oh, please, don't pick up the shells."

Looking up, I saw two teenagers, a boy and a girl, arm-in-arm on the top of the sandbank. The girl, in her beach wrap, said, "Please leave the shells. They're for my grandmother."

"Are you serious?" I asked, with some confusion.

She was. I replaced the shell and continued my walk. At the end of the beach, I turned and retraced my steps. Now I could see the sheer majesty of the Ko'olau Mountains. When I reached the same stretch of sand, the young people were gone. Instead, I saw a solitary, silver-haired woman with winter-white skin, wearing a blue pantsuit and closed-toe shoes. She stooped to pick up a shell and put it into the plastic bag in her other hand.

As I passed her, the woman spoke. "I think I've got all the pretty shells. Would you like to see them?" She held out the bag to me. "This beach is just as I imagined it. Shells and all. A dream come true, and at my age! Look at this one!" She pulled out a cowry with dappled brown edges.

"It's very beautiful," I agreed.

"Here, take it. I have so many. I should have left some

for others," she said. Her frail, freckled hand trembled as she held out the shell.

"No, you keep it. I think these shells were waiting just for you." I smiled, hoping she could somehow tell that I, too, had found something rare and lovely on the beach that day. I walked home grateful for the love in the world. My depression was gone.

~Norma Gorst
*Chicken Soup from the Soul of Hawaii*

# How Do You Talk to God?

*My grandson was visiting one day when he asked,*
*"Gramma, do you know how you and God are alike?"*
*I mentally polished my halo while I asked,*
*"No, how are we alike?"*
*"You're both old," he replied.*
*~Author Unknown*

W hen I was a little boy, I thought that my grandmother was God. You see, in Sunday school they taught us that God was very old, older than the whole world, and my grandma was the oldest person I knew. She would sit in a faded yellow, shellback chair in the corner of the room and gaze upon her visitors, and I would sit on the floor in front of her and wonder what she was thinking about up on her throne.

The teacher taught us that no one knew what God looked like, but that was just because she hadn't met my grandmother. God had quiet gray hair that was set in curlers and styled every Tuesday at 9:00 A.M., and thick glasses that allowed her all-knowing eyes to focus on you, and the softest cheeks that you always wanted to nuzzle when you hugged her. God always dressed frumpy, and she wore the same orthopedic shoes forever, probably since she walked across the desert with the twelve tribes. She walked with a cane that I always assumed was the one Moses had turned into that snake that ate Pharaoh's snakes. That was Grandma's style after all. No one argued with her because she was always right.

The rabbi taught us in Sunday school that God was wise and knew everything, and that God was respected by the entire world for his wisdom. Well, my grandma knew everything and everybody, even stuff like math, and my whole family came from all over just to seek her advice. She knew what was wrong with people's marriages and the answer to every question on *Jeopardy*.

No one was smarter than she was. They said God could create anything just by thinking about it. Well, every time we would visit her, I would start getting hungry for her famous meat loaf and blueberry pie. Please, I'd hope as the car moved along the highway, let there be meat loaf and pie at Grandma's! Don't you know the first thing she would say to me as I hugged her was, "Your meat loaf and blueberry pie are over on the table. Go eat it while it's hot." And I would look over and there it was, just like that! How did she know? To my child's mind, there was no doubt; Grandma had to be God.

As I got older, I began to appreciate my grandma as a person and not just as God. She was a refined Southern lady who had been one of the founders of her synagogue. She was a pillar of the community, and everyone knew her. We would go to services on Friday night, and she always walked with great dignity to her seat on the third-row aisle. We would follow her down the center of the congregation as all of the folks rose to greet her. "Good Shabbos, Miz Aaron!" "How ya feelin', Miz Aaron?" "Good to see your family with ya, Miz Aaron!" She would nod her head in greeting to everyone and address them by name.

She was one of the oldest members of the shul, and she took great pride in her role there as a community matriarch. Even when she could no longer walk, I would wheel her down the aisle with her head held high and her jaw set firm. Sometimes when we followed Grandma down the big center aisle with everyone rising as we passed, I felt like I was following Moses through the Red Sea.

On one special occasion, though, I truly came to know how both holy and human my grandmother was. I was about six or seven, the age you start to learn the main Hebrew prayers in the Shabbat service. I was so excited to go to shul with my grandma and show her what I had learned in religious school! We took our seats in the congregation and when the services reached the Shema and v'ahavta (Deuteronomy 6:4-9), I excitedly started to sing along with everyone else. I turned to my grandma to show her what I knew and saw her smiling down at me very proudly. But then I also noticed that her lips were not moving; she was not singing along with us but rather humming!

"Grandma," I whispered, "how come you are not singing along with us?"

"I don't know the words, dear," she replied and continued to hum. I was totally amazed. How could this be? How could my wise and all-knowing Grandma not know the words?

"But Grandma," I said, "the words are right here on the page."

She smiled at me, one of the few times I remember her smiling. "Dear," she said, patiently, "I don't know how to read Hebrew."

Utter confusion. My little mind almost exploded as it

tried to understand what she was saying. My grandma, my Jewish hero, was Jewishly illiterate?

What I did not know then was that women raised in the South in the early part of the century were often not given a Jewish education or taught any Hebrew. It was not a time where a woman's mind was valued like a man's, and this woman who founded a synagogue and kept Judaism alive in our family was never given a Jewish education. But as a kid, I couldn't comprehend any of this; all I knew was that God couldn't read Hebrew! I leaned over to her and tugged on her sleeve to interrupt her humming. "Grandma! Grandma!"

"Yes, dear?" she whispered.

"If you can't read the Hebrew in synagogue, how do you talk to God?"

She looked at me with her all-knowing eyes as she reached down to take my face gently in both of her soft, aged hands. She bent down, kissed me on the cheek and whispered into my ear, "Don't worry, sweetheart, God knows what I'm saying."

~Rabbi Scott Aaron
*Chicken Soup for the Jewish Soul*

# 61

# Green Power

W hen I arrived to retrieve my two granddaughters Halle and Maddie for a sleepover, Halle was in "time-out" in her bedroom, while Daddy was playing with Maddie in the family room.

Hearing my arrival, Halle began begging Daddy through the air vent in her bedroom floor, which connected with the air vent above Daddy's head in the family room, "I love you, Daddy; I'm sorry I kicked Maddie, Daddy; I won't do it again, Daddy; is my time-out over, Daddy?"

Had Daddy not needed me to take his daughters overnight so he and Mommy could both make early-morning meetings, I would have been forced to leave without Halle. As it was, Daddy released Halle from time-out and counseled with her.

"Why did you kick Maddie?" Daddy asked four-year-old Halle about her one-year-old sister, Maddie. "Because she bugs me," Halle answered matter-of-factly, as though her actions were perfectly justifiable and Daddy's question was too stupid to answer.

As an involved and observant grandmother who often takes care of my two granddaughters, I can vouch for Halle's claim. Maddie bugs her all the time, mainly because Halle is not yet used to sharing her world with a new baby sister.

I have a younger sister who grew up in my shadow, which was never easy for her. When Maddie was born, I very much feared she would experience the same thing growing up in Halle's long and large shadow, Halle having been the only child of her parents and the only grandchild in our family for three whole years. But from the beginning, Maddie let us know that she is her own woman. As soon as she was able, she was crawling over the top of Halle to get at whatever she was pursuing, not to mention slapping Halle's face and pulling Halle's hair for the sport of it, I hoped, but sometimes wondered.

Halle, on the other hand, having had her own life, toys and schedule for three years, was having a very hard time sharing anything with Maddie, particularly Bama.

I never held Maddie that Halle didn't also demand to be held. (Fortunately, I have a lap and arms big enough and a back strong enough to accommodate both.) I never fussed over Maddie that Halle didn't also demand some fussing (which I never failed to provide). But, no matter how equal I kept things, Halle regularly complained, "You don't love me anymore, you love Maddie more."

So, when Maddie crossed her path, Halle would sometimes kick at her, for which she was always punished.

Daddy asked again, "Why do you kick Maddie?" Halle answered again, "She bugs me." Daddy counseled, "She is not bugging you, she wants to play with you," to which Halle replied, "Well, I don't want to play with her," to which Daddy counseled, "You have to play with her; she's your little sister and it's your job to take care of her."

The counseling session could have gone back and forth for some time because Halle is not one to admit she's wrong or to be told what to do, but Halle wisely knew her responses were tied to going home with Bama, so she let it go.

While we were driving home, we paused to admire the various Halloween decorations along the way. One yard had a giant-sized, inflated and lighted green-faced Frankenstein monster, something Halle had never seen before. "What's Frankenstein?" she asked. Knowing she was not ready for the deep psychological story of the famed literary character, I answered simply, "Oh, just a Halloween monster" and we drove on.

Always wanting to reinforce Mommy's and Daddy's teachings, I asked Halle, "Why are you mean to your baby sister Maddie, who loves you?" She thought for some time before replying, "It's the 'green power' in me."

One of the things I enjoy most about being a grandmother is seeing in my grandchildren what I was too young and inexperienced to see and appreciate in my own babies and children. In fact, I have been so fascinated by my first grandchild that I have recorded her every word and action since birth, filling 700 pages before her fourth birthday. The thing that fascinates me the most is Halle's "take" on life, her "theories," her "logic," her own unique way of looking at and understanding the world around her.

Halle has very long hair that she has never liked having shampooed or rinsed. The older she gets, the better she gets at rinsing it herself, but she never quite gets the bubbles out without help. When I offered to help her recently, she snapped, "No, you can't help me." When I asked, "Why not?" she replied, "Because you don't have girls, you have boys." (I am the mother of four sons, while her mother is the mother of two daughters.) "If you had girls," she chattered on, "you could help me, but you have boys, so you can't, only Mommy can, because she has girls." A strange, but reasonable theory, I thought. But she didn't stop there.

"That's why you're fat, because you had boys; Mommy's skinny because she had girls; if you had girls, you'd be skinny, but you had boys, so you're fat." I roared with laughter.

Not only did Halle's frankness delight me, but her "logic" fascinated me. If Bama has boys and is fat, and Mommy has girls and is skinny, then surely when it comes to weight, the deciding factor is the gender of your children. (Had I known, I would have prayed for all girls.)

And so go countless of my conversations with my delightful four-year-old granddaughter.

When Halle made reference to "the green power" inside of her, I knew I was in for another one of her delightful "takes" on life.

"What green power?" I asked.

"The green power inside me that makes me do bad things," she replied absently, having already moved on in her thoughts.

Thinking now would be a good time to introduce the concept of Satan, I launched in, only to remember that Satan has no power over children until they are of the age of accountability, so I shelved that thought and asked more about the green power.

"You know, Bama," Halle impatiently replied, as though I should already know what she was just figuring out, "like the green monster. When I do bad things, the green power's in me."

Once again, I was amazed by her logic. If that inflatable, lighted, green-faced Halloween decoration is a monster, and monsters are bad (she had seen, after all, the

Disney movie Monsters, Inc.), then Halle must have that same green power inside of her when she's bad.

Odd concept though it was, it was also pretty darn smart and logical for a four-year-old and a far better explanation than I could have come up with on the spur of the moment.

But Halle was way beyond me. While I was still contemplating green power, she was vowing that she would never kick Maddie again, emphasizing her commitment with a concluding and dramatic "ever."

Oh, that we all had such logic and discipline.

~Peg Fugal
*Chicken Soup for the Latter-day Saint Soul*

# 62

# The Last Puppy

*Everything has beauty, but not everyone sees it.*
*~Confucius*

It had been a very long night. Our black cocker spaniel, Precious, was having a difficult delivery. I lay on the floor beside her large four-foot-square cage, watching her every movement. Watching and waiting, just in case I had to rush her to the veterinarian.

After six hours the puppies started to appear. The first-born was black and white. The second and third puppies were tan and brown. The fourth and fifth were spotted black and white. One, two, three, four, five, I counted to myself as I walked down the hallway to wake my wife, Judy, and tell her that everything was fine.

As we walked back down the hallway and into the spare bedroom, I noticed a sixth puppy had been born and was now lying all by itself over to the side of the cage. I picked up the small puppy and lay it on top of the large pile of puppies, who were whining and trying to nurse on the mother. Precious immediately pushed the small puppy away from rest of the group. She refused to recognize it as a member of her family.

"Something's wrong," said Judy.

I reached over and picked up the puppy. My heart sank

inside my chest when I saw the puppy had a cleft lip and palate and could not close its tiny mouth. I decided right then and there that if there was any way to save this animal, I was going to give it my best shot.

I took the puppy to the vet and was told nothing could be done unless we were willing to spend about a thousand dollars to try to correct the defect. He told us that the puppy would die mainly because it could not suckle.

After returning home Judy and I decided that we could not afford to spend that kind of money without getting some type of assurance from the vet that the puppy had a chance to survive. However, that did not stop me from purchasing a syringe and feeding the puppy by hand—which I did day and night, every two hours, for more than ten days. The little puppy survived and eventually learned to eat on his own, as long as it was soft canned food.

The fifth week after the puppies' birth I placed an ad in the newspaper, and within a week we had people interested in all the pups—except the one with the deformity.

Late one afternoon I went to the store to pick up a few groceries. Upon returning I happened to see the old retired schoolteacher who lived across the street from us, waving at me. She had read in the paper that we had puppies and was wondering if she might get one from us for her grandson and his family. I told her all the puppies had found homes, but I would keep my eyes open for anyone else who might have an available cocker spaniel. I also mentioned that if someone should change their mind, I would let her know.

Within days all but one of the puppies had been picked up by their new families. This left me with one brown and tan cocker, as well as the smaller puppy with the cleft lip and palate.

Two days passed without my hearing anything from the gentleman who had been promised the tan and brown pup.

I telephoned the schoolteacher and told her I had one puppy left and that she was welcome to come and look at him. She advised me that she was going to pick up her grandson and would come over at about eight o'clock that evening.

That night at around 7:30, Judy and I were eating supper when we heard a knock on the front door. When I opened the door, the man who had wanted the tan and brown pup was standing there. We walked inside, took care of the adoption details, and I handed him the puppy. Judy and I did not know what we would do or say when the teacher showed up with her grandson.

At exactly eight o'clock the doorbell rang. I opened the door, and there was the schoolteacher with her grandson standing behind her. I explained to her the man had come for the puppy after all, and there were no puppies left.

"I'm sorry, Jeffery. They found homes for all the puppies," she told her grandson.

Just at that moment, the small puppy left in the bedroom began to yelp.

"My puppy! My puppy!" yelled the little boy as he ran out from behind his grandmother.

I just about fell over when I saw that the small child also had a cleft lip and palate. The boy ran past me as fast as he could, down the hallway to where the puppy was still yelping.

When the three of us made it to the bedroom, the small boy was holding the puppy in his arms. He looked up at his grandmother and said, "Look, Grandma. They found homes for all the puppies except the pretty one, and he looks just like me."

My jaw dropped in surprise.

The schoolteacher turned to us. "Is this puppy available?"

Recovering quickly, I answered, "Yes, that puppy is available."

The little boy, who was now hugging the puppy, chimed in, "My grandma told me these kind of puppies are real expensive and that I have to take real good care of it."

The lady opened her purse, but I reached over and pushed her hand away so that she would not pull her wallet out.

"How much do you think this puppy is worth?" I asked the boy. "About a dollar?"

"No. This puppy is very, very expensive," he replied.

"More than a dollar?" I asked.

"I'm afraid so," said his grandmother.

The boy stood there, pressing the small puppy against his cheek.

"We could not possibly take less than two dollars for this puppy," Judy said, squeezing my hand. "Like you said, it's the pretty one."

The schoolteacher took out two dollars and handed it to the young boy.

"It's your dog now, Jeffery. You pay the man."

Still holding the puppy tightly, the boy proudly handed me the money. Any worries I'd had about the puppy's future were gone.

Although this happened many years ago, the image of the little boy and his matching pup stays with me still. I think it must be a wonderful feeling for any young person to look at themselves in the mirror and see nothing, except "the pretty one."

~Roger Dean Kiser
*Chicken Soup for the Dog Lover's Soul*

# 63

# Sacred Cows

Last weekend my grandson noticed for the first time the cow skull I have hanging on the living room wall. As a longtime admirer of Georgia O'Keeffe, painter-laureate of the Southwest, I came home from Santa Fe several years ago with one of those bleached skulls that have become a trademark, of sorts, for her and her desert art. It hangs on the wall just to the left of my front door, and I use its horns as a hat rack.

One day I walked into the room and found four-year-old Bennett standing stock-still beneath it, a dead-serious expression letting me know his little mind was whirling. So I stood by him, not saying a word, just to give him moral support wherever he was going with this new discovery.

It was a full minute before he turned to me and asked: "Did you kill it?"

Before I could say a word, he shot a mouthload of more questions: "Did you shoot it with a gun or stab it with a knife?"

"How did you get the skin off?" And, finally: "Why do you have dead things on your wall?"

I tried to explain, going into way too much detail, about Georgia O'Keeffe and how she painted pictures of the desert; and because deserts are so dry, lots of cows and other animals die in the heat; and the sun beats down on the bones and turns them white and blah blah blah.

Bennett didn't get it.

"Did a cow die in your yard and turn white, and so you picked it up and hung it on your wall, so you could think about O'Creep?"

One of the things Bennett and I like to do together is drive over to the pasture about half a mile from my house and visit the cows. Occasionally one of the cows in that pasture gets loose and wanders around in the neighborhood. He and I had found one in the middle of the road and had to go knock on the owner's door to tell him to come get his cow before somebody ran over it. Bennett's question was not all that far-fetched.

I explained that actually I'd bought the cow skull at a flea market, that out West there are lots of cows, and people sell their skulls to tourists as a kind of souvenir of the desert. We then made a short detour in the conversation while I explained what a flea market was. He wanted to know why there were no fleas at a flea market, but there were cows. Why wasn't it a cow market?

"Good question," I said.

"I live in the West," says Bennett when we got back on the subject of skulls, "and we don't have cows."

"Well," said I, "Houston is not the desert. The cows I was talking about were desert cows that died in the sun and a famous artist painted them as a symbol for her part of the country—its austerity and its beauty."

"I don't think a dead cow is very beautiful," Bennett says. "I think it's really sad." He looked up at me, such a mournful expression in the drop-dead beautiful eyes he got from his mother and grandfather. "I think you should take it down and bury it in the backyard and put a nice sign over it so God can take it up to heaven with all the other cows."

I was stumped. What's a grandmother to do? Should I rip it off the wall and have a cow funeral? I hate to admit it, but the skull cost me eighty dollars. It makes a great hat rack, and to me it really does represent a part of the country I love for its hard edges and sun-baked magic. To me that landscape is about life, its challenges and sacrifices. I think of it as the workshop of creation, with its blazing lights and fearful clouds, its muscular, bone-bare mesas and flowers that surprise with their audacity to bloom where they are planted, no matter what. That skull means a lot to me. Besides it makes a great conversation piece.

Except in this case.

"When you get a little older, you'll understand," I said, wanting to kick myself the minute I said it. I had hated that phrase when I was a kid. "When you grow up you'll understand" was a cop-out for adults too lazy or too dumb to explain things properly. But leave it to Bennett to get the last word. "My daddy's a grown-up and he wouldn't like dead cow heads hanging on the wall...."

If you're curious as to how this situation worked itself out, well, I don't know if I did the right thing, but I didn't take it down. He and I met several more times under the hat rack to chat about it—like where the eyeballs were and what happened to all its teeth, and is that why his mom puts sunscreen all over him when he goes to the beach—so he won't get bleached and his skin dry up and fall off?

But the only thing I convinced Bennett of in all my explanations was this: his grandmother is slightly crazy.

~Ina Hughs
*Chicken Soup for the Every Mom's Soul*

# The Fishing Lesson

Fishing with my dad was a big event for me, but this trip was going to be extra special, because my grandfather was joining us. Dad and I were in our old Ford truck heading over to pick up Grandpa on our way to the lake. I was so excited to be included in this trip.

"Dad, does Grandpa know how to fish?" I asked.

Dad looked at me and smiled. "Your grandpa taught me how to fish," he said. "And you should know this — Grandpa doesn't like horsing around in the boat."

"Okay," I said. Wow, I thought, Dad catches most of the fish when we go fishing together, and Grandpa taught him how to fish. Grandpa must be the best fishermen ever!

It was a little crowded in the pickup, but I felt pretty important sitting there between the two of them. They talked most of the way, and I didn't mind much because it was fun listening to them talk about work, and even about Mom and Grandma.

As we pulled up along the lake, Grandpa nudged me and asked, "Who's going to catch the biggest fish today?"

"Me!" I answered.

"Well, we will just have to see about that," Grandpa replied.

While Dad and Grandpa had talked most of the way

in the truck, they were very quiet in the boat. Grandpa hooked the first fish, then Dad bested him by two. Me? Not even a nibble.

"Grandpa," I began chattering. "Do you think something is wrong with my bait? I'm not even getting any bites. Maybe I need to do something different. Grandpa, I think I need a new worm. Grandpa, can...?"

Grandpa interrupted me. "Raymond, the reason you're not catching fish is because you aren't holding your mouth right." His comment was perplexing to me.

Grandpa ended the day with five fish on the stringer and Dad had four. Dad told Grandpa that it was a tie because one of his had dropped off the hook and bounced inside the boat, but ended up back in the water, so it still counted. Grandpa argued that it's what you end up with that counts, and you can't count fish you can't eat.

Well, needless to say, I had an empty stringer again, and according to our fishing rules the one who catches the least cleans all the fish. It was a chore I didn't mind, but I would have enjoyed it more if just one of the fish had been mine.

Later that evening after supper, while Dad was cleaning out the boat, I went over to him. "Dad, what does holding your mouth right have to do with catching fish?"

Dad stopped hosing out the boat and looked at me, seeming rather surprised I had asked the question.

"Raymond, I will let you in on a little secret that I had to learn the hard way from Grandpa. But don't tell him I told you, okay?" he said.

We sat down and he explained that when he was about my age and wasn't catching fish, Grandpa told him he wasn't holding his mouth right. So one day while fishing, Dad began making all kinds of faces. After a few minutes of silence, Grandpa turned to see why my dad had become so quiet and saw him making all those silly faces.

"Charles," he asked my dad, "what in the name of God is wrong with your face?"

Dad explained that he was trying to find which way to hold his mouth so he could catch fish. Grandpa started laughing so hard he nearly tipped the boat over.

My dad finally explained it to me: "Raymond, what your grandpa meant was that I was talking too much. When you're fishing, the way to hold your mouth is closed."

"Why?" I asked.

He explained that when I talk too much, the noise moves my fishing pole, making the line vibrate and scaring the fish. At least that was Grandpa's theory.

"But don't tell Grandpa I told you so," Dad warned me again.

"How long was it before Grandpa told you?" I asked.

Dad chuckled again. "Well," he said, "I can tell you I got pretty good at cleaning fish, just like you."

All that winter I thought about what Dad had told me, and it felt pretty cool that I knew the secret. When spring came, all three of us once again went fishing. Dad and Grandpa were quietly talking in the back of the boat and I was in the front when I felt a fish strike, so I gave my line a little tug. They never even noticed. I knew I had one hooked, but I didn't call out to them just yet.

It was then I started making all the weird faces I could muster. Finally, they both stopped talking and looked at me.

"Look at your son's face," Grandpa said. "What in the world is he doing?" They both started laughing.

At that moment, I jerked back on my pole and yelled out, "I GOT ONE!" They both stopped laughing.

I was even in for a little surprise. That fish jumped

clean up out of the water and skipped across the top of the lake, then my reel screamed as it took out more line. I fought that fish back and forth for what seemed forever. When I finally got the fish in the boat, Grandpa and Dad were both speechless.

"Yep, guess you just got to hold your mouth right!" I said.

Grandpa cleaned fish that night, including my five-and-a-half-pound rainbow trout. Dad said later that it was bigger than anything either he or Grandpa had ever caught.

~Raymond Morehead
*Chicken Soup for the Fisherman's Soul*

# 65

# Hershey's Dark Chocolate

*Grandfathers are just antique little boys.*
*~Author Unknown*

I guess we all know of the one person in the neighborhood who stays by himself, or herself, and has very little to do with everyone else in the community. You know the type, right? Well, that is not exactly me, although I am not far from it.

I have been married too many times to talk about. In fact it would be embarrassing to say the exact number. All of the marriages were very good, as far as I was concerned, yet ended because I was unable to fully show love or affection. I found it very easy to be nice, kind and responsible. I mean, what else is there other than being good, kind, honest and responsible? That is all I ever knew or was even taught as an orphan in the orphanage in Jacksonville, Florida.

One day this little girl showed up at my door with dirty hands and chocolate all over her face. "Don't move, and I mean don't move a muscle," I yelled at her, as I ran to get a washrag. Darn kids can't do anything without making trouble for me, I thought, as I returned to wash her hands and face. For the remainder of the day I worked as a prison guard making sure this little troublemaker did not touch any of my personal stuff. All day long all I heard was, "Can I have this?" and "Can I have that?" I thought I would pull out what little bit of hair I had left before the day was over. Thank God, the phone finally rang and they were on their way to pick her up. But, oh no! They had not made it back to town and wanted to know if I would keep her for the night. Reaching for the aspirin, I shook my head and told them, "I guess I have no choice."

Later that evening I put Chelsey to bed, and as I was about to leave the room she looked at me and said, "Poppa, do you love me?"

"Of course, I love you!" I hollered. "I'm your Poppa!" and then I closed the door.

"I love you, too, Poppa," I heard through the door. I stood for several seconds with my head leaning against the wall. I immediately opened the door and just stood there looking at her at the end of her bed. She walked over and kissed my hand. I grabbed that three-year-old little baby girl and I hugged her as tightly as I could. I had never known, until that very moment, what the feeling of love felt like, and I never realized that — I hadn't known.

Now Poppa and his little sweetheart eat Hershey's dark chocolate in Granny's favorite recliner, until Granny gets the broom and chases Poppa and Chelsey to the bedroom where they watch cartoons together and get chocolate all over everything. That little baby will never have to ask her Poppa, ever again, if he loves her.

It is true that we must learn to love before we can truly begin to live, even at age fifty-three.

~Roger Dean Kiser (Poppa)
*Chicken Soup for the Grandparent's Soul*

# Grand and Great

## Special Connections

*Grandchildren are lovely reminders of*
*what we're really here for.*
*~Janet Lanese*

# 66

# Orange Cheeks

Willie was six years old. He lived in the country. The phone rang, and Willie picked it up. He had a habit of breathing into the phone instead of talking.

"Hello, Willie," his grandmother's voice said to the breathing.

"How'd you know it was me?"

"I just knew, Willie. Willie, I want you to spend the night."

"Oh, Grandma! I'll get Momma!"

His mother took the phone, talked a while and hung up.

"Willie," his mother said, "I never let you spend the night at your grandmother's because you get in trouble."

"I won't get in trouble," Willie burbled. He shone with excitement so his mother spoke quietly, seriously, "I don't want to get a call tonight and have to drive thirty miles to pick you up."

"No troubllllllllle," he said.

"I'll tell you this: Your grandmother can be difficult late in the day," she went on. "She can be a bit of a grump."

"I'll be good. I promise."

"Well, if there's any trouble you won't go overnight again for a year. Go up and pack your bag."

Willie had won. He ran upstairs and put six t-shirts and a toothbrush in his bag.

He and his mother drove all the way into Cambridge. Willie loved Cambridge because all the houses were squeezed together. They drove around Harvard Yard, down Trowbridge Street and took a left on Leonard Avenue. The houses were all wooden triple-deckers, and his grandmother lived at number nine. They parked and Willie ran up the outside stairs, pushed the outside door open and pressed the buzzer inside.

Zzzzzzzzzzzzzzzzzttt! The door wouldn't open until his grandmother pressed another buzzer from the inside. It made a click, then the door unlocked. It was magic. Willie pushed the door in and stood at the bottom of the stairs. The stairs were narrow and dark and filled with the wonderful smells of his grandmother's house. He could have spent the whole weekend right here, but his grandmother was standing at the head of the stairs calling him.

"Come on up, Willie."

"Here I come, Grandmaaaaaaa," he sang out.

He rushed up to the top and his grandmother leaned down for a hug. He kissed her on those wrinkled, crinkled cheeks. He loved those cheeks, but never said anything about them.

"You'll be in the guest room upstairs," his grandmother said. "There's a prize up there for you."

"Thank you, Grandmaaaaa," he said, hurrying up the stairs. His mother's voice caught up with him, "You remember what I said, Willie."

"Don't worry. No troubllllle."

When Willie ran into the guest room he saw his grandmother had done something wonderful. She had pasted six large silver stars to the ceiling. He loved those.

The prize lay on the table. Two pieces of orange paper, a small pair of scissors, glue and a sharp pencil. Willie took the scissors and cut two circles from the paper and put glue on the back of the circles. He pasted the circles to his cheeks. Now he had orange cheeks.

Looking out the window he saw his mother driving off. "Goodbye, Mommaaaaa," he shouted with a victorious grin.

He ran downstairs and his grandmother said just the right thing: "Wonderful cheeks."

"Thank you, Grandmaaa," he smiled, jouncing his shoulders.

"We'll have tea in the dining room, but first I'll hang out wash and you'll go on an errand to Mr. Murchison's. You know him."

"The fruit man."

"Yes. He's right next door. He's expecting you. Get four pounds of bananas. Here's a dollar. Do a good job."

Willie went down the dark narrow stairs, the secret stairs, and on outside to the fruit store. He had never gone on an errand by himself before. He bravely stepped into the old-fashioned fruit store. Dark. The floor was dark and wooden and oily. Mr. Murchison stood there. He was older than the bananas. And he was curved like the bananas. "Hello, Willie," he said in a long, dark voice. "Your grandmother told me you were coming. Nice to see you again." He reached to the top of the banana rack. "I've got four pounds of bananas for you."

Willie shook his head back and forth. "I don't want those."

"What's the trouble?" Mr. Murchison asked.

"They're rotten."

"They're not rotten," moustached Murchison insisted, laughing. "They're ripe. Best way to have 'em."

"I want the yellow ones," Willie said.

Mr. Murchison replaced the bananas and took yellow ones from the rack. "Someday you'll know better," he growled.

"Think I know better now," Willie replied.

Mr. Murchison seemed to be chewing something distasteful. "I like your cheeks," he finally grunted.

Willie looked up, "I like your cheeks, too."

"Arrrrrrr."

Willie took the bananas to the backyard where his grandmother was hanging clothes on the line. "Good for you, Willie. You're a regular businessman. You go up and play till I finish, and we'll have tea."

Willie was a businessman! To him a businessman was someone who made pencil marks on the walls. Secret ones. But they were real. Willie went up and down the back stairway making small pencil marks. Then he decided to make a secret mark in the dining room.

He pushed a chair against the white wall in the dining room, stood on the chair, reached way up and started to make a tiny dot. Willie heard something. Terrified, he turned, "Grandma!" In his panic he made a scratch mark two feet long on the wall. "Oh, no. I have to go home now." He tried to erase it, but that made it worse. He spat on his hands and tried to wipe the mark off. Now it was all over the wall. It was horrible. Now he was in trouble. He jumped off the chair and ran to the window. His grandmother was hanging the last few socks. He had to do something or he'd have to go home. Willie opened the drawer in the pantry and saw a hammer and two nails. He took them into the dining room. He pulled the dining room cloth off the table and climbed onto the chair. He nailed the cloth to the wall. Now you couldn't see the scratch mark — but you could see the dining room cloth.

His grandmother made the tea and put everything on a tray.

"Come on, Willie. We'll have tea in the dining room."

His head seemed to be sinking into his shoulders. "Let's have the tea here," he said.

"We always have tea in the dining room," she said and went into the dining room alone.

"Willie, the dining room cloth is not on the table," she said curiously. Then, "Willie, the dining room cloth is nailed to the wall."

After a silence Willie said, "Which wall?"

"You come in and see which wall."

Willie came slowly in. His head sank further into his shoulders. "Oh, that wall," Willie said. "I nailed it to that wall."

Suddenly, he began to shake. His whole body trembled, and he burst out crying. "Now I have to go home." He was crying so hard the tears ran down onto his orange paper cheeks. He began to rub the cheeks, and the paper was shredding. That overwhelmed his grandmother. "Willie!" she said, rushing over, kneeling down to hold him. She was crying now, and her tears were falling onto his orange paper cheeks. She held him close, then breathed deeply, saying, "Willie, look at the two of us; this is absurd. It's all right."

"No, it isn't," Willie sobbed. "Now I have to go home. I can't come for a whole year."

"You don't have to go home," she said, standing and straightening her dress. "It's perfectly all right."

"No, it isn't," Willie persisted. "Momma says late in the day you're a grump."

His grandmother's eyes opened rather wide. "Hmmmmm, she does, does she?" His grandmother's lips pursed in thought for what seemed forever. "Well! I'll tell you this, Willie, your mother's no prize either."

They sat down at the table. "Now we'll have tea, and then we'll take care of the wall. How many sugars, Willie?"

"Five."

"One," she corrected.

The tea seemed to calm his whole body.

His grandmother took the hammer and pulled out the nails. She put the cloth on the table, saying, "I'll sew the holes up another time. For now we'll put a bowl of fruit over one hole and flowers on the other. Your mother will never know." Then his grandmother put putty in the nail holes, and she and Willie painted over the scratch mark.

In three hours, the paint was dry and the mark gone. "Now your mother won't know about this," she said with assurance. "It's our secret."

"She'll know," Willie pouted. "She always knows."

"She's my daughter. She won't know."

"She's my mother. She'll know!"

The next morning Willie was scared to death as his mother came up the dark, secret stairs. The three of them would have tea before leaving.

They sat at the dining table drinking tea. Willie was quiet as long as he could be. Finally, he looked at his mother and said, "Don't pick the bowl of fruit up."

"Why would I pick the bowl of fruit up?" she asked.

An extraordinary look of total innocence filled his face, "I don't knoooow."

Tea continued, and Willie was staring at the wall.

"What are you staring at?" his mother said.

"The wall," Willie replied. "It's a nice wall."

"Ahh!" his mother sighed. "There was trouble. What was the trouble?"

Defeated, Willie said, "Tell the trouble, Grandma."

"Well, there was trouble. The trouble was we didn't have enough time. Is that what you mean, Willie?"

"That's what I mean," he bounced.

A few minutes later his grandmother stooped over at the top of the stairs, and Willie kissed her on those wrinkled, crinkled cheeks. And then he and his mother went down the dark, narrow stairway with the wonderful smells. His mother didn't know what had happened. It was a secret.

When he got home Willie ran up to his room, unzipped his bag and took out the orange paper. He cut two circles and put them in an envelope with a note saying, "Dear Grandma. Here's orange cheeks for you. Love, Willie."

~Jay O'Callahan
*Chicken Soup for the Grandparent's Soul*

# 67

# The Shawl

*Grandchildren are the dots that connect
the lines from generation to generation.*
~Lois Wyse

Most children are put to bed with cozy bedtime stories, but not so for me. At bedtime, my grandmother Bea would tell me the story of how she, her mother and her five siblings had escaped the Russian pogroms. As told by my grandmother, the Russian Cossacks stormed into their town and killed many Jews.

When the Cossacks stormed into my grandmother's house, my great-grandmother screamed, "Run, Kinder, Run!" My grandmother and her sister fled and were hidden by a non-Jewish neighbor in a cold and dark potato cellar. They stayed there for over two days, with rats crawling on them while the neighbor risked her life by telling the soldiers that she had not seen any Jewish children. Later, the neighbor took them out of the potato cellar and told the soldiers that they were her own children, again risking her own life to save the lives of my grandmother and her sister. Eventually, the family was reunited and my great-grandmother, Sara, led her six children on a journey away from Russia. This journey took over two years, during which they traveled and hid.

On a bitter cold, blustery night in 1910, Sara and her six children arrived in Buffalo, New York. They were tired, cold and hungry. The only warm item of clothing they possessed was Sara's winter coat. Sara cut her coat into six pieces, so that each child would have some warmth. Sara had nothing to keep her warm.

A kind woman named Esther Mintz heard of Sara's plight, as the Jewish community was very small and supportive of the newly arriving immigrants. Esther stayed up an entire night and knit Sara a beautiful and warm black shawl. She gave Sara the shawl and a basket of freshly cooked food. The food was quickly eaten, and the shawl saw Sara through her first cold winter in America. Sara never forgot the kindness of this stranger.

Forty-six years later, Renee, the American-born grandchild of Sara, told her grandmother that she was engaged to be married. Renee was to marry a man named Joseph Mintz. Sara quickly realized that Joseph was the grandchild of the woman who had knit her a shawl so many years ago when she arrived in America, a cold and hungry immigrant. Sara had saved this shawl, and she took it from her attic and showed it to Renee. Holding the shawl to her heart, Sara spoke in Yiddish, telling her grandchild that this marriage was beshert, meaning that Renee and Joseph's marriage was planned in heaven before Renee's birth, and the shawl was a sign of this destiny.

Renee and Joseph are still married—they are my parents. Sara and Esther died years ago and I never knew them. My grandmother Bea, who told me the story of her escape from Russia, died when I was pregnant with my own daughter, Jennifer. While dying, she symbolically, but likely unconsciously, continued a family tradition: She knit a blanket to give warmth to the great-grandchild she would never meet. Today, I am writing this story with Jennifer sitting beside me. The blanket, first knit for Jennifer, has since sheltered my youngest daughter Allison and my sister's son Steven. While the original shawl has unfortunately been lost, its story, and the new knitted blanket, keep us warm inside and connected to the pain, kindness, love and perhaps even the destiny of past generations.

~Laurie Mintz
*Chicken Soup for the Jewish Soul*

# 68

# Abuela's Magic

*Dreams are nature's answering service—*
*don't forget to pick up your messages once in a while.*
~Sarah Crestinn

My grandmother was one of the most influential people in my life. She moved in with us right after my grandfather died, and she lived with us from the time I was five years old. Every day when I got home from school, she was there to make my world magical. No matter what we were doing, she turned it into something bigger and brighter than it was.

Before my grandmother moved in with us, she lived in a little house in Wilmington, California. Behind her house was a shallow creek, dry usually, with a tiny wood bridge. When we visited, my grandmother would take my sister and me over that little bridge, which for anybody else was probably no big deal. But because there were no ordinary moments or events for my grandmother, she always got us ready for our walk by talking about our difficult "journey" over the bridge and about how we needed to pay close attention to every step we took. She praised us in advance and after our trip for our "courage" in walking over the dangerous deep creek, and she reminded us that by taking this daily journey we were preparing ourselves for life's bigger challenges.

My sister and I grew up with the impression that we were extraordinarily brave for performing this death-defying act; we felt proud of ourselves and confident. Years later as adults, we had the chance to revisit the "deep creek" and the bridge, and we were amazed to see that it was really just a small puddle covered by an ornamental bridge. My grandmother had created another world for us through her storytelling and her imagination, a world much more intriguing than anything our daily lives offered us.

My grandmother loved to tell me stories about growing up in Puerto Rico, stories about her brothers and sisters and her mother. To her, psychic experiences were just part of everyday life. When her brother Tito died in Puerto Rico, his shadow appeared to her in New York as she sat sipping coffee at the kitchen table. When her first great-grandson was born, she said an angel had appeared blowing a trumpet, saying that the baby was a boy. She wrote down the time, and it was just minutes after my nephew John was born. Just before my grandfather died, she and my mother had identical dreams about him.

So when my adored grandmother died four years ago, I thought that in some way I would "hear" from her, but I never did. I had been trying to have children and had become pregnant several times, but miscarried each time. I had been receiving fertility treatments, and two years after my grandmother's death I was in the process of taking treatment again. I came home from the doctor's office one day and took a nap. While I was sleeping, I heard the phone ring. When I didn't pick up the phone, the answering machine went on. It was my grandmother, and she was saying: "Hola, Chinita!" ("Chinita" was her nickname for me.) "I just called to tell you happy birthday; I love you."

When I got up I remembered the dream, and then I thought how weird it was that my grandmother had mentioned my birthday because my birthday wasn't near. The following week I went to the doctor, and they told me that I was pregnant. I was so happy, I couldn't believe it. When I asked them my due date, they said October third.

October third is my birthday.

~Michele Capriotti
*Chicken Soup for the Latino Soul*

# 69

# Thoughts from a Three-Year-Old

*What children need most are the essentials
that grandparents provide in abundance.
They give unconditional love, kindness, patience, humor,
comfort, lessons in life.
And, most importantly, cookies.*
~Rudolph Giuliani

Because of adult perspectives, our expectations from children, when they answer us, can be quite different than what actually takes place.

My three-year-old son had been told several times to go into the bathroom to get washed for bed. The last time I told him more assertively. His response was "Yes, Sir!" Being his mother, I didn't expect the "sir."

"You say, 'Yes, Sir,' to a man. To a lady you would say, 'Yes, Ma'am.'" So to quiz him on his lesson I queried, "What would you say to Daddy?"

"Yes, Sir!" came the reply.

"Then what would you say to Mama?"

"Yes, Ma'am!" he proudly remarked.

"Good boy! Now what would you say to Grandma?"

Being used to his usual question posed to Grandma, he lit up and said, "Can I have a cookie?"

~Barbara Cornish
*Chicken Soup for the Grandparent's Soul*

# 70

# Food for Thought

*A child needs a grandparent, anybody's grandparent,*
*to grow a little more securely into an unfamiliar world.*
*~Charles and Ann Morse*

Heart failure had robbed her of her husband, and now macular degeneration was stealing her eyesight and osteoporosis was plundering her body.

I worried about my elderly neighbor's loneliness and her diet. Lack of appetite and motivation kept Gwen from cooking. More than a quiet street separated the two of us. Her life had been derailed, while mine was a locomotive on a fast track as I raised a house full of kids and maintained a demanding time schedule to match. So I turned to Koy, our little redheaded caboose, for help.

"Do you think you can carry these muffins over to Mrs. Potter's?"

"I fink I can," he nodded.

With me watching from our front door and Gwen waiting at hers, three-year-old Koy cautiously crossed the street, carrying the plate of fragrant goodies. And so began their long relationship.

"I fink Grandma Potter needs me," he would say. Or, "Don't you fink Grandma Potter wants some of those cookies?" And, "I fink Grandma Potter likes cupcakes." Then off he would go, thoughtfully bearing a plate of this or a sandwich bag of that, and always taking time to settle in for a nice little talk. Well, Koy talked; Gwen listened. A lonely last child; a lonesome lost widow.

Those regular visits continued through the years, sometimes at her invitation and other times at his instigation. As his age, sensitivity and caregiving expertise grew, Koy did more than take food. He ran her errands, did light chores and drove her to doctor appointments. On prom night, he and his date even dashed through the rain to model their finery before an admiring Grandma Potter.

Finally, as we stood arm-in-arm in the street waving Koy off to college, Gwen turned to me.

"I'm certainly going to miss that young man and his visits. You know, when he was little, he rarely came empty-handed."

I nodded agreement, remembering all the baking I used to do.

"But, when you didn't send something, our little Koy must have raided the pantry." She winked. "No matter what, he always took good care of me."

"What do you mean?"

"Over he would come, his pocket filled with raisins, pretzels, popcorn or even Cheerios. Whatever he could scavenge."

I laughed in motherly embarrassment. "Oh, good grief." I could just imagine grubby little boy hands and fists full of crumbs. "What did you do?"

"Why, I got out a serving plate," she smiled at the memory. "I watched as he proudly piled his offerings on the kitchen table. Then... well... then the two of us sat down and ate them, pocket lint and all."

~Carol McAdoo Rehme
*Chicken Soup for the Caregiver's Soul*

# 71

# We'll Never Divorce You

*When doubts filled my mind,*
*your comfort gave me renewed hope.*
*~King David*

D ear Grandchild,
Grandma and Grandpa know that you're hurting right now because Mommy and Daddy are breaking up. It's called "divorce," and you probably know some other children who have gone through this, too. It happens a lot, more than anyone would like, but we want you to know that you're not alone. When you're at school, ask around, and you're sure to find lots of other kids who have been through what you're going through. And they are surviving. You'll survive, too, although Grandma and Grandpa know that you probably don't feel that way right now.

It's no fun at all, is it? Just a little while ago, things looked fine, everything seemed to be just right, and now everything seems to have fallen apart. We really wish we could somehow "kiss all the boo-boos" and make everything right, but, sadly, Honey, we can't.

We want you to know that this time is difficult for us, too. It makes us very sad to see the hurt and uncertainty in your eyes. When we sense that you are hurting, we hurt, too.

Mommy and Daddy have found that, for whatever reasons, they can't go on living together. You must know that Mommy and Daddy still love you very much even if they are having problems with each other.

We want you to know several important things, things that we hope will help you to go through this scary and difficult time.

The first thing that we want to tell you is this: It is not your fault! You know, whenever a divorce happens, almost all children think that they did something that made it happen. And we want to promise you this — that is almost never true! Mommies and daddies who break up are doing so because they are having some big problems in their relationship. And you are not to blame. If you are blaming yourself, even a little bit, please let us know. Talk to us or write us, and we'll be your special friends and listen to your feelings.

The second thing we want you to know is that you probably can't fix it. Lots of kids imagine that they might be able to find just the perfect thing to say or do and, magically, Mommy and Daddy will start loving each other again. We're sorry to tell you, that almost never works. Sometimes mommies and daddies do get back together again after a time apart and some time for healing, but that happens because they found their own reasons to do so.

The third and maybe the most important thing we want to tell you is this: We will never divorce you! We will always be there for you when you need us. Sometimes we may be far away, but you can call or write us. We'll answer as soon as we can. And you can always talk to us because we promise to be the very best listeners we can for you.

You need to know that we won't ever take sides between your mommy and your daddy. The only "side" we're going to be on is yours. Instead, we'll be good listeners, and we'll also help you find good things to do and great ways to spend your time. We'll search for fun, and we'll make some of our own, too.

You might think that you'll never be happy again or that things will never feel right again. We can understand those feelings. But we want you to know something that we've learned because we've lived so long and seen and experienced so many things—you will laugh again; it will get better. You'll laugh and grow and experience joy again. Good things will happen. You will have many good times with Daddy and many good times with Mommy again, we assure you. It won't be the same as it was, but your life will be a good one. And the love that surrounds you—from your parents, your grandparents and the rest of the family, and all your friends—will heal and help.

Now here's a list of the things you can count on:

Nothing you can ever do or say will make us stop loving you. We'll love you forever. When we're in heaven, we'll still love you. There are things you can count on now, when the world seems so shaky, and one of them is our love for you.

We'll be good listeners for you. Share your feelings, both good and bad. It is a healthy way to help yourself get past these rough times.

We'll give great hugs and warm, long back rubs.

And we'll still make your favorite foods whenever you ask us.

You can contact us easily. We're enclosing a card with our address, home phone number, cell phone number and e-mail address. So no matter where you are, you'll always be able to reach us. If you have to, you can call us "collect." We've also included a pack of stamped postcards addressed to us, so you can always send us a card. And there's a stack of stamped, addressed envelopes for when you have bigger, longer things to write or a nice picture to send us.

Honey, you're not alone. Your mommy and daddy still love you, even if they are breaking up. And we'll always love you, no matter what. And remember: We will never divorce you. Never.

Love,
Grandma and Grandpa

~Hanoch and Meladee McCarty
*Chicken Soup for the Grandparent's Soul*

# Grand and Great

## There Is No Place I'd Rather Be

*The best thing to spend on children is your time.*
*~Joseph Addison*

# Grandma's Soup Night

*Our grandchildren accept us for ourselves, without rebuke or effort to change us, as no one in our entire lives has ever done, not our parents, siblings, spouses, friends—and hardly ever our own grown children.*
*~Ruth Goode*

It had been a busier than usual week, and trying to cope with a stiff neck had made it worse. By Thursday afternoon I had used up my supply of energy and patience. All I wanted to do was to get home, put on a comfortable robe, fix a bowl of good hot soup and collapse with my feet up.

So when I pulled into the driveway and saw my daughter-in-law Wanda's car, I groaned in despair. I had forgotten it was Bryan's night.

Since his parents' separation, I had tried to have my six-year-old grandson spend a few hours with me at least once a week. I always tried to make it a special time for him. We cooked his favorite meal—chicken and cranberry sauce—or went to his favorite hamburger place. Then either a movie or a walk through the park, and home for some fun together. We'd get down on the floor and have car races. Sometimes we'd make candy, or maybe read some silly or scary book. Bryan delighted in all these activities, and so did I. Usually.

Tonight there was no way I could handle it. I was going to have to postpone our evening together until next week. I hugged them both and then explained how badly I was feeling.

"Bryan, honey, I'm sorry," I said. "Tonight your Grandma Joan isn't up to any fun and games. Just a nice hot bowl of soup, a lazy hour of TV and then early to bed. We'll have our night together some other time."

Bryan's smile faded, and I saw the disappointment in his eyes. "Dear Lord, forgive me," I prayed, "but I'm really not up to it tonight. I need this night to relax and renew myself."

Bryan was looking up at me solemnly. "I like soup, Grandma."

My grandmother's heart knew what he was really saying. In his own way, he was saying, "Please don't send me away. Please let me stay."

I heard Wanda say, "No, Bryan. Grandma Joan's too tired tonight. Maybe next week."

But in Bryan's eyes, I saw the shadow, the uncertainty. Something else was changing. Maybe Grandma Joan wouldn't want to have him come anymore. Not tonight, not next week, not ever.

I hesitated and then tried again. "Just soup and TV, Bryan. No car games on the floor for me tonight, no baking cookies, no books. I probably won't be awake very long."

"I like soup," he repeated.

With a sigh of resignation, I gave in and placed my hand on his shoulder. "Then you are cordially invited to dine at my castle. The meal will be small, but the company will be delightful. Escort the Queen Mother in, please, Sir Bryan."

It was worth it to see his eyes light up and hear him

giggle as he made a mock bow and replied, "Okay, your Royal Highness."

While I put the soup on the stove and changed into my robe, Bryan set up trays and turned on the television set.

I must have dozed off after the first few sips of soup. When I woke up, there was an afghan over my legs, the bowls and trays were gone. Bryan was sprawled on the floor, dividing his attention between a coloring book and a television show. I looked at my watch. Nine o'clock. Wanda would be coming to get Bryan soon. Poor boy, what a dull time he must have had.

Bryan looked up with a smile. Then, to my surprise, he ran over and gave me a big hug. "I love you, Grandma," he said, his arms still around my neck. "Haven't we had a nice time together?"

His big smile and happy eyes told me that this time he meant exactly what he was saying. And, to my surprise, I knew he was right. We really had had a nice time together.

That was the key word—together. We had done nothing exciting or special. I had slept in the chair. Bryan had colored and watched TV. But we were together.

That night I realized something important. Bryan's visits don't have to be a marathon of activity. The important thing is that he knows I love him and want him. He knows he has a place in my life, which is reserved particularly for him. A time that is just for us to be together.

Bryan still comes once a week. We still bake chicken or eat out, make cookies or go for a walk in the park. But every now and then we enjoy our favorite together time, our special feast of love—soup night.

~Joan Cinelli
*Chicken Soup for the Mother's Soul 2*

# 73

# Digging in the Dirt

*Grandmother-grandchild relationships are simple.*
*Grandmas are short on criticism and long on love.*
*~Author Unknown*

"Dig in the dirt with me, Noni."

My three-year-old grandson, Ethan, stood in the kitchen with pleading eyes and a big spoon. I had two large clay pots with soil that needed changing, and he needed something to do—a perfect match. After getting the necessary digging utensil from the junk drawer, he'd rushed to the deck and sent dirt flying everywhere. I could just imagine my daughter's reaction to his dirty clothes, but that was okay with me. As the grandma, I'm allowed to spoil.

It was hard to resist his invitation to play, but I had a meeting that night and I still had to fix supper.

"I can't right now, honey. Noni's busy."

Ethan hung his head and stared at his shoes all the way back outside. Guilt hovered over me while I chopped celery and onions for meatloaf. Some grandma! But, I reasoned, it's different being a grandmother these days. I'm younger, busier. I don't have time to play like mine did when I was a child.

As I watched Ethan through the window, memories of

a tea party with my grandmother surfaced. I remembered how Mammie filled my blue plastic teapot with coffee-milk and served toasted pound cake slathered in butter. She carried the tray as we walked to the patio and sat under the old magnolia tree that was full of fragrant, creamy-white blooms. I served the cake, poured the coffee into tiny plastic cups and stirred with an even tinier spoon. Our playtime probably lasted less than thirty minutes, and yet, after all these years, I still remembered.

Ethan saw me watching him and pointed to the pot. He had emptied it. I waved and nodded to him. Just then it dawned on me that my love for flowers came from Mammie. She had dug in the dirt with me. I recalled the new bag of potting soil and flower seeds I had in the garage. It would be fun to plant seeds and watch them grow with my little grandson.

I left my knife on the chopping block, found another old spoon and went outside.

"Noni can play now."

Ethan clapped his dirty hands as I plopped down beside him. What fun we had that sunny afternoon. Supper was on time, and so was I for my meeting.

I learned the important life secret that Mammie always knew: there's always time to play.

~Linda Apple
*Chicken Soup for the Grandma's Soul*

# 74

# What's
# a Grandma to Do?

One of the most pressing problems for grandparents these days is knowing how to be a grandparent. I certainly don't wear cotton flowered dresses and big full-sized aprons and bake molasses cookies every week like Grandma Kobbeman did. I don't sit on a porch swing and rock the evening away or watch soap operas like my Grandmother Knapp did. When I was fifty and a grandmother, I water-skied behind my brother's boat in Kentucky and snorkeled for hours in the ocean off the coast of two Hawaiian islands. The next year I rode every scary roller-coaster ride at Disneyland.

Grandparents are different nowadays. We have full-time careers. We run corporations and marathons. We belong to clubs, watch the stock market, eat out a lot, exercise regularly and still have the energy to do the Twist at wedding receptions.

My five grandchildren live out of town, and I don't see them on a daily or weekly basis. In fact, since their parents have busy careers and whirligig lives like I do, I'm lucky if I get to see my grandchildren once or twice a month.

When Hailey was four years old she came for her very first "all alone" visit. She would be alone with me Saturday night, all day Sunday, all day Monday and half of Tuesday before her mother arrived to take her back home. Saturday night and Sunday were a breeze. Hailey, her favorite blankie, latest Beanie Baby and I, snuggled together in my big bed. We slept just fine until Hailey sat up in the middle of the night and whispered, "Gramma, you were snoring."

All day Sunday we kept busy with my daughter-in-law and other granddaughter who were visiting for the day. But on Monday morning when Miss Hailey and I woke up and she assured me that I didn't snore at all that night, I began to fret. It's Monday, a workday. I have books to read and review and a book proposal to get out. I need to be in my home office! How am I ever going to get it all done if I have to entertain Hailey all day?

I'll worry about it later, I thought. For at that moment there were little girl hugs to be had, waffles to toast, and birds to feed on the deck with my four-year-old helper.

And so we hugged and rocked and ate, and I held the bird feeder while Miss Hailey scooped up six big cups full of tiny seed into the feeder and only a half-cup or so landed on the deck.

As we sat in the glider swing on the deck watching the squirrels eat the bird feed I began to worry again. I have a column to write and a talk to prepare. And yet I wanted to be with Hailey. After all, we only had a day and a half left before her mother came. But my work. I needed to work. Or did I?

"Grammie, can we put up the hammock? We could take a nap in it!"

"Let's go to the shed and find the hammock," I said gleefully. We hung the chains on the hooks in the big trees in the backyard and hopped aboard. As we watched a yellow finch and two cardinals flit around the branches high above us as we lay on our backs in that big double-wide hammock, I knew for certain that I was taking the next day and a half off work. Completely.

Hailey and I drew huge pictures on the driveway, using up a whole bucketful of sidewalk chalk. Then she wanted to climb up into her Uncle Andrew's old tree house. She swept all the leaves off the tree house floor and only about half of them landed on my head. We took a long bike ride on the bike path near my house. I walked while Hailey rode her tiny two-wheeler with the training wheels.

"Grammie, can we go down by the creek?" Miss Hailey squealed when she saw the water.

"Sure! Maybe we'll catch a frog!"

Later that morning we jumped in the car, went shopping for shoes and found just the perfect pair for my wide-footed grandchild. Then we headed to the playland at McDonald's for lunch. Later that afternoon we ate Combos and candy at the $1.99 movie as we giggled at the funny songs in *Cats Don't Dance*.

"Grammie, are you sure there aren't any rules at your house?"

"I'm sure."

"No bedtime?"

"Nope."

"I can stay up until you go to bed?"

"Yup."

"Until late?"

"Sure. We can sleep late tomorrow. You just sit here in my lap so we can snuggle, and I'll read you a couple of books."

"I love you, Grammie."

And so, that's how I learned the true meaning of the words I have laminated on top of my computer: WRITE

THINGS WORTH READING OR DO THINGS WORTH WRITING.

I learned that doing things like spending an entire day and a half playing with a granddaughter is infinitely more important than sticking to a work routine and getting things done in the office. I learned that grandmothers today often need to abandon their schedules, meetings, clubs, activities, workload and appointments, and sometimes spend hours at a time drawing silly animals on the driveway or staring at the leaves from a hammock with a four-year-old's head snuggled in the crook of your arm.

~Patricia Lorenz
*Chicken Soup for the Grandparent's Soul*

# A Day at Grandmom's House

*A grandmother is a babysitter who
watches the kids instead of the television.*
~Author Unknown

My eleven-year-old grandson Ryan was on his way to the school bus when, as he told his mother, his stomach began to bother him. It felt queasy. He didn't feel he should go to school. My daughter had a doctor's appointment in another city, so Ryan came to Grandmom's house.

He looked a bit pale when he walked in, and a bit taller, as if he had grown inches during the night. I settled him down in my big, king-sized bed, put on his favorite TV cartoons, puffed up his pillows as I once did for my own son at his age and asked him if he was hungry. That's the first thing grandmoms ask under any circumstances.

"I think I could have an orange," he said listlessly. Usually he was full of energy. Today, his body seemed limp, unable to withstand any physical activity.

So I cut up an orange and delivered it to him on a plate. He gulped it down.

Soon after I asked him again, "Would you like something else to eat?"

"I think I could have two pieces of toast," he said. "And maybe two hard-boiled eggs."

"Wonderful," I responded. I boiled some eggs, buttered some toast, put some jelly on the side and carried it on a tray to his bed.

He gulped it down.

An hour later we were both munching on our favorite cookies.

Followed by potato chips.

Followed by pretzels.

We finished just in time for lunch.

"Would you like a turkey sandwich?" I asked about noon. "With sliced tomatoes?"

"That would be great," he said.

He had some color in his face now. In fact, he seemed quite content. He lay beneath the blankets, my dog at his feet, the cats by his shoulder, the cartoons playing in the distance.

When lunch was over we attempted a game of cards, but we didn't have an entire deck. Usually, we find something to talk about, sharing things we don't share with anyone else. Today, neither one of us seemed in the mood for conversation. So we turned the cartoons back on and had an ice pop, a few more cookies, some water and some cold cereal.

He didn't move for eight hours. He just ate. And ate. And ate.

It occurred to me during this eating orgy that I had witnessed the same behavior with my son at the same age. I called it the growth spurt. He would complain about his stomach, saying that he didn't feel good. And he would stay home from school. And then eat for an entire day. It seemed he grew taller as he devoured the food. Just sprouted up. When you're eleven, it's difficult to understand that growing taller takes energy. And food. Grandmoms know exactly what to do about growth spurts—and eleven-year-olds whose bodies are changing as rapidly as the world around them.

An apple, watermelon, lollipops... all followed.

My daughter called to inquire about Ryan's health. "How's his stomach?" she asked.

"Fine," I answered.

"Be careful what he eats," she cautioned.

"I'm being very careful."

We ended the day with a game of Scrabble. Finally, he turned to me and said, "I'm feeling better, Grandmom. I think I've got to get out of here and get some air."

I smiled. I had done my job. Ryan was ready to go out and face the world again.

Probably two inches taller.

~Harriet May Savitz
*Chicken Soup for the Grandma's Soul*

# Why Not?

A CD player headset drowned out the background noise as I worked in the living room at my computer. My fingers rushed over the keys as fast as my mediocre typing skills would allow, and my unblinking eyes stared at the monitor. Working in the living room of a small house that is home to three adults and two young children has forced me to develop a new level in my ability to concentrate. I was busy, very busy with my work. I had achieved that state of concentration that allowed me to block out just about anything, a tornado vacuuming up the room around me, if need be.

Then it happened. A tiny rift opened in my concentration as my eye caught a glimpse of an object flying upward through the air. I pulled my mind back to my work. I didn't even look to see what the object was, or what became of it as I sealed the rift. No sooner had I resumed my work, then laughter opened another rift in my concentration. Now I was getting annoyed. My seven-year-old grandson, Zach, was sitting across the room on the couch. His smile faded as I gave him my most stern, "Hush, I'm working" look.

Although I couldn't hear him, I could see that he said, "Sorry, Nana."

Success—another rift sealed and concentration restored. Sometimes children don't understand that there is a time for play and a time for work. This time is work time and I must get back to it. Clickety, clickety over the keys my fingers raced.

Another object whizzed past my peripheral vision, and the music wafting through my headset was no match for Zach's hearty laughter. Now I was really annoyed. Zach was too busy to see my sternest "Hush, I'm working" look. I followed his gaze to the ceiling as he launched another object, a hair scrunchy. With a quick slingshot motion, the hair scrunchy was airborne—whiz, bump, stuck to the popcorn ceiling. Some people like popcorn ceilings. To me, they look as if someone forgot to smooth out the Spackle. I never had any use for a bump-filled ceiling. Zach, on the other hand, had found a use for the ceiling, which now was adorned with a half a dozen hair scrunchies.

Red, purple and green circles clung to the ceiling, some flat up against it and some hanging down.

I lightened up my stern look a bit. "That's very funny but you have to stop now. Scrunchies don't belong on the ceiling."

"But why not? It's fun! I won't break anything."

I was about to tell him to go get the broom so that I could remove the scrunchies, when his words sunk into my head and reminded me of a time when I would have said, "why not?"also. When had I gotten so serious and so busy that I couldn't revel in the joy of a moment? What happened to the woman who would send her young children's friends into fits of giggles upon meeting them for the first time by asking them what they did for work and if they were married and had any children? What happened to the woman who laughed herself silly when her children and husband got into a snowball fight in the kitchen with cookie dough? When did I become so rigid? When did I forget, "Why not?"

Why not indeed! I looked at Zach and couldn't help but smile.

"Can you show me how to do that?"

His face lit up as he showed me how to launch a scrunchy. His laughter filled the air and his eyes sparkled. The ceiling never looked so colorful and happy with all those red, green, purple and yellow circles, some laying flat and some hanging down. I have to admit, Zach was better at it than I. Most of his attempts hit their mark. Most of mine ended up on the floor.

The following morning, I sat at the computer, ready to begin my work. I looked at the scrunchies still clinging to the ceiling and smiled. I certainly had enjoyed our time putting them up there. I decided I would take them down later. That is, until the ceiling lost its grip on one, and it fell, bounced off my shoulder, and onto the floor. Zach's smiling face flashed in my mind's eye. I smiled again. I felt like that woman of years ago who laughed at the cookie dough fight. I picked up the scrunchy and plopped it into my pocket.

When Zach came home from school that day, I was ready. He had given me a precious gift, now it was time to show him that I appreciated it.

"Zach, I've been waiting all day for you. Look what I found on the floor. It's no wonder I can't find these scrunchies when I need them. Please put this away." I handed him the scrunchy and he headed toward the door.

"Zach," I called out to him, "where are you going?"

He turned to me, "I'm going to put the scrunchy away, Nana."

"Please put it where I can find it." I shifted my gaze from

his sweet little face to the ceiling. A broad smile spread across his face as he realized what I was asking him to do. Whizzzzzz, bump—up it went. It was perfect!

If you come to my house, beware of falling scrunchies. You may wonder why I keep my scrunchies on the ceiling. Zach knows the answer to that question, and now, so do I— "Why not?"

~Christina Coruth
*Chicken Soup for the Grandparent's Soul*

# 77

# A Coke and a Smile

*What a bargain grandchildren are!*
*I give them my loose change,*
*and they give me a million dollars' worth of pleasure.*
*~Gene Perret*

I know now that the man who sat with me on the old wooden stairs that hot summer night over thirty-five years ago was not a tall man. But to a five-year-old, he was a giant. We sat side by side, watching the sun go down behind the old Texaco service station across the busy street. A street that I was never allowed to cross unless accompanied by an adult, or at the very least, an older sibling. An unlikely pair, we sat together, perched on the top step. His legs reached down two stairs; mine dangled, barely reaching the first. The night was muggy and the air thick. It was the summer of 1959.

Cherry-scented smoke from Grampy's pipe kept the hungry mosquitoes at bay while gray, wispy swirls danced around our heads. Now and again, he blew a smoke ring and laughed as I tried to target the hole with my finger. I, clad in a cool summer nightie, and Grampy, in his sleeveless T-shirt, sat watching the traffic, trying to catch the elusive breeze. We counted cars and tried to guess the color of the next one to turn the corner. I was luckier at this game than Grampy.

Once again, I was caught in the middle of circumstances. The fourth born of six children, it was not uncommon that I was either too young or too old for something. This night I was both. While my two baby brothers slept inside the house, my three older siblings played with friends around the corner, where I was not allowed to go. I stayed with Grampy, and that was okay with me. I was where I wanted to be. My grandfather was babysitting while my mother, father and grandmother went out.

"Thirsty?" Grampy asked, never removing the pipe from his mouth.

"Yes," was my reply.

"How would you like to run over to the gas station there and get yourself a bottle of Coke?"

I couldn't believe my ears. Had I heard right? Was he talking to me? On my family's modest income, Coke was not a part of our budget or diet. A few tantalizing sips was all I had ever had, and certainly never my own bottle.

"Okay," I replied shyly, already wondering how I would get across the street. Surely Grampy was going to come with me.

Grampy stretched his long leg out straight and reached his huge hand deep into the pocket. I could hear the familiar jangling of the loose change he always carried. Opening his fist, he exposed a mound of silver coins. There must have been a million dollars there. He instructed me to pick out a dime. I obeyed. After he deposited the rest of the change back into his pocket, he stood up.

"Okay," he said, helping me down the stairs and to the curb, "I'm going to stay here and keep an ear out for the babies. I'll tell you when it's safe to cross. You go over to the Coke machine, get your Coke and come back out. Wait for me to tell you when it's safe to cross back."

My heart pounded. I clutched my dime tightly in my sweaty palm. Excitement took my breath away.

Grampy held my hand tightly. Together we looked up the street and down, and back up again. He stepped off the curb and told me it was safe to cross. He let go of my hand and I ran. I ran faster than I had ever run before. The street seemed wide. I wondered if I would make it to the other side. Reaching the other side, I turned to find Grampy. There he was, standing exactly where I had left him, smiling proudly. I waved.

"Go on, hurry up," he yelled.

My heart pounded wildly as I walked inside the dark garage. I had been inside the garage before with my father. My surroundings were familiar. My eyes adjusted, and I heard the Coca-Cola machine motor humming even before I saw it. I walked directly to the big old red-and-white dispenser. I knew where to insert my dime. I had seen it done before and had fantasized about this moment many times. I checked over my shoulder. Grampy waved.

The big old monster greedily accepted my dime, and I heard the bottles shift. On tiptoes I reached up and opened the heavy door. There they were: one neat row of thick green bottles, necks staring directly at me, and ice-cold from the refrigeration. I held the door open with my shoulder and grabbed one. With a quick yank, I pulled it free from its bondage. Another one immediately took its place. The bottle was cold in my sweaty hands. I will never forget the feeling of the cool glass on my skin. With two hands, I positioned the bottleneck under the heavy brass opener that was bolted to the wall. The cap dropped into an old wooden box, and I reached in to retrieve it. It was cold and bent in the middle, but I knew I needed to have this souvenir. Coke in hand, I proudly marched back out into the early evening dusk. Grampy was waiting patiently. He smiled.

"Stop right there," he yelled. One or two cars sped by me, and once again, Grampy stepped off the curb.

"Come on, now," he said, "run." I did. Cool brown foam sprayed my hands.

"Don't ever do that alone," he warned firmly.

"Never," I assured him.

I held the Coke bottle tightly, fearful he would make me pour it into a cup, ruining this dream come true. He didn't. One long swallow of the cold beverage cooled my sweating body. I don't think I ever felt so proud.

There we sat, side by side, watching the sun go down behind the old Texaco service station across the busy street. A street I had been allowed to cross by myself. Grampy stretched his long legs down over two stairs. I dangled mine, a bit closer to the first step this time, I'm sure.

~Jacqueline M. Hickey
*Chicken Soup for the Woman's Soul 2*

# Grand and Great

## Gifts and Gratitude

*God gave us loving grandchildren
as a reward for all our acts of kindness.*
*~Roger Cochran*

# 78

# Piano Music

*Kindness is more than deeds. It is an attitude, an expression, a
look, a touch. It is anything that lifts another person.*
~C. Neil Strait

There are advantages and disadvantages to coming from a
large family. Make that a large family with a single parent,
and they double. The disadvantages are never so apparent
as when someone wants to go off to college. Parents have cashed
in life insurance policies to cover the cost of one year.

My mother knew that she could not send me to school
and pay for it. She worked in a retail store and made just
enough to pay the bills and take care of the other children
at home. If I wanted to go to college, it was up to me to
find out how to get there.

I found that I qualified for some grants because of the
size of our family, my mom's income and my SAT scores.
There was enough to cover school and books, but not
enough for room and board. I accepted a job as part of a
work-study program. While not glamorous, it was one I
could do. I washed dishes in the school cafeteria.

To help myself study, I made flash cards that fit perfectly
on the large metal dishwasher. After I loaded the racks, I
stood there and flipped cards, learning the makeup of atoms

while water and steam broke them down all around me. I learned how to make y equal to z while placing dishes in stacks. My wrinkled fingers flipped many a card, and many times my tired brain drifted off, and a glass would crash to the floor. My grades went up and down. It was the hardest work I had ever done.

Just when I thought the bottom was going to drop out of my college career, an angel appeared. Well, one of those who are on earth, without wings.

"I heard that you need some help," he said.

"What do you mean?" I asked, trying to figure out which area of my life he meant.

"Financially, to stay in school."

"Well, I make it okay. I just have trouble working all these hours and finding time to study."

"Well, I think I have a way to help you."

He went on to explain that his grandparents needed help on the weekends. All that was required of me was cooking meals and helping them get in and out of bed in the morning and evening. The job paid four hundred dollars a month, twice the money I was making washing dishes. Now I would have time to study. I went to meet his grandparents and accepted the job.

My first discovery was his grandmother's great love of music. She spent hours playing her old, off-key piano. One day, she told me I didn't have enough fun in my life and took it upon herself to teach me the art. My campus had several practice rooms with pianos where music majors could practice. I found myself going into those rooms more and more often.

Grandma was impressed with my ability and encouraged me to continue. Weekends in their house became more than just books and cooking; they were filled with the wonderful sounds of the out-of-tune piano and two very out-of-tune singers.

When Christmas break came, Grandma got a chest cold, and I was afraid to leave her. I hadn't been home since Labor Day, and my family was anxious to see me. I agreed to come home, but for two weeks instead of four, so I could return to Grandma and Grandpa. I said my goodbyes, arranged for their temporary care and returned home.

As I was loading my car to go back to school, the phone rang.

"Daneen, don't rush back," he said.

"Why? What's wrong?" I asked, panic rising.

"Grandma died last night, and we have decided to put Grandpa in a retirement home. I'm sorry."

I hung up the phone feeling like my world had ended. I had lost my friend, and that was far worse than knowing I would have to return to dishwashing.

I went back at the end of four weeks, asking to begin the work-study program again. The financial aid advisor looked at me as if I had lost my mind. I explained my position, then he smiled and slid me an envelope. "This is for you," he said.

It was from Grandma. She had known how sick she was. In the envelope was enough money to pay for the rest of my school year and a request that I take piano lessons in her memory.

I don't think "The Old Grey Mare" was ever played with more feeling than it was my second year in college. Now, years later, when I walk by a piano, I smile and think of Grandma. She is tearing up the ivories in heaven, I am sure.

~Daneen Kaufman Wedekind
*Chicken Soup for the College Soul*

# 79

# Help for the Helper

At age eighteen, I left my home in Brooklyn, New York, and went off to study history at Leeds University in Yorkshire, England. It was an exciting but stressful time in my life, for while trying to adjust to the novelty of unfamiliar surroundings, I was still learning to cope with the all-too-familiar pain of my father's recent death—an event with which I had not yet come to terms.

While at the market one day, trying to decide which bunch of flowers would best brighten up my comfortable but colorless student digs, I spied an elderly gentleman having difficulty holding onto his walking stick and his bag of apples. I rushed over and relieved him of the apples, giving him time to regain his balance.

"Thanks, luv," he said in that distinctive Yorkshire lilt I never tire of hearing. "I'm quite all right now, not to worry," he said, smiling at me not only with his mouth but with a pair of dancing bright blue eyes.

"May I walk with you?" I inquired. "Just to make sure those apples don't become sauce prematurely."

He laughed and said, "Now, you are a long way from home, lass. From the States, are you?"

"Only from one of them. New York. I'll tell you all about it as we walk."

So began my friendship with Mr. Burns, a man whose smile and warmth would very soon come to mean a great deal to me.

As we walked, Mr. Burns (whom I always addressed as such and never by his first name) leaned heavily on his stick, a stout, gnarled affair that resembled my notion of a biblical staff. When we arrived at his house, I helped him set his parcels on the table and insisted on lending a hand with the preparations for his "tea"—that is, his meal. I interpreted his weak protest as gratitude for the assistance.

After making his tea, I asked if it would be all right if I came back and visited with him again. I thought I'd look in on him from time to time, to see if he needed anything. With a wink and a smile he replied, "I've never been one to turn down an offer from a good-hearted lass."

I came back the next day, at about the same time, so I could help out once more with his evening meal. The great walking stick was a silent reminder of his infirmity, and, though he never asked for help, he didn't protest when it was given. That very evening we had our first "heart to heart." Mr. Burns asked about my studies, my plans, and, mostly, about my family. I told him that my father had recently died, but I didn't offer much else about the relationship I'd had with him. In response, he gestured toward the two framed photographs on the end table next to his chair. They were pictures of two different women, one notably older than the other. But the resemblance between the two was striking.

"That's Mary," he said, indicating the photograph of the older woman. "She's been gone for six years. And that's our Alice. She was a very fine nurse. Losing her was too much for my Mary."

I responded with the tears I hadn't been able to shed

for my own pain. I cried for Mary. I cried for Alice. I cried for Mr. Burns. And I cried for my father to whom I never had the chance to say goodbye.

I visited with Mr. Burns twice a week, always on the same days and at the same time. Whenever I came, he was seated in his chair, his walking stick propped up against the wall. Mr. Burns owned a small black-and-white television set, but he evidently preferred his books and phonograph records for entertainment. He always seemed especially glad to see me. Although I told myself I was delighted to be useful, I was happier still to have met someone to whom I could reveal those thoughts and feelings that, until then, I'd hardly acknowledged to myself.

While fixing the tea, our chats would begin. I told Mr. Burns how terribly guilty I felt about not having been on speaking terms with my father the two weeks prior to his death. I'd never had the chance to ask my father's forgiveness. And he had never had the chance to ask for mine.

Although Mr. Burns talked, he allowed me the lion's share. Mostly I recall him listening. But how he listened! It wasn't just that he was attentive to what I said. It was as if he were reading me, absorbing all the information I provided, and adding details from his own experience and imagination to create a truer understanding of my words.

After about a month, I decided to pay my friend a visit on an "off day." I didn't bother to telephone as that type of formality did not seem requisite in our relationship. Coming up to the house, I saw him working in his garden, bending with ease and getting up with equal facility. I was dumbfounded. Could this be the same man who used that massive walking stick?

He suddenly looked in my direction. Evidently sensing my puzzlement over his mobility, he waved me over, looking more than a bit sheepish. I said nothing, but accepted his invitation to come inside.

"Well, luv. Allow me to make you a 'cuppa' this time. You look all done in."

"How?" I began. "I thought...."

"I know what you thought, luv. When you first saw me at the market... well, I'd twisted my ankle a bit earlier in the day. Tripped on a stone while doing a bit of gardening. Always been a clumsy fool."

"But... when were you able to... walk normally again?"

Somehow, his eyes managed to look merry and contrite at the same time. "Ah, well, I guess that'll be the very next day after our first meeting."

"But why?" I asked, truly perplexed. Surely he couldn't have been feigning helplessness to get me to make him his tea every now and then.

"That second time you came 'round, luv, it was then I saw how unhappy you were. Feeling lonely and sad about your dad and all. I thought, well, the lass could use a bit of an old shoulder to lean on. But I knew you were telling yourself you were visiting me for my sake and not your own. Didn't think you'd come back if you knew I was fit. And I knew you were in sore need of someone to talk to. Someone older, older than your dad, even. And someone who knew how to listen."

"And the stick?"

"Ah. A fine stick, that. I use it when I walk the moors. We must do that together soon."

So we did. And Mr. Burns, the man I'd set out to help, helped me. He'd made a gift of his time, bestowing attention and kindness to a young girl who needed both.

~Marlena Thompson
*Chicken Soup for the Golden Soul*

# 80

# Monday Night Tea

*To everything there is a season,*
*a time for every purpose under heaven.*
*~Ecclesiastes 3:1*

"**M**om!" my exasperated eight-year-old pouted glumly. "That's your 'no' look. All the other kids go see the Cookie Lady every day. Can't I go, please?"

This same request had punctuated every afternoon since shortly after we'd moved to this new area of town. A lady who gave away cookies to small children made me wonder if we had made the right move. But surely, I reasoned silently, all of these children's parents must know this person if they allow daily visits. Sighing reluctantly, I looked at the five eager faces outside our screen door. I took my daughter's hand, bowing playfully. "Okay, Princess. I am your royal subject. Lead me to the Cookie Lady."

Giggling in delight, the children pulled and led me, like a Pied Piper in reverse, I thought, hopping and skipping down the street past other homes that were similar in size and status to ours. The children teased to see if I could identify their homes as we walked on, laughing and creating silly rhymes to help me remember whose home was whose, and making up names when I didn't know. Our entourage must have been quite the sight. "Blue, blues, that house is Sue's" and "Christmas red without the green, that house belongs to Imogene" were completed with groans and more laughter.

Looking up for the next home, I realized we were heading around the bend and stopped in my tracks, suddenly shy. Our family had walked the neighborhood and noticed the half-dozen imposing, column-fronted homes on the bend. We had not yet seen or met any of their owners, and my neighbors and I were in awe of the social and financial power these homes represented. It was almost as if the bend contained an imaginary boundary.

"Come on," the children urged, pulling me toward the most elegant home.

As they raced past me to the door, I was awed that the children had no concern of status as they listened to the beautiful multitoned chimes harmonize a welcome while I weakly compared it to the ding-dong of our doorbell.

I was completely disarmed, however, by the tall, elegant older woman who answered the door. Loving. The description came to me unbidden and remained as she gave us each an obviously homemade sugar cookie centered with a pecan half.

Business done, the little ones lined up on her porch and munched happily, allowing Magdalene Veenstra to introduce herself and smilingly guess whose mom I was. Imagined social barriers melted with her charming story of once offering "store bought" cookies, which were instantly rejected by several children who announced they would return "when you feel better and make Cookie Lady cookies again." Five minutes later I left, bemused and wondering over a warm invitation to join her for a cup of tea the following Monday.

A junior-high home-economics class was my only preparation of protocol for that first visit, and I wore a skirt to honor her generation and her genteel nature. I was grateful for the sense of smell when she opened the door; my aproned hostess did not need to tell me she had been baking. I followed her to the kitchen with an anticipation that never dimmed over the following fifteen years of Monday night teas.

Leading me past her blue delft collection and through a luxurious formal dining room to the kitchen, she directed me to a seat at a porcelain-topped table from another era. From there I watched "the ritual," as I came to think of her tea preparations, while drooling (inwardly only, I hoped) over the freshly baked delicacies that she'd placed on our English rose china plates.

A small but pleased surprise filled me as she sat and bowed her head in prayer. Realizing that this longed-for grandmother figure also shared my faith instantly drew our hearts closer.

From that Monday on, recipes filled our conversations—recipes for her famous pecan cookies and the almond-filled tarts known to other generations as bridesmaid tarts—then other "recipes," for living, for walking the faith, for loving our families and eventually even for dying. Each cup of tea opened a chapter of a living history book with tales of war, the Depression, numerous presidents, life on several continents and the inventions of radio, airplanes, automobiles and television. But history came only after our time of prayer for family, including present and future generations.

Being accepted taught me to accept others; her childlike faith ("I asked God to keep me safe while I slept—should I now insult him and stay awake worrying?") taught me to keep things simple. A favorite adage of hers, "Use it or lose it," gave me inspiration to utilize my talents and energy. It was this very adage that gave me a final lesson.

Grandma V, as I'd come to call her, had asked me to read. Her hearing and vision were now limited, so I was sitting on a cushioned footstool at her feet, but the book lay closed in my lap. She had recently ceased most cooking and had shocked the motor vehicle department by voluntarily giving up her license with a simple, "It's time." I was distressed by her inactivity, so I sat gently chiding her to "use it or lose it" when she caught me by surprise. She leaned forward until we were practically nose-to-nose and effectively stopped my thoughtless chatter. I gave her my full attention as she looked me straight in the eye, paused for effect and said, "You ever been ninety-three?"

We laughed the rest of the night over her remark and my shocked reaction. As usual, though, I was on the way home when I realized the lesson amid the humor. I cannot lead where I have not gone. Ecclesiastes' "a time for everything" formed the refrain to memories of ageless wisdom from the kids and the Cookie Lady.

Surely there is a time to walk before and a time to walk behind, but the time is always right to walk beside.

~Delores Christian Liesner
*Chicken Soup for the Grandma's Soul*

# 81

# The Dress

*Real generosity is doing something nice for someone*
*who will never find out.*
*~Frank A. Clark*

The security clerk pretended to check tickets on the dress rack nearest the door. Her eyes carefully scanned a woman who stood hesitatingly just inside the boutique door. The clerk took a quick mental snapshot—old shoes with run-over heels, a small run in her right stocking, out-of-style leather handbag, crinkly black nylon dress at least fifteen years old and straggly hair. Not the image of this store's usual clientele. She approached the woman, asking the mundane, "May I help you?"

The elderly woman smiled and whispered, "Yes, I need a dress." The surprised security clerk quickly signaled a nearby salesperson who hurried over to the waiting customer. Store policy toward the less desirable was, "Wait on them quickly; get them out of sight."

"How may I help you?" the salesclerk asked. This would only take a moment, and then she could go on her morning break.

"My only granddaughter is getting married. I need a complete outfit for the wedding. I want her to be proud of me. Just tell me what I should wear."

"You mean you want to see a bridal consultant?" the clerk asked incredulously. The woman nodded her head and followed the clerk to a small oval room filled with fancy clothes.

"Why did you bring her in here?" the consultant whispered angrily.

"She wants to be outfitted for a wedding," the clerk said as she laughed and walked away.

The bridal consultant had been a model in her younger years and still affected the haughty look she believed implied sophistication. She asked the woman to sit down at the small desk opposite her and took out a pad and pen.

"First, I must know how much you are prepared to spend," she asked. She was eager to get this over with and might as well cut to the chase.

"I have been saving my money for this outfit ever since their engagement was announced last spring. Annie sent me an airplane ticket so I can spend it all on something nice to wear." Her slightly palsied hand pulled the envelope from her handbag. "I think there is seventy dollars here. You may count it if you like. I can spend it all if need be."

The consultant quickly counted the money. "Actually, there are seventy-two dollars. Perhaps you should visit our basement thrift shop. They have a few dresses for around fifty dollars."

"I went there first. They suggested I come to see you," she said smiling. "They said you would be glad to help me."

(Oh, that Miriam. She loves a good joke. Wait until I get the chance. I will pay her back for this, the haughty one thought to herself.)

Just then the elderly woman spotted a powder blue dress on a nearby rack. She stood and walked quickly toward it. Before the consultant could stop her, she held the dress before her in a mirror. "Now, this one I like. It is beautiful, but not too showy." It was a plain dress with a long-sleeved jacket edged with just a touch of matching lace. "I should have matching shoes, of course. I will wear my strand of pearls. Afterward, I will give them to the bride as a wedding present. They belonged to my grandmother. Look, the dress is just my size."

The consultant gulped. She was suddenly feeling a mix of frustration, sympathy and anger. How could she tell this sweet old lady that the price of the dress she wanted was three hundred dollars? Matching shoes would be another seventy-five dollars. Sometimes life just wasn't fair.

A young, beautifully dressed bride-to-be stood nearby watching the scene. She had just picked up the custom veil she had ordered for her own wedding next week. Her family was well-off and had told her to spend whatever she wished on her wedding. She interrupted the consultant before she could speak to the grandmother about the dress.

"Excuse me a moment," she said as she led the consultant aside and whispered. "Let her have the dress, shoes, whatever else she needs. Just add it to my bill. Tell her they are on sale. Just take fifty dollars of her money. That will leave her with a little spending money—and her pride."

"But why?" the consultant asked. "You don't even know her."

"Just call it a wedding present to myself. I never knew either of my grandmothers. As I walk down the aisle, I will think of her and pretend she is my grandmother, too."

~Lee Hargus Hunter
*Chicken Soup for the Soul Stories for a Better World*

# 82

# Gifts of the Heart

y eleventh birthday was just a week away when we arrived in the refugee camp on that bleak and cold November day in 1947. My grandparents, who were raising me, and I had fled our Soviet-occupied Hungary with only the clothes we were wearing. The refugee camp, called a displaced persons camp, was in Spittal, Austria.

To cold and hungry people like us, the refugee camp was a blessing. We were given our own space in a barrack, fed hot soup and given warm clothes, so we were grateful. But as for my upcoming birthday, I didn't even want to think about it. After all, we had left our country without any possessions or money. So I had decided to forget about birthday presents from then on.

My grandmother, the only mother I ever knew, had taken over my care when I was a baby because her only child, my mother, had died suddenly. Before the war intensified, my birthdays had been grand celebrations with many cousins in attendance and lots of gifts. The cake had always been a dobosh torte, which my grandmother prepared herself.

My eighth birthday was the last time I received a bought gift. Times were already hard, money was scarce and survival the utmost goal. But my grandmother had managed to buy me a book. It was a wonderful book, full of humor and adventure, and I loved it. In fact, *Cilike's Adventures* had transported me many times, from the harshness of the real world of war and strife to a world of laughter and fun.

After that, birthday presents were usually crocheted or knitted items, made lovingly by my grandmother—but there was always a present. However, in the refugee camp, I was resigned to the inevitable.

On November 25, when I woke in the barrack, I lay there on my little cot beneath the horsehair blanket and thought about being eleven. I was practically a grown-up, I told myself, and I would act accordingly when Grandma and Grandpa awoke. I didn't want them to feel bad because they couldn't give me a present.

So I dressed quickly and tiptoed out quietly. I ran across the frosty dirt road to the barrack marked "Women's Bathroom and Shower," washed, combed my hair and took my time, even though it was chilly, before returning to the barrack. But finally, I returned.

"Good morning, sweetheart. Happy birthday," Grandfather greeted me.

"Thank you. But I would rather forget about birthdays now," I replied, squirming in his generous hug.

"You are too young to forget about birthdays," Grandmother said. "Besides, who would I give this present to if birthdays are to be forgotten?"

"Present?" I looked at her surprised, as she reached into her pocket and pulled something out.

"Happy birthday, honey. It's not much of a present, but I thought you might enjoy having Cilike back on your eleventh birthday," she said with tears in her eyes.

"My old Cilike book! But I thought it was left behind

with all our other things," I exclaimed, hugging the book to my chest, tears of joy welling up in my eyes.

"Well, it almost was. But when we had to leave so quickly in the middle of the night, I grabbed it, along with my prayer book, and stuck it in my pocket. I knew how much you loved that book; I couldn't bear to leave it behind. Happy birthday, honey. I'm sorry it's not a new book, but I hope you like having it back."

"Oh, thank you, Grandma. Having this book again means so much to me. So very much," I said, hugging her, tears streaming down my cheeks. "It's the best birthday present I ever received!"

And it truly was, because I realized that day how blessed I was.

Gifts of the heart are always the best gifts. They are true gifts of love.

~Renie Burghardt
*Chicken Soup for the Grandma's Soul*

# 83

# Gramma Jan

*When one door of happiness closes, another door opens;*
*but often we look so long at the closed door*
*that we do not see the one which has opened for us.*
*~Helen Keller*

When I drove into the park, I noticed and recognized Grace right away. She sat on a bench watching the children romp and play. Why did she have to come? I thought. Couldn't she let me be "Gramma" for the day? I'd waited so long.

When I walked up, Grace looked at me tenderly. "I've thought about you so much these last few years."

She was constantly in my mind, too — the woman who is grandmother to my daughter's child.

My mind went back to when Amy, just seventeen, told me she was pregnant. I had struggled as a single mom after Amy and Jennifer's dad left us seven years before, and I thought the worst was behind us until that day.

Amy decided to place the baby for adoption. I agreed it was the right thing for this confused, young girl, and I was touched that she asked me to help her choose the parents through an open adoption process. I was fine until I saw the ultrasound, the life growing inside Amy. Then it hit me. In a few months I would have to let go, say goodbye to my granddaughter.

Leslie, the prospective adoptive mom, assured me, "We want you to be a part of her life." But what role could I possibly have? Leslie's mother, Grace, waited sixty-three years to spoil a grandchild. How much would she want me involved?

After little Nicole was born, Amy insisted on bringing her home for a week. "I need time to say goodbye." Those were special days, days to make memories with her first child, hold her, sing to her, write her a loving letter and then let her go. Yet, I couldn't even cuddle her as I wanted, fearful that bonding with this child would only increase my sorrow when she left us.

The first time I met Grace, she came to my house for the adoption ceremony. "I know you'll love her very much," I said, stiffly, biting my lip as they were about to leave with the baby. Grace said nothing but just hugged me. After everyone left, Amy and Jennifer couldn't stop crying, and I kept assuring them it was the right thing to do, that blessings would come from it.

Amy's tears started coming right away when she shared her story with other pregnant girls.

The first year I saw Nikki often, fussing over her like any grandparent does, buying frivolous department store dresses she'd only wear once. Then it happened—the family moved to Florida. What would I do now?

Leslie promised endless pictures and videos of special moments, but what did it matter? I was bonded with Nikki, and they were whisking her away. How would she ever get to know me at three thousand miles away?

The years went by, and as I tore open every letter I ached as I put the photos in an album. Why did Nikki have to look exactly like Amy? Suddenly, I was struck with baby radar, tuning in to every toddler with brown eyes and dark curls, struggling to squash the tears.

Then came the telephone call. The family was coming to California for a visit. Would I like to meet them at the park? Of course! All week I was as anxious as a grasshopper. It had been five years!

As my car sped down the freeway, I wondered, would Grace be there? Was it selfish to hope not? Couldn't I have Nikki to myself just for a few hours and make believe I was her only grandmother?

Nearing the off ramp, I thought, how will Nikki respond to me? I'm just a stranger to her. Should I hug her or play it cool?

"She knows she's adopted," Leslie had told me earlier on the phone. "We're not sure now much she understands, but to her, you are her Gramma Jan."

What a delightful, loving child I met that day. We played "hide n' seek" and fed the ducks. She sat on my lap and let me fuss with her ponytail. Grace didn't say much. She sat quietly in the background and let me relish those precious hours.

In the afternoon, she nudged my side. "You've done better than I thought you would, Jan. I know how hard this must be for you."

The tears stung. Oh, Grace, this is making me cry.

"She's a special child, Jan. She's such a blessing to me."

It was easy to see. Nikki was secure, adored by her father and thrilled with two little brothers. (Six months after the adoption, Leslie was miraculously pregnant.)

"Please come and see us in Florida when you can," Keith said as he gave me a big bear hug. It was as if God reached down with comforting arms to say, This day was my gift to you, Jan. She will know you, and you will be an influence in her life. Just be patient.

As Grace said her goodbyes to me, she glanced over at

Nikki feeding the squirrels. "Thank you," she said, squeezing my hand.

She was thanking me?

I pondered that for a moment, then I understood. Nikki was a gift to Grace from God, a gift that came directly through me. Sitting back to watch me connect with Nikki was Grace's way of honoring me.

To think I almost missed the blessing.

That day in the park I finally let go.

As I glanced back at Nikki chasing another squirrel, I put my arm around Grace. "Thank you for having room in your heart to let me be 'Gramma Jan.'"

~Jan Coleman
*Chicken Soup for the Grandparent's Soul*

# 84

# Ripples in the Pond

There have been times in my life when I've felt insignificant. Sometimes it was because I felt stuck in unfulfilling jobs or empty relationships. Sometimes I felt as though I wasn't connecting with other people and that I didn't make much difference on the planet. Sometimes it seemed I had no real effect on the rest of the world, as though my coming and going didn't matter to anyone. When I start to buy into that feeling, I remember a story that was told to me by a stranger over a decade ago at a wake for my grandfather George.

As I stood in the center of the room, mourning his passing, I noticed someone who seemed out of place. He looked like an old weathered farmer, rumpled and wearing a suit coat that hadn't been in style for many years. His shoes were old and worn, but I could see that he had taken the time to polish them. His unkempt hair was as white as snow, and he had the bluest eyes I'd ever seen.

He noticed my stares and approached me and told me his name was Paul. He had met my grandfather more than sixty years ago, but never knew his name nor ever exchanged a word with him. Grinning at the curious expression on my face, and in a voice that sounded as worn and as old as he looked, Paul told me the most compelling story.

"I was just a little boy. Me and Momma and my little

sister were on our way home from visiting my momma's people. It was a hot August morning. The Chevy broke down in the middle of nowhere. Momma tried to tinker with it, but she didn't know about cars. I was just a little boy and I knew even less. Me and my baby sister were hot and thirsty. Seems like we'd been there for days off on the side of the road.

"Finally around noontime, we heard a car. We felt great relief, believing that help was coming. 'Course that was until the car got closer and we could see it was a colored man in it, your granddaddy. See, in those days we didn't have much exchange with colored people. They stayed on their side and we stayed on ours, no mixing. He pulled his car right up to us and asked if he could help. I knew Momma didn't want any part of that, but God, it was so hot that day and she had her babies to think about. She had no choice but to accept help from him.

"As he approached our car I was so scared I memorized every line on his face. I figured the time would come when I'd have to identify him since I just knew he meant to do us harm. I wasn't sure exactly what I was going to do, but I was ready to fight to protect my momma and baby sister. I tried to keep my eyes on him while he was under our hood. It had to be 120 degrees under there. Well, he worked for what seemed like hours but he couldn't bring the old Chevy back to life.

"Finally he says, 'I'm sorry, I can't fix your car, ma'am, but why don't you let me ride you and your children home?'

"We were terrified at the thought of getting into that colored man's car. Momma agonized over it, but it was so hot and her babies so thirsty, she decided she had no better choice. She piled us all into the backseat of his car, trying to stay as far away from him as possible. It must have been a good forty miles out of his way, but he didn't even ask for money. He drove us all the way home, then just dropped us off as sure as you please. He never even tried nothing.

"Later that night when Daddy heard about it, he nearly beat Momma to death for getting into a car with a colored man. We were forbidden to ever talk about it again. Your granddaddy was an angel that day. Imagine, an angel that looked just like a colored man."

Paul smiled and continued, "You know, when you get to be my age, you start to read the obituaries 'cause that's where all your friends are. Just two days ago, I saw your granddaddy's face staring back at me after all those years. It came back to me all at once. I never even knew his name, but I'd never forgotten his face. The way he just smiled at us even when we never even thanked him for all he did that day. I had to come here to pay my respects because it turned out to be more than just a ride home on a hot August day. Something about that day changed the way I saw the world despite what my daddy said.

"Today, I got two grown boys I'm proud of. They're good boys. Both became civil rights lawyers. They work in Chicago, and they have a partner who's a black man. My daddy would turn over in his grave if he saw that. I'm old and sick. It won't be too long before I'm laying there just like your granddaddy. You know, when my time to cross comes, I'm gonna find your granddaddy and thank him for that ride, put my arms around him and tell him all about my boys."

Paul had a far-off look in his eyes as he turned and walked away.

By now, my tears streamed freely as I stood there frozen, filled with pride and love for the man in the coffin. Even now he was teaching me.

After all of these years I still become lost sometimes. When that happens I close my eyes and see my grandfather's face with that huge smile. I hear his voice reminding me how much I matter, how much we all matter.

~Tyrone Dawkins
*Chicken Soup for the African American Soul*

# 85

# The Grandma Video

From the day of my first grandchild's birth, my daughter thoughtfully has sent frequent pictures and videos of him. Even though we live over three hundred miles apart we have always felt we are an active part of his life. As Matthew's second birthday approached, we knew we could not be with him to celebrate it, so we made a short video wishing him a happy birthday. We ended it by setting the camera on a tripod so my husband and I could sing (a bit off-key) a happy birthday duet to him. Even at two, Matthew seemed to understand the video and watched it over and over again.

It doesn't take much to encourage me, so when my daughter reported back the success of the video, I began to do videos periodically whenever we saw or did something that we would have shared with Matthew had he lived closer. It was an interesting turn of events from them sending us videos of Matthew!

Our videos are short, often with just a single subject. We have one of a pasture, not far from our house, filled with cows. We are showing the cows to Matthew and talking about them. We ask him questions, which his mother reports he eagerly answers from his seat on the couch as he watches the video. "Look at that one chewing his food. Isn't he silly?" I ask. Matthew nods and laughs as Grandpa zooms in for a close-up of the cow's face. Just then the cow unexpectedly moos, and it is perfect.

Then I tell Matthew when he visits we can go to see the cows together. It's a good way to keep from being strangers and is also a learning experience as we show him things that might not be readily available in his area.

When the almond trees in our yard bloom, we take a short video of the trees with a close-up of the flowers, explaining that they will turn into almonds and assure him we will send him some to taste when that happens in the months ahead.

For Christmas, we toured our house as Grandpa pointed out the items his mother had made as a child and I showed him my special nativity collection. We saw the lights outside our house after dark and the crackling fire in the fireplace. Our younger daughter was home from college that weekend, and she even got into the act by showing us the cookies she was baking. Matthew especially liked that part.

We watched snowflakes drifting down around our swimming pool in a rare desert snowfall and a shepherd tending his flock of sheep a few miles from our home. Matthew has watched his grandpa hammering and sawing in the garage and Grandma washing dishes. As the camera roams around our home, Matthew sees the bed he will sleep in when he visits and the stack of special books we saved for him from his mother's childhood. "We'll read these books together again when you visit our house, okay?" I ask. I'm told that Matthew smiles and says, "Yes," every single time he sees that part.

The videos are obviously unprofessional, the camera bounces around a bit and sometimes I can't find the object I want to zoom in on. "Oops," you can hear me say.

"Where did those flowers go?" My husband and I laugh, but Matthew certainly doesn't mind.

The "Grandma Videos" have continued for over seven years now, and four more grandchildren are viewing them. We enjoy taking the videos and sometimes wonder if we enjoy them more than the grandchildren do! It's fun for us to look at things from a child's perspective again, and I find we have a renewed interest in the simple little objects we often took for granted. We delight in sights we would normally drive past and barely notice. We literally stop and smell the California poppies when they bloom because we want to share them with our grandchildren on a video. The flowers take on a more intense beauty as we walk among them for the very best shot. While on vacation, instead of driving along the beach, we stop and examine the seashells and write the children's names in the sand.

These videos only take half an hour or so from start to finish and cost a minimal amount to mail. My own children saw their grandparents only once a year, but ours can literally have their grandparents at their fingertips anytime they wish.

Oops! I gotta go. It's time to star in another chapter of the Grandma Video!

~June Cerza Kolf
*Chicken Soup for the Grandparent's Soul*

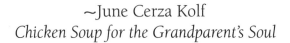

# 86

# An Unexpected Moment

*Sometimes someone says something really small,*
*and it just fits right into this empty place in your heart.*
*~From the television show*
My So-Called Life

It was hard to watch her fail. Physically she was growing thinner and more stooped. Mentally she was losing her ability to sort out reality. Initially, my grandmother had railed angrily against the symptoms of Alzheimer's disease that were eroding who she had always been. Eventually, the anger gave way to frustration, and then resignation.

My grandmother had always been a strong woman. She had a career before it was common for women to have careers. She was independent. In her eighties, she was still dragging out her stepladder every spring to wash all the windows in her house. She was also a woman with a deep faith in God.

As my grandmother lost her ability to live alone, my father moved her into his home. Grandchildren and great-grandchildren were often in the house. She seemed to enjoy being surrounded by the noise and activity of a large, extended family.

As she slipped further away from us mentally, my grandmother would occasionally have moments of lucidity when she knew where she was and recognized everyone around her. We never knew what prompted those moments, when they would occur or how long they would last.

Toward the end of her life she became convinced that her mother had knit everything she owned. "Mama knit my boots," she would tell strangers, holding up a foot clad in galoshes. "Mama knit my coat," she would say with a vacant smile as she zipped up her raincoat. Soon we were putting on her boots for her and helping her zip up her coat.

During my grandmother's last autumn with us, we decided to take a family outing. We packed up the cars and went to a local fair for a day of caramel apples, craft booths and carnival rides. Grandma loved flowers, so my dad bought her a rose. She carried it proudly through the fair, stopping often to breathe in its fragrance.

Grandma couldn't go on the carnival rides, of course, so she sat on a bench close by and waited while the rest of the family rode. Her moments of lucidity were now a thing of the past — having eluded her for months — but she seemed content to sit and watch as life unfolded around her. While the youngest members of the family ran, laughing to get in line at the next ride, my father took my grandmother to the nearest bench. A sullen-looking young woman already occupied the bench, but said she wouldn't mind sharing the bench. "Mama knit my coat," my grandmother told the young woman as she sat down.

We didn't let my grandmother out of our sight, and when we came back to the bench to get her, the young woman was holding the rose. She looked as though she had been crying. "Thank you for sharing your grandmother with me," she said. Then she told us her story. She had decided that day was to be her last on Earth. In deep despair and feeling she had nothing to live for, she was planning to go home and commit suicide. While she sat on that bench with Grandma, as the carnival noises swirled around them, she found herself pouring out her troubles.

"Your grandmother listened to me," the young woman informed us. "She told me about a time in her own life, during the Depression, when she had lost hope. She told me that God loved me and that He would watch over me and would help me make it through my problems. She gave me this rose. She told me that my life would unfold, just like this rose, and that I would be surprised by its beauty. She told me my life was a gift. She said she would be praying for me."

We stood, dumbfounded, as she hugged my grandmother and thanked her for saving her life. Grandma just smiled a vacant smile and patted her arm. As the young woman turned to leave, she waved goodbye to us. Grandma waved back and then turned to look at us, still standing in amazement. "Mama knit my hat," she said.

~Sara Henderson
*Chicken Soup for the Christian Woman's Soul*

# Grammy's Gifts

*I think sometimes a person's spirit is so strong that it never
completely leaves the Earth but remains scattered forever
among all those who love them.*
~Chris Crandall

"What are you looking for?" my husband, Peter,
asks, watching me dig through a box in one
of our closets.

"Stuffed cabbage," I reply. It was always a family
Hanukkah tradition, served with crisp latkes. I haven't
seen my grandmother Miriam's recipe in years, but I know
exactly where to find it: in the large cardboard box of
mementos I had labeled "From Grammy" when I was thirteen years old.

The box contains photos of a chubby toddler splashing
around in a pool in water wings. When I was terrified I
would drown in the deep end, Miriam taught me how to
float on my back, supporting my shoulders and assuring
me she'd never let go.

The box also contains a graduation card with the words
"You always make me so proud. Love, Grammy" scrawled in
a thin, shaky hand. And it has her gold wedding band, the
one I wore when I took my marriage vows last January.

Miriam knew the most amazing things. She could spell

Mississippi backwards. She could keep an omelet from sticking to the pan. She could comb the knots out of my long, matted hair without it hurting one bit.

When I was six and she was in her sixties, she showed me how to Charleston. "I was an extra in a Gloria Swanson movie, you know," she'd say, swinging one leg high out in front of her to demonstrate. "It was a party scene with lots of people dancing, and the director put me up front because he thought I had great legs."

On the nights when my parents went out to dinner and she was babysitting, we'd dress up in bangles and boas, and belt out "Boogie Woogie Bugle Boy" to an imaginary audience. My grandmother and I were kindred spirits. We laughed and cried at the same things, and we understood each other. I told her we'd travel around the world together, and she showed me how to touch the stars by closing one eye and balancing them on my fingertips.

She taught me how to paint my toenails a perfect shade of Redcoat Red and never gave away my secret when I stalked around the living room in sweat socks. When my mother would scold me for hanging upside-down on the monkey bars or riding my bike with no hands, Grammy would nod and wink. "Go on," she'd whisper in my ear. "Do something spectacular with your life."

She was the first person who ever encouraged me to dream and to put those dreams down on paper. When she became almost completely bedridden and shook with Parkinson's disease, I would sneak into her room — a makeshift space we had walled off from the dining room — in the middle of the night and crawl under her covers. We'd stare up at the ceiling, watching the darkness fade into dawn, and tell each other stories. We called the cracks in the plaster our cloud pictures and squinted to see an assortment of characters take shape in the shadows.

"Right there's a one-legged ballerina," she told me once, pointing her chin in the direction of a paint splatter. "Do you see it?"

I nodded, straining to make out a woman in a tutu en pointe. "She lost her leg because she danced too much in tight shoes," she whispered so my parents down the hall wouldn't hear us and chase me back to bed. "She should never have bought them on sale at Macy's."

Miriam's lessons are the ones that stuck with me — not all the algebra formulas or Spanish verb conjugations I studied for years. She taught me important basics: how much constitutes a pinch of salt; how to use seltzer to get a stain out of a silk blouse; how to sew a button on so it stays put. She helped me appreciate the simple things, like cream cheese and tomato sandwiches, towels warm from the dryer, and the quiet moments at dusk when the whole world is draped in a curtain of blue light. She liked the springtime most of all, when the air was warm and the breezes gentle. "This is soft weather," she explained to me. "Not too hot, not too cool, just soft."

But I don't need to rummage through my box to recall Miriam's lessons. My senses often bring them and her back to me: the gardenia fragrance of her hand lotion at a department store counter; an Andrews Sisters tune playing on Muzak in the dentist's office; the taste of her favorite sticky-sweet cherry cordial. Sometimes I see the back of a head on a bus and recognize the snowy-white hair falling in soft waves. Or I catch myself laughing her laugh, a hearty, joyous cry that makes my shoulders shake and my cheeks ache.

I'm reminded of all those little words of wisdom she

instilled in me, about life, love and loss: "Every time a door closes, a window opens," "There's a lid for every pot," "Don't cry over spilled milk."

My husband calls these little phrases old wives' tales and teases me when I tug on my left ear each time I sneeze as she advised me (to ward off bad luck). But I cherish her sayings. Miriam's lessons have gotten me through many terrible times—when I lost my job, when I broke up with a boyfriend, when I failed a test or when I simply burned dinner.

As I stir a big, boiling pot of stuffed cabbage on my stove, I can picture the past as if it were yesterday: My sister, Debbie, and I are spinning a dreidel and snacking on Hanukkah gelt, as my mother and grandmother work diligently in the kitchen. Miriam sprinkles a dash of sugar into the pot of cabbage for sweetness and squeezes in just enough lemon juice to "give it a kick."

And I can't help thinking that "life is like that"—sometimes sweet, sometimes sour, and always a challenge to blend both parts perfectly.

~Sheryl Berk
*Chicken Soup for the Grandparent's Soul*

# That Sunday Afternoon

I t was the first warm day of spring, about 20° C with a clear Calgary sky and full afternoon sun. Only a handful of people were around as I jogged through the park. Ahead was an elderly gentleman in a worn cardigan, sitting on a wooden bench a few feet off the path. He was somewhat secluded, nestled among the poplars and aspens, which were leafing out and stretching their wings. He had found a shaft of sunlight wending its way among the branches; he was enjoying the radiant sun on his face.

I was ready for a break to catch my breath and check my pulse. I sat next to him, looked at my watch, and started counting my heartbeats. After a few seconds, he interrupted my focus by asking how often I jogged. Being somewhat preoccupied with counting, I responded without making eye contact and muttered, "Two or three times a week." He persisted and attempted to engage me in the small talk that one engages in with a stranger.

His genuineness and comfortable smile eventually won me over, and soon we were talking about everything under the sun. We first discussed the timing of spring, our favourite television programs and great places we had visited in Canada. Unexpectedly, we began revealing our politics, exchanging our different experiences as parents, and expressing deeper feelings about the people we loved. He mentioned that his daughter and her ten-year-old son, Jason, were coming to Calgary in a couple of weeks to visit him; he hadn't seen them for two years. How he looked forward to their visit! "You know," he said, touching my arm, "family shouldn't be separated. We should be with people we love and who love us." I nodded.

In-and-out, back-and-forth we went, revealing meaningful moments in our lives, paths taken and not taken, laughing, and occasionally misting at the corners of our eyes. We touched one another, emotionally and physically; a sense of mutual "knowing" washed over us. I learned that he was a widower and gently poked him when he mentioned a certain woman he had recently met in the nearby retirement village. He smiled at the compliment; I could see the face of a young man in his eyes.

I think it was the late afternoon chill that broke the moment between us. I looked down at my watch. What seemed like a half-hour had actually been three hours! We had been captured in a moment, totally unaware of time and place. We who were strangers had somehow become soul mates. It was a serendipitous meeting and yet magical in the "connection" that occurred.

We bade our gentle farewells, "See ya around," smiling and waving as we parted. We knew we probably wouldn't meet again, and why should we? We had never met before despite having engaged in the same activities in the same park many times before.

Several days later, while putting newspapers into a recycling bin, I chanced to see the old man's picture in *The Calgary Herald*, on the back page, in the obituaries: "Mr. — is survived by.... In lieu of flowers, please send donations to the Canadian Heart and Stroke Foundation." Tears welled up in my eyes. They trickled down my cheeks as I drove home; I didn't brush them away. I was also crying for his daughter and her not having had that moment of closeness with him that I just had on that Sunday afternoon. Arriving home, I sat down and wrote her a brief letter, describing the chance meeting and what we had talked about. I hoped it might ease her grief knowing that she was loved and in his thoughts before his passing. I addressed it in care of the funeral home.

It was almost eight months later when an envelope arrived postmarked "Brandon, Manitoba." I didn't know anyone from Brandon, at least that I could recall. As I began reading, I realized it was from the old gentleman's daughter. There was a carefulness and kindliness in the letter that brought him vividly back to mind:

*Dear Mr. Fouts,*

*Please excuse the tardiness of this letter. I'm sure you can understand. I wish to acknowledge your warm generosity of spirit for letting me know that Dad had Jason and me in his thoughts just before he died. You were probably the last person that he talked to in his life, since he was found in the park later in the day where you said you had met. It was close to his apartment. I wish to thank you for being the kind of person you are to talk to an old man sitting alone on a park bench. I take comfort in knowing that you were there with him—if only for a brief time—to share the sunshine and a few thoughts. Thank you so much.*

I put her letter away with the picture of the old gentleman from the paper. Later, as I went for my jog through the park, I approached the same bench where we had met eight months before. No one sat there now on this cold December day, but as I jogged past, I was filled with the memory of our special connection and all the things we had shared on that Sunday afternoon. With a warm feeling in my heart, I gave a little salute and carried on.

~Gregory Fouts
*Chicken Soup for the Canadian Soul*

# 89

# A Gift from Nana

*Wherever there is a human being,
there is an opportunity for a kindness.*
*~Seneca*

On the morning of March 22, 1995, my sister-in-law went into Los Robles Medical Center to be induced into labor. My husband and I arrived at the hospital in the late afternoon to be there for the exciting event. When we got to her room, everyone present seemed to be in a state of shock.

At the change of shifts, the head nurse, Charlotte, noticed my sister-in-law's last name and immediately paused. The last name brought back a memory of a woman she had once cared for twenty years ago at a hospital fifty miles away. Consequently, she decided to assign herself to my sister-in-law's care that evening. She entered the room and hesitantly asked my brother if he knew of a JoAnn. Stunned, he answered, "Yes, she was my mother."

Although we were excited for the birth of our niece, we could not forget that the next day would be exactly twenty years since my mother had passed away after battling cancer. Charlotte's eyes grew wide as she realized that she was assisting in the delivery of JoAnn's first grandchild.

To our amazement, Charlotte actually remembered my

father, brother and me, and throughout the evening she shared several endearing stories of the friendship she had developed with my mom for over a year. The commonality of having children the same age made their relationship especially close.

Well past midnight, my sister-in-law was not making progress, so a C-section was performed and Kylee Ann entered the world. For the first time in twenty years, the sadness I so often felt on this day, the anniversary of my mother's death, was replaced with the joy of new life.

Two days later, as Kylee Ann was being discharged, Charlotte came in holding a delicate white porcelain figurine of a large bird perched on a branch looking down at a smaller bird.

"Your mother gave this to me as a thank-you gift when I took care of her twenty years ago. I've cherished it all these years. Now I pass it on to Kylee Ann"—a gift from her Nana.

~Terri Murcia
*Chicken Soup for the Nurse's Soul*

# 90

# A Treasured Gift

"Grandpa's dying," Mom called to tell me. The hospital had sent her father home with little time left. My aunt and cousin had already moved in to provide around-the-clock care. Mom felt she should be there, but we'd been estranged from her family for more than twenty years. I agreed to go with her for moral support.

Instead of being tense and awkward, however, the visit turned out to be warm, loving and special.

After we arrived, my grandfather gestured at the wall. "Kimmie, see that?" he said, struggling to sit up. "I tell all my friends my granddaughter drew that for me!"

A framed piece of art hung over the television. I didn't recognize it. Keeping my smile as I crossed the room to get a closer look, I mentally ran through diplomatic ways of telling him he was mistaken. Getting closer to the drawing, my eyes widened. There was my signature, plain as anything! Stunned, I tried to recall any information about this picture. How could I have completed such detail but not remember it?

Like an open door allowing a flood of light into a dark closet, I suddenly remembered. I was sixteen when I'd drawn this chalk pastel picture of a goldfish for him—a man I didn't know well, except as my mother's father.

Everything became clear, and I remembered why I'd drawn this for him. That Christmas I had purchased a Bible for my grandmother. I'd added a box of colored pencils with instructions for marking special verses. I felt excited about this personal, significant gift.

Then I puzzled over what to do for my grandfather. It would look odd giving a Christmas gift to one grandparent but not the other. I prayed for a solution. Then I realized I could give him something personal as well—a gift of my artwork. I drew a goldfish on a black background, because that seemed adequately masculine. I worried over whether my grandfather would care about a silly fish picture. But as I worked on all of its colorful oranges, with a tinge of white in the flowing tail and a touch of blue in its darting eyes, I prayed that my gift would touch his heart.

With little contact before or after that Christmas long ago, I'd assumed my grandfather didn't care for my siblings and me. I wasn't offended, but accepted it pragmatically. Some men simply aren't comfortable around children. I assumed that was true for him.

Now I stared at the fish hanging on my grandfather's paneled wall. Shame filled me and tears blurred my vision. He had treasured my gift all those years, and I never knew.

Needless to say, I returned for several more visits, getting acquainted with Grandpa. He shared with me about his service in World War II. He told me about his work building prototypes for Boeing's commercial jet airplanes. He met my sons—his great-grandsons—before he died.

After the funeral, my aunt and cousin approached me. "We want you to have this," my aunt said, smiling through tears. In her hands she held the goldfish picture.

The treasured drawing now hangs on my kitchen wall. When I tell visitors about it, and I tell them about my grandfather, my voice always catches when I share about the error of assumption, the mystery of relationships—and the amazing power of a treasured gift.

~Kimn Swenson Gollnick
*Chicken Soup for the Christian Woman's Soul*

# Grand and Great

## Treasured Moments

*Live so that your children and grandchildren model your
understanding of joy, laughter and love as elixirs of life.*
*~Laura Spiess*

# Grandma's Catfish

*Success seems to be largely a matter of
hanging on after others have let go.*
~William Feather

I was living my dream, working as a state park ranger in Lake Tahoe, California. I spent my spare hours cross-country and downhill skiing during winter and fishing the nearby Sierra streams all summer and fall.

My mother lived in Sacramento, the hot valley a short two-hour drive from the high country. She called me one day and said that my grandmother's already frail health had taken a major turn for the worse. My grandfather had died years before, and now the doctors were saying they didn't expect Grandma to live past the end of the day. I headed down the mountain.

When I arrived at the nursing home, I was welcomed by several members of the staff who told me of a near miracle. When informed about the promised arrival of her first and favorite grandson, Grandma suddenly grew stronger. When I entered her room, she looked up at me, her eyes instantly brightened, and she squeezed my hand as I hugged her. Her voice grew stronger as she spoke to me, telling me how excited she was to see me. We chatted for a while as my mind raced back over the years. She and

Grandpa had taught me to fish, first on the local rivers and sloughs, then at Clear Lake where they lived following Grandpa's retirement, a two-hour drive west into the coastal mountains from Sacramento.

Her smile suddenly broke into a big grin. "Do you remember that big old catfish that broke my fishing line?" she asked.

I assured her that it was a summer morning I would always remember. She insisted that I retell the story for the benefit of the staff who had gathered around to witness her miracle recovery. I thought about that day more than twenty years earlier and launched into the tale:

Early one summer morning, Grandpa, Grandma and I loaded ourselves and our fishing gear into their small wooden boat. The air was crisp and clean as I let my hand hang over the side and splash in the cool water during the torturously slow, five-mile-per-hour ride out of the marina toward the main lake. My ten-year-old patience was really being tested. Soon enough we were speeding through the open water, finally turning up into a narrow, tule-lined slough where we coasted to a stop. Grandpa tossed the homemade anchor—a coffee can full of concrete—into the water.

We baited our hooks and cast them into the water, setting the bright red and white plastic bobbers so the chunks of old, smelly bait hung just off the bottom of the shallow greenish water—there was nothing clear about Clear Lake's water. We soon caught several channel cats, some reaching a pound or so.

Suddenly, Grandma's bobber dove underwater. A huge blue catfish had grabbed her bait and headed up the slough. Grandma got really excited having such a big fish on her line, yelling for Grandpa to grab the net. It was the biggest fish she'd caught since the five-pound bass she'd landed the year before. Just as the battle got going, she moaned disappointment when her line snapped—but it broke above her big red and white plastic bobber. After it appeared that the bobber and her trophy catfish had headed for deeper water and safety, it happened! Her bobber popped back to the surface and began circling about ten feet from the side of our boat. Grandma still had her fish!

"Grab my bobber, Kenny, hurry!" Grandma frantically yelled to me. "Get him before he gets away!" She was trying to stand in the small rocking boat, pointing to the erratically darting bobber. I was stretching out as far as my short arm could reach, but the bobber was starting to move farther away, and with it any chance of me grabbing her errant fish.

"Walter, you start that motor!" she yelled at my grandfather in her excitement. "Get us closer so Kenny can grab it!"

Grandpa rolled his eyes, but after several yanks on the starting rope, fired up the boat motor.

"Hurry up, Walter, you're going to let him get away!"

Grandpa began maneuvering around closer to the fleeing bobber that periodically disappeared underwater, only to reappear farther away several seconds later. Every time the bobber reappeared, Grandma pointed in another direction and yelled at Grandpa that he was going the wrong way. Grandpa would mumble something about not being able to read Grandma's mind, let alone the fish's mind, then he'd reverse direction and head toward the bobber's last known location. Finally Grandpa got lucky: The fish turned the wrong way and headed at us.

"Kenny, grab the bobber, grab the bobber!" Grandma yelled repeatedly. "Grab the bobber! You be careful and don't fall in, now. There it is again, get it!" She was jumping up and down in her seat and rocking the boat as she pointed at the approaching bobber. "Walter," she ordered my grandpa, "you get Kenny closer now. Don't let my fish get away."

After a couple of near catches, with Grandma continuing to yell directions to which the fish paid no attention, I managed to stretch my arm out far enough over the side of the boat and grabbed the fleeing bobber. By some miracle, the fishing line didn't slip through the bobber as I tugged and strained to pull the huge catfish to the water's surface. Grandpa netted the monster and dropped the huge, flopping, whiskered cat into the middle of the boat, adding to the water and fish slime that already covered the floor. We all yelled in celebration as we watched that monster catfish flop around, not the least bit aware that he was going to be dinner in a few hours.

The retelling of her favorite fishing story had worked its magic, putting the biggest smile imaginable on Grandma's face. But it was one of her last smiles. Grandma only lived a couple of days more, but they were days the doctors had not originally given her. I still smile when I think about the joy derived from fishing with my grandparents, and especially that single summer fishing adventure. I'm sure Grandma's still smiling—and Grandpa's still mumbling something about not being able to read minds.

~Ken McKowen
*Chicken Soup for the Fisherman's Soul*

# 92

# A Sister's Visit

*Is solace anywhere more comforting than
in the arms of a sister?*
~Alice Walker

Gram and her sister, Acq, were close in age, and the bond between them was so strong they visited each other almost daily. But when she was ninety-three, Gram's health deteriorated, and she finally became homebound. Although they lived only sixteen miles apart, visits were no longer possible for them; they were both too ill to make the trip. I was privileged to be my grandmother's major caregiver, and I knew how desperately they missed each other and longed to be together again. It was always on my mind.

One cold winter day, Gram sat up in bed and said, "I want to see my sister." She was still weak from her last hospitalization; her face was pale and drawn from the weight she had lost.

"You can see her in the spring," I soothed.

Her eyes widened. "No, that's too long."

I knew Gram's time on earth was limited. She and Acq needed to see each other... but how? Then I had an idea. The next morning, I brought out the video camera.

"Gram, you can talk to your sister through this." I showed her how it worked. She threw her head back, laughed a little and said, "Okay." She went into the bathroom, washed her face and combed her hair. Then she held the camera and looked deeply into the lens. Gram spoke softly, "Acq, I'm too sick to come over and see you.... I miss you and we will be together again soon." Gram smiled. "When the garden is ready, I'll send you some of my tomatoes."

Her eyes sparkled and her voice became stronger. "Bye-bye, Acq."

I drove over to visit my aunt and told her I had a message for her. I helped her into the bedroom, where a picture of her and Gram sat next to the bed. I handed her the camera and turned it on. As soon as Gram started talking, my aunt sat up straight, excited, and answered her back. "Lizzie, you look good. I have missed you too, it's been so long." She sat back and listened to the rest of Gram's message to her. She looked at me as she wiped a tear from her eye. "If I talk, will Lizzie hear me?"

I told her yes, and she combed her hair just like Gram had, while displaying a renewed sense of spirit. When I pressed the record key, Aunt Acq's voice grew stronger. "Hi, Lizzie, it was nice to see you today." She turned to me. "Maybe she can't hear me." She held the camera with both hands and shouted, "I'd like some of your Italian beans from the garden, too."

We walked to her closet and opened the door while I continued to film. "You know my grandson Gerry's getting married in a few weeks. This is my new dress and shoes. I hope I'll be well enough to go."

As I left, I told my aunt I would return in a few days. I was not sure if either of them truly understood this method of communicating, but Aunt Acq hugged me and said, "Thanks for bringing Lizzie here to me."

Gram and I settled in on the couch, next to a picture

of the sisters from last summer's family picnic. I draped my arm over her shoulder and showed her the whole video. When she saw herself talking, she giggled with excitement, "That's me!" We both laughed at the same time. When Aunt Acq started talking, Gram's eyes brightened and her whole face lit up. She reacted the same way my aunt had, holding the camera up close. "Hi Acq, it's good to see you again."

When Gram said that and looked up at me, tears streamed down my cheeks. At dinner that night, Gram said, "It was nice to see Acq today, she looks pretty good."

For the next few months they "visited" each other regularly. While they were never physically together again, they were "close" to the end.

~Paula Maugiri Tindall
*Chicken Soup for the Grandma's Soul*

# 93

# Porch Swing Cocktails

*We can do no great things,*
*only small things with great love.*
*~Mother Teresa*

This is not one of those "when Grandma was alive she used to..." stories you often read. No, my grandmother is alive and well and kicking at eighty-four and so, I guess you could call this one of those "let's see if my memory is as good as hers" stories:

When I was growing up, my parents went out on Saturday nights and my grandmother babysat for me. For their big night out, Dad always wore a shirt with a very 1960s ruffled collar and puffy sleeves and had neatly trimmed sideburns. Mom dressed in a miniskirt and shiny white go-go boots. It was the only night my parents were free to go out and have some fun for themselves, but I knew I had just as much fun as they did.

My grandmother went all out for my weekly visits. Shortly after Mom and Dad dropped me off, dinner would be served. I loved her carrots. Sliced thick and never mushy, they swam in a sea of butter and melted in my mouth like candy. "Orange wheels," I called them, which always made her laugh.

Grandma's other specialty was a steaming platter

heaped with succulent chicken and rice. Being a five-year-old boy, I was too young to know that this was the only meal of the week Grandma actually cooked anymore. With her arthritis, it was hard just to open the can of Campbell's mushroom soup, which she stirred in the rice to give it that special "oomph." And skinning and deboning the chicken breasts (they were cheaper that way) was a nearly Herculean effort for the little old lady who spent the rest of the week zapping Lean Cuisine dinners and sipping tea with blueberry muffins for dessert.

Grandma had a special set of dishes she'd purchased, one dish a week, at the local grocery store. They were white and covered with blue windmills and little wooden shoes. Grandma told me that she had bought them just for our special dinners, and that I was the only person she ever used them for. This always made me feel ten feet tall. (It was years later before she finally confessed that the real reason she only used them with me was that she'd skipped a few weeks down at the grocery store, and the set was incomplete.)

Dinner was usually over by the time *The Lawrence Welk Show* came on, and even though it was her favorite show, Grandma said she preferred spending time with her "little man." So we'd retire to the wooden porch swing.

Grandma's husband, my grandfather, had died years earlier. The two of them had spent countless hours in this very porch swing, rocking back and forth and admiring the Florida sunset while the neighbor children played, dogs barked and flowers bloomed. Now it was my turn to sit next to Grandma and help her while away her lonely Saturday evenings. It never felt creepy, taking my grandfather's place in that creaky, old porch swing. To me, it just felt right.

While champagne music bubbled through the screen

door from the TV, Grandma and I would sit and swing, swing and sit. Sometimes I'd draw, and she would sew. Other times, we'd just talk about the neighbors or what each of us had done that day. She'd share stories about growing up in the Great Depression until the closing strains of champagne music were corked for yet another week. Then it was time for dessert, which, in the best of all grandmotherly traditions, was something Mom would never give me at home: a bottle of Coca-Cola, the short kind that fit perfectly into a young boy's hand, and a can of fancy mixed nuts. Grandma showed me how to drop the salty Spanish peanuts inside the bottle and watch the soda foam, then take a sip, chomping the slimy nuts and tasting the salty sweetness of the fizzy soda.

Grandma called this concoction our "porch swing cocktails," and not only were they delicious, but they made me feel grown up. Imagine a five-year-old drinking a cocktail!

When the Cokes were gone, we'd chomp on cashews and almonds and listen to dogs bark in the distance. Grandma would light a citronella candle to ward off the mosquitoes, so big and plentiful that she called them "Florida's State Bird"!

As the night got darker, the tempo of our rocking would gradually slow down, until our feet just dangled in the warm air. We hardly moved at all, simply enjoying the smooth ocean breeze from the beach flowing over us. Living half a block from the Atlantic Ocean, there wasn't a night of her life that Grandma didn't enjoy falling asleep to the sound of ocean breakers crashing against the sandy beach. She said she wouldn't trade that sound for anything in the world....

So you see, this is not a "boy, I miss my grandmother"

story. It's a story about good times past, but still possible today. I think I'll call Grandma and tell her it's time for some porch swing cocktails. And even though I'm old enough now to enjoy an alcoholic drink, I'll go buy some Cokes and nuts—and get ready for my favorite Saturday night date.

~Rusty Fischer
*Chicken Soup for Every Mom's Soul*

# 94

# Through the Windowpane

*If you look for a way to lend a hand,*
*you will be lifting yourself as well.*
*~Source Unknown*

Riding the crest of a desert arroyo, our property becomes a passageway for wildlife. We keep our eyes open for the animals and birds that come to visit. One season, a mother quail nested on the ground of our open atrium, where we could eavesdrop on her developing brood through the windowpanes.

When our Midwestern grandchildren came to visit, it was seven-year-old Hannah who pressed her nose against the glass and became resident companion to the mother quail. Hannah sat on the tile floor, guarding the nest from inside the house for long stretches of time. Whenever we wanted to find Hannah, we knew just where to look. I sat there a fair amount, finding the tranquil time often not available when grandkids' visits are brief and energy rides high. Sitting together and watching the quail family cast a special aura around us. We were inches away from the birds, yet we didn't frighten them because of the glass that separated us. If we were still, if we were quiet, we could see the chicks bob and scratch around their mother as they learned the ways of nature.

Hannah and I were watching together on the day the mother quail began to lead the chicks over the four-inch ledge out into the desert. Hop. Skip. Up and over. Hop. Skip. Up and over. Each little bird did the calisthenics required to leave the protected nest and proceeded to conquering the unknown. The mother called to each one softly, offering encouragement. All went according to the designated plan until the turn of the tiniest chick. The little bird hopped again and again but couldn't make it over the concrete ledge to reach the rest of the family. The height was too great. The mother coaxed and cajoled, then finally abandoned the last bird in the window well to care for the rest of the youngsters who foraged for seeds nearby. Hannah and I listened to the heartbreaking cheeping sounds of the forlorn, feathered babe. We were upset, too. I'd been told that once quail leave the nest, they do not come back, but I didn't want to share this information with Hannah. I knew she expected me to solve the problem. Her eyes held mine, searching for my answer.

Then I did have an idea. I grabbed a sturdy piece of heavy cardboard and explained the plan to Hannah. We hurried outside with the makeshift material. I let Hannah slip the ramp into place for the last chick, angling it to present an easy slope to the top of the ledge. We quickly retreated back to the inner window.

When the little bird scrabbled up the cardboard and scooted out to join the others, we sighed in relief. It was a matter of cardboard and common knowledge, sympathy and simple wisdom.

The words of a poem by Emily Dickinson came to mind, and we went to the bookshelf and found her words. Now the lines could be understood in a new light, for Hannah and for me.

> *Or help one fainting robin*
> *Unto his nest again,*
> *I shall not live in vain.*

On that sunny desert morning, my granddaughter Hannah and I had not lived in vain.

~Connie Spittler
*Chicken Soup for the Grandparent's Soul*

# 95

# The Holly Trees

*A garden of Love grows in a Grandparent's heart.*
*~Author Unknown*

Growing up in the sixties wasn't easy when your parents were divorced and your dad seemed to have disappeared off the face of the planet — especially when everyone else seemed to be living like Ozzie and Harriet. And although my mom worked hard to keep us clothed and fed, when Christmastime rolled around, life suddenly seemed rather bleak and barren. About the time of the school Christmas party, all I could think about was making that three-hour drive to my grandparents' house where Christmas was really Christmas. Where food and relatives abounded, and artificial trees, like the cheesy tin-foil job in our tiny living room, were not allowed. You see, every year, my grandpa cut down a tree tall enough to touch the high ceiling in their old Victorian house. We often got to help; but some years, especially if we arrived just before Christmas, the tree would already be up, but we'd still help decorate it.

One year, just two days before Christmas, we arrived and the tree wasn't up. I asked Grandpa if we were going out to the woods to get one. He just smiled his little half smile, blue eyes twinkling mischievously, and said we weren't going out to the woods this year. I worried and watched my grandpa all afternoon, wondering what we were going to do about the tree, but he just went about his business as if nothing whatsoever was unusual. Finally just after dinner, Grandpa went and got his axe. At last, I thought, we are going to cut down a tree. But in the dark?

Grandpa grinned and told me to come outside. I followed him, wondering where he could cut a tree down at night. My grandparents' large home was situated on a small lot in the middle of town, with no U-cut trees anywhere nearby. But Grandpa went out to the parking strip next to their house and began whacking away at the trunk of one of his own mature holly trees—the tallest one, a beautiful tree loaded with bright red berries. I stared at him, in silent shock. What in the world was he doing? And what would Grandma say?

"The city says I gotta cut these trees down," he explained between whacks. "They're too close to the street. I figure if I take one out each Christmas, it will keep us in trees for three years." He grinned down at me, and the tree fell. Then my sister and I helped him carry it into the house, getting poked and pricked with every step of the way. I still wasn't sure what I thought about having a holly tree for a Christmas tree. I'd never heard of such a thing.

But when we had the tree in the stand and situated in its place of honor in one of the big bay windows, I knew that it was not a mistake. It was absolutely gorgeous. We all just stood and stared at its dark green glossy leaves and abundant bright red berries. "It's so beautiful," said Grandma. "It doesn't even need decorations." But my sister and I loved the process of decorating, and we insisted it did. We began to hang lights and ornaments—carefully. It isn't easy decorating a holly tree. But with each new poke we laughed and complained good-naturedly.

For three years, we had holly trees for Christmas. And now, whenever I get pricked by holly, I think of Grandpa. Later on in life, after my grandpa passed away, I learned about the symbolism of holly and why we use it at Christmas—and how the red berries represent droplets of Christ's blood. I don't know if my grandpa knew about all that, but he did know how to be a father to the fatherless. And he knew how to salvage good from evil. My grandpa didn't like to waste anything.

~Melody Carlson
*Chicken Soup for the Soul Christmas Treasury*

# 96

# Pudgy

In 1975, my grandparents brought home a new pup and named him Pudgy. This came as no surprise since they always named their dogs Pudgy. In the course of their extremely long lifetimes, my grandparents must have had a dozen or more dogs named Pudgy.

At the time, Grandpa was ninety-two and Grandma was eighty-nine, and they had been married since she was thirteen. That seems shocking today, but it was quite ordinary in the small village on the Polish border where they were born, met and fell in love in the late 1800s. They emigrated to the United States and made a life together that lasted through the coming of the first automobiles, the Roaring Twenties, the Great Depression, four wars—and many Pudgys.

When anyone asked Grandpa why Pudgy was the only name he would ever give to his dog, he answered, "He's the same dog, come back."

Relatives told him that was crazy and that he should give new dogs new names, but he always stood firm. Rather than debate the issue, people simply accepted that "Pudgy" was Grandpa's dog.

Each Pudgy was about the size of a fox terrier and white with black spots or patches. For the little kids in the family, like me, who lived in other states and traveled across the country to visit them in their big old brownstone in Chicago, using the same name for each dog did make it a lot easier to remember. And many of us believed it was the same dog, although I did wonder once why the Pudgy I saw when I visited them in 1949, 1950 and 1951 had shaggy, floppy ears and the Pudgy I played with over Easter vacation in 1952 had short, pointed ones. Since the Pudgy of 1952 was still black and white and about the same size, I simply assumed my grandfather was telling the truth when he told me that the dog had accidentally stuck his tail in a light socket and his ears had shot straight up and had never gone down again. It didn't explain where all the shaggy hair on his ears had gone, but at seven, I simply decided the electricity must have burned it off.

Looking at an old family album with photos from the various decades, one could see the dog change a little in height and definitely in bone structure. He went from having a long, slim nose to a short, puglike one and then back to something in between. In some photos he had curly hair; in others, smooth. One decade he had small black spots on the white coat; and the next, large, pinto-pony-type patches. One time he had no tail at all. It didn't matter: he was always Pudgy.

This last Pudgy was a short-legged, potbellied pup, a mixture of too many breeds to try to put a finger on any dominant one. He was the first "Pudgy" that really looked as if the name belonged.

About two weeks after the pup arrived at the house, Grandpa decided it was time to take him on his first walk. Grandpa was a great walker, and even in his nineties, he did a good two miles several times a week. His favorite destination was the park, a great place to let his dog run after a nice long walk down the busy city streets. He could sit and talk with his friends while their dogs romped together. That day, when Grandpa didn't come back at his usual time, Grandma simply thought he was spending more time at the park with his friends, showing off the new pup. Then she heard yapping at the front door. She opened it and there was the pup, leash dragging behind him. A panting boy ran up to the door. He'd been chasing the pup all the way to the house. Grandpa had been hit by a car!

The rescue unit that had come to his aid found no identification on him—only the pup, licking the unconscious man's face. They had taken Grandpa to the general hospital. But when they'd tried to grab the pup, he'd run away. The boy followed him over a mile and a half back to the house. How could this pup, who had lived in the house only two weeks and had never been out walking in the city, have made a beeline right back to the front porch? It amazed everyone.

Grandpa had been admitted to the hospital as a John Doe and did not regain consciousness for several days. Thanks to Pudgy, Grandma was able to go immediately to see Grandpa and ensure that he received the best care possible instead of being relegated to languish in the charity ward until relatives could be found and notified.

Within two months, Grandpa was back walking with Pudgy and sharing with his friends at the park the story of how his Pudgy brought help when it was needed the most. Of course, the story grew in heroic proportions every time it was told, but nobody seemed to mind. One thing was certain: nobody ever again contradicted Grandpa when he told them that Pudgy was, "The same dog, come back."

~Joyce Laird
*Chicken Soup for the Dog Lover's Soul*

# 97

# The Locket

L ydia went up into the attic to get the old dehumidifier for Grandma Ruth's bedroom. Once she'd opened the trapdoor and climbed the rickety old ladder into the crawl space, she couldn't resist rummaging through some of the family heirlooms stored up there. Her attention was drawn to an old locket resting on top of a photo collection, stacked neatly in an attractive but faded hatbox. Lydia's curiosity got the better of her, so she carefully picked up and examined the tiny piece of jewelry. It didn't look expensive, but it was well made and charming. She knew it must have been a special present to a child.

She gingerly snapped the clasp open, taking care not to break the delicate hinges. Hidden inside were two miniature photographs of smiling little girls, perhaps eight or nine years old. One of the happy young faces looked just like her Grandma Ruth. But who was the other young lady? Could it be that Lydia had a secret, long lost great aunt? Who was this stranger in the locket and what had become of her?

Forgetting the dehumidifier and clutching the locket, Lydia scurried down the ladder and burst into Grandma's sewing room. Grandma was busy at work on her entry in the town's annual quilting bee.

"Grandma," Lydia exclaimed, "look what I found. Is this you?"

Grandma slowly took the trinket from Lydia's hand and cupped it gently in her palm. She examined it quietly for a moment. A sad, wistful smile passed over her face. "It's me," she nodded.

"But who's the other little girl? You look so much alike. Was she... was she your sister?"

"Oh, no," Grandma laughed, "No... but we were as close as any sisters could be, Emma and I."

"But who was she?" Lydia asked eagerly.

"We grew up together right here in town. Went everywhere together—we wore the same clothes, rode the same bikes. We even got the same haircut. I remember the day these photos were taken, down at the old Imperial Theater—of course, that's a laundromat now."

"Sounds like you two had a very special friendship."

"We were like peas in a pod," Grandma agreed, "until Emma's family moved away to Akron. Her father was a doctor, and he took a job at a clinic in the city. We wrote every day, then every week, then a few times a year—all through high school, and even after I met your Grandpa Bill. But somehow we lost touch after that. It's been more than fifty years since I've heard from her."

Grandma's story made Lydia think of her own special friendships, how much they meant to her and how she would hate to lose touch with the "Emmas" in her own life.

"I wonder whatever happened to her," sighed Grandma, "I guess I'll never know."

But Lydia was never one to give up hope, and seeing Grandma's reaction to the locket, she was determined to find out. She spent the remainder of her stay poring over

Emma's old letters—she didn't want to miss a single one. Fortunately, Grandma had saved many of them, pressed between the pages of a heavy copy of the young friends' favorite book, *Little Women* by Louisa May Alcott. Like the book, Emma's letters also told a moving story—the story of two great friends coming of age together. But the story of Ruth and Emma wasn't a tale of fiction; it was all true.

Lydia was struck by one letter in particular. It was among the latest in Grandma's collection, and it contained a clue she thought might help them learn of Emma's whereabouts. One of Emma's last letters announced that she had taken a teaching position at a school in the city. Perhaps that school still existed and might have some record of Grandma's old friend.

Some amateur detective work on the Internet quickly revealed that the school was still in operation, but had relocated to a new building in 1963. Lydia was worried. Had Emma's records survived the move? It was time to make some phone calls.

The principal was reluctant to share any details over the phone, but when Lydia explained the unique circumstances, she agreed to meet in person. Lydia bought a round-trip bus ticket and was on her way to Akron later that same week.

Lydia's meeting with the principal was more successful than she had dared to hope. Emma had retired before the principal had come to the school, but a few of the older teachers had fond memories of her. The French teacher still visited with her regularly. She could arrange a meeting.

Two weeks later, on the day of the annual quilting bee, Emma made the journey all the way from Akron, driven by her son Steve. Lydia had spent the morning calming Grandma, who paced nervously about the house, straightening and restraightening the doilies.

Emma entered quietly. "Ruth," she said with a shy smile. Without a word, Grandma handed Emma the locket. No words were needed.

Emma's son Steve was an accomplished photographer, and his cameras captured beautifully the meeting of the two friends. When they left, he asked to borrow the locket. Nobody was quite sure why, until a package arrived at Grandma's house a few weeks later. Steve had enlarged, restored and framed the original photos of the young friends in the locket, and added two more—the old friends, reunited at last.

As for Lydia, she made a special lifelong friend of her own. She and Steve are expecting their first child this spring.

~Tal Aviezer and Jason Cocovinis
*Chicken Soup for the Grandma's Soul*

# 98

# Pumpkin Magic

*Each day of our lives we make deposits*
*in the memory banks of our children.*
*~Charles R. Swindoll,*
The Strong Family

The heat is just beginning to rise, steaming the earth lightly under my feet. It smells of fresh-turned dirt and young corn, heavy ripe blackberries and climbing beans, sunflowers and peonies and pine trees.

The scent clears the sleep from my head, and I breathe in deeply, drinking it down to the bottom of my lungs. I scuff my toes in the soft grass on the edge of the garden.

Grandpa is strolling through the rows of young growing plants, pulling a weed here, plucking a bean there, testing and touching and studying. I love it here, out in the huge growing field that seems to stretch for miles beyond the acre lot. I watch as Grandpa paces his domain.

"Come here, Sweetheart. I have a surprise for you." I hurry after him, stumbling a little in my attempt to keep up with his long-legged stride. He's headed to the far left edge of the garden, past the rows of corn and tomatoes and cabbage, past the beans and peas and cucumber. He stops at the last row, pausing in front of several low, flat-leaved viney plants. I stand back as he lifts the broad leaves aside, searching for his surprise. Then he nods and beckons me forward.

It is a small, still-growing pumpkin, slightly green, not fully ripe. Its stem is still attached to the vine, and it lies on the ground at an angle. I can see a scar on the far side, and I'm slightly disappointed, sad for Grandpa that his surprise is damaged.

Then he turns the pumpkin over, brushing the dirt away, and I can see that it's not a scar at all; it's my name, growing there along with the pumpkin! MY NAME, borne on this fresh and growing plant, living there in the dirt and sun and wind. I stare at it, run tiny fingers along the edge of the letters. They are rough and solid. When Halloween comes, this pumpkin will be mine and no one else's. I turn wide eyes to Grandpa, standing in the field with the sun behind him. "How did you do that?" I asked.

"Well, it's a long process," he begins. "First, you take a pumpkin seed and a very small knife...."

His eyes sparkle as he discusses magnifying glasses and special planting techniques. I turn and look at the house. Grandma is standing in the doorway waving. "How about breakfast?" Grandpa asks. "I'll make oatmeal with raisins cooked in."

We begin the long walk back to the house. I think about the fresh peas with dinner and the just-picked blackberries over vanilla ice cream, the ripe plums in the bowl on the counter and the corn that won't be ready until the next visit. And I think about my very own pumpkin and my grandpa who can work magic in his special garden. I place my hand in his and walk up the hill to breakfast.

~Kati Dougherty-Carthum
*Chicken Soup for the Grandparent's Soul*

# 99

# The Burning of the Leaves

*Winter is an etching, spring a watercolor,*
*summer an oil painting and autumn a mosaic of them all.*
*~Stanley Horowitz*

Papa, my grandfather, loved the fall. Every year, at the end of October, he would gather all the yard's leaves in neat piles along the curb and begin burning them.

All along the avenue, as far as one could see, leaves would be burning. I used to wonder if it were prearranged, this ritual of disposal. Yet I never heard Papa phone anyone and say, "Well, today is the day. I'll see you at the curb." No, it just sort of happened. The fires would start in the late afternoon, when the winds were low, and continue into the early hours of dusk, the dying embers barely discernible by the time we children had to go in.

Leaf burning was a family affair, a part of autumn I looked forward to every year. Adults raked all day, trying to keep the laughing children from running and jumping into the leaves before they got to the curb. At an early age, I delighted in the crackling sounds the flames made, and learned respect for fire, as well.

Neighbors talked and caught up with the latest

goings-on. The men said things like, "Seems like there are twice as many as last year." Nana baked pies and invited folks in for food and company. The visitors lingered long after the embers were cold, and spoke of the coming winter. Papa, though, stayed outside, standing guard lest some stubborn leaf try to reignite and escape.

As a child, I never asked Papa why he seemed to love the burning of the leaves. I just assumed that everyone burned leaves in October and he was just doing what was expected of him. As I grew into adolescence, I found myself sitting at the curb, talking into the evening with him. And I became aware that it was more than a yearly chore for him. He once shared with me the times his dad had burned leaves on their small plot in the Pennsylvania hills. My great-grandfather was a coal miner and had little time to relax with his family. Papa and his ten brothers and sisters all looked forward to spending precious time with their dad during the burning of the leaves.

Papa was a quiet man, not given to a lot of talk. After years of working in open steel pits, he was still in great shape, but he moved slowly and always with a purpose. He and Nana were the anchors in my formative years, always there: same house, same comfortable routines. My parents and I lived a migratory army life. My grandparents rarely traveled. They were a constant I held even more dear as I grew into adulthood.

Then, early one summer, Nana died. That fall, Papa moved in with my parents. With his flowers, his hobbies and his family, he seemed content. But then one weekend when I was home from college, I noticed that Papa was raking the leaves out to the curb. Mom hadn't told him. I realized that I was going to have to be the one to break the news. I went out and explained that here, in this new town, there was an ordinance against burning leaves. All that smoke wasn't considered environmentally sound, and the authorities were worried about spreading fires.

Papa never said a word. He walked away, shoulders as low as they had been at Nana's funeral. He put the rake against the house and went inside. The leaves remained at the curb until late fall winds scattered them back into the yard. A feeling of sadness stirred within me that autumn; I, too, had lost something that could not be replaced. For many autumns after that, Papa pruned, repotted and did other garden chores, but he never again raked leaves.

The year I got pregnant with my second son was also the year we learned Papa had cancer. The doctors didn't think he would make it to Thanksgiving. Papa was thinner and moved slower than ever, but we all lied to him and to ourselves, saying how good he looked and making plans for joyful, not empty, holidays.

In the middle of October, I took Papa out to the farm my husband and I had just bought. The air was crisp, and Indian summer was at its peak. Papa walked the few acres with Adam, his great-grandson, as if he were patrolling an estate, with a measured step and head held high. I watched from the yard as he delighted in my four-year-old's exuberance.

When they returned, I told Papa that out here in the country, we wouldn't get fined for burning leaves. Could he please give me a hand with the task? He smiled widely for the first time in a long time, hugged me and said, "Thank you, I'd be glad to help." Tears began to fill my eyes, and the closeness between us was cemented for all time to come.

I raked, Adam ran through the leaves and Papa supervised the careful placement of the leaves along the gravel drive. He instructed Adam on the hazards of fire. The lesson was like a favorite bedtime story heard and loved so many times before.

Then Papa lit the match and the first pile began to burn. The colors moved quickly together, swirling around. Leaves tried to escape, only to be brought back in by Papa's deft control of the iron rake. The pile burned into the early hours of the evening.

The pie and coffee Papa had that night before retiring were, he said, the perfect end to one of the best days he had had in a long time.

He died one week later in his sleep.

A few days afterward, I received a letter from the Department of Sanitation. It had a warning and a copy of the local ordinance against leaf burning. But I hadn't really lied to Papa; there was no fine.

I shall miss my grandfather always... and the burning of the leaves.

~Edie Cuttler
*Chicken Soup for the Gardener's Soul*

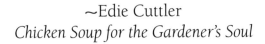

# The Marriage License

*Carry laughter with you wherever you go.*
*~Hugh Sidey*

Grandpa was a practical joker. He was a successful businessman, farmer and entrepreneur, but his most memorable trait was his sense of playfulness. He made you want to be around him, and if nothing else, you wanted to see what was going to happen next.

Grandpa Eric, at eighty-seven, needed to renew his notary license and called upon his friend and partner Terry Parker to drive him to the Sacramento County recorder's office to complete the task. Terry and her father had worked with Eric in the real estate business for years and were well acquainted with his shenanigans. They knew to look for the twinkle in his eye, which was their cue to go along with anything Eric said or did. The payoff for going along with the practical joke was a guarantee of a good belly laugh and a terrific story to tell anyone who came into the office.

Terry and Eric must have been a comical sight together. Eric's mobility was questionable, his sight was undependable, he was sporting a big Stetson hat, two hearing aids and an unlit cigar. Terry supported his arm walking up the steps of the county recorder's office, but it was challenging for the two of them to maneuver through the door. Terry was nine months pregnant with a sixty-inch waist, swollen feet and a bladder reduced by pressure to the size of a small cocktail olive. They just barely made it through the office door only to notice the long, long line up to the records and licenses window. Eric didn't mind waiting because he was already working on how to turn the wait into a little fun.

It was a busy day in the recorder's office and the staff were working as quickly as they could, fielding many questions, some ridiculous, handing out numerous forms and directing people who were completely lost to other offices.

After about a thirty minute wait, Terry and Eric made it to the front of the line only to be coolly greeted by an exasperated state employee. Sighing impatiently, she asked, "How can I help you?" From her attitude, it was clear that she was thinking that this old man had probably come in with his daughter to get a power-of-attorney form and could have saved everybody a lot of time if they'd just called ahead and picked one up at their local stationery store. In spite of his age, Eric was a very sharp guy and figured out the woman's impression of him at first glance and couldn't resist the chance to have a little fun. He was thinking, Let the games begin!

"We're here for a marriage license!" he demanded loudly as he pounded his fist on the counter. "And speed it up! We've been waiting in line for a half an hour and as you can see my bride-to-be here can't stand much longer." The look of total shock (and negative judgment) on the clerk's face as she processed this bit of surprising information could have stopped a speeding locomotive in its tracks. She was so befuddled that she couldn't even muster up enough composure to cover her shock and said, "Why I thought

I'd seen everything in my thirty years of working here, but this takes the prize!"

Eric pulled himself up to his full height, puffed his chest out, looked her in the eye and said, "I'm not getting any younger here, so let's not take all day about it." Terry had a decision to make: let this gal off the hook or go along with the joke. She was also doing everything in her power not to burst into laughter at the ridiculous request, not to mention the hilarious look on the clerk's face. She went for it. She put on her best game face, one that resembled a desperate gold-digging bride who'd found her sugar daddy at the eleventh hour of the game. She also looked very uncomfortable — which was not part of the joke, since she was afraid she was going to laugh so hard that her "tears" would run down her legs.

Eric let that poor clerk run all over that office looking for a marriage license. She was so disconcerted that a simple daily task turned into the search for the Lost Ark. The clerk stopped at each secretary's desk, soundlessly whispering to them, shaking her head and pointing to Terry and Eric. Shocked stares and rolled eyes refocused on the odd couple.

At long last the clerk came back with the necessary paperwork and with an incredulous expression asked Eric if he knew that in the state of California he needed blood tests to get married in case of infectious diseases. "I don't know where she's been before I got hooked up with her, but at my age I guess I'm ready to take the leap of faith. What do you think?" An unrecognizable sound came from the clerk's mouth as she shoved the paperwork in his direction. Eager to go to the ladies' room, Terry was wondering just how long Eric was going to keep the clerk in suspense when suddenly he smiled and said, "Gotcha! We're really here to renew my notary license!"

At this point Terry was sure the practical joke had run its course and dashed to the ladies' room, not a moment too soon. When she returned to collect Eric and his renewed license, the entire office was laughing with him, including the clerk who was a good sport considering the joke was at her expense. After that day, whenever he had any business in the recorder's office he asked for her by name.

~Meladee McCarty
*Chicken Soup for the Grandparent's Soul*

# Grandma-Great

She was twelve when Teddy Meyer gave her a ring. His mistake was asking for it back. First, she took a hammer to it—slamming it flat. Then she marched across a damp field to deposit it smack in the middle of a cow paddy. "There's your ring," she said. That was seventy-eight years ago. My maternal grandmother, Barbara Cecilia Dutra LaFleur, just turned ninety. She's a full-blooded Portuguese powerhouse of a woman who taught me the two most important things I ever learned about God.

She's a painter, usually on large canvases, in oils, though once she painted a pine plank that hangs in my kitchen, gleaming the words of my first lesson: "Pray to God, but Row toward Shore." It sports a man in a rowboat heaving against the tide. "You can't just sit around on your fanny expecting God to fix all your problems," she'd say. "You've got to row." It seemed so refreshingly heretical to me as a child. I somehow knew she was speaking in opposition to someone or something that advocated God fixing everything so long as you were good enough, quiet enough, nice enough or some measure of "enough." Grandma is not always quiet, nice or good. And she never just sits on her fanny amidst a flurry of waves. She's a rower.

The second lesson came when I was much younger. It

was a time of strictness and gloves every Sunday. Parents stood straight in church and children stood beside them pulling at the elastic bands of their hats or the itch of their small ties. I remember the hiss of mothers reprimanding their charges from under their breath, the building edge of threat — behave, sit up straight, the shooting stare of "stop that or else." Sunday was serious.

Grandma was babysitting all four of us kids, ages seven, six, five and four, one weekend. I don't remember the morning unfolding that Sunday when we were lost in the lollygaggle of grownups orchestrating the day. I don't remember dressing for church or driving to church. My siblings were probably little aware of it either, riding the tune of morning play and wresting into our socks, unaware of what came next, just happy and fed and twirling.

What came next was the four of us emptying out of the car and my two little brothers looking up the steps of the church in horror and then down at themselves and then up again. They began to cry and buried their faces in their hands, ashamed.

My sister and I were vaguely interested and looked them up and down. Grandma fluttered about, a sputtering of "What's wrong?" "Boys — What's happened?" My sister, the oldest, exclaimed, "Those are their pajamas!" She pointed to the neat and matching short set Grandma had dressed the boys in. That era was the heyday of matching pajamas — always purchased at Penney's or Sears. My brothers were indeed wearing their new pajamas and had been far too busy playing to notice.

So there in the parking lot where even my sister and I could commiserate with how utterly unthinkable it was to show up for church improperly dressed, there in the parking lot with two embarrassed, tearful little boys, my grandmother once again cut through all the blithering nonsense of what we so often think is paramount. "Oh, boys—God doesn't care if you go to church in your pajamas. God loves you. He doesn't care how you look. He loves you anyway."

And they stopped crying, empowered even as they marched into church heads held high and a little thrilled. They were loved and in their pajamas.

This—to me at six—was, again, blazingly heretical. I was wowed by her power to say such a thing, to proclaim it as if she knew, as if she could make the rules at a time when rules were so very important.

And of course she knew. As she said the other day when I called to ask her the cow-paddy boy's name, "I was always very definite." You sure were, and you still are. I tell her often that she is my hero. Each time she says the same thing: "No. I'm not. I'm very definite." Bingo and Amen.

~Natalie Costanza-Chavez
*Chicken Soup for the Christian Soul 2*

# Chicken Soup for the Soul

# Share with Us

We would like to know how these stories affected you and which ones were your favorites. Please e-mail us and let us know.

We also would like to share your stories with future readers. You may be able to help another reader, and become a published author at the same time. Please send us your own stories and poems for our future books. Some of our past contributors have launched writing and speaking careers from the publication of their stories in our books!

Your stories have the best chance of being used if you submit them through our web site, at:

## www.chickensoup.com

If you do not have access to the Internet, you may submit your stories by mail or by facsimile. Please do not send us any book manuscripts, unless through a literary agent, as these will be automatically discarded.

Chicken Soup for the Soul
P.O. Box 700
Cos Cob, CT 06807-0700
Fax 203-861-7194

**Chicken Soup for the Woman's Soul**
1-55874-415-0

**A Second Chicken Soup for the Woman's Soul**
1-55874-622-6

**Chicken Soup for the Golden Soul**
1-55874-725-7

**Chicken Soup for the Veteran's Soul**
1-55874-937-3

**Chicken Soup for the Grandparent's Soul**
1-55874-974-8

**Chicken Soup for the Grieving Soul**
1-55874-902-0

**Chicken Soup to Inspire a Woman's Soul**
0-7573-0210-6

**Chicken Soup for the Grandma's Soul**
0-7573-0328-5

**C**heck out our great books for

We know how it is to cross the magic 60-year mark and feel young at heart despite a few new wrinkles. We wouldn't trade away a bit of our wisdom and experience to get rid of all those life markers. This is the first Chicken Soup book to focus on the wonders of getting older, with many stories focusing on dynamic older singles and couples finding new careers, new sports, new love, and new meaning to their lives. This inspiring, amusing, and heartwarming book includes the best 101 stories for today's young seniors from Chicken Soup's library.

978-1-935096-17-7

# Seniors

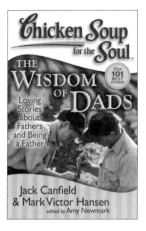

### The Wisdom of Dads

Children view their fathers with awe from the day they are born. Fathers are big and strong and seem to know everything, except for a few teenage years when fathers are perceived to know nothing! This book represents a new theme for Chicken Soup – 101 stories selected from 35 past books, all stories focusing on the wisdom of dads. Stories are written by sons and daughters about their fathers, and by fathers relating stories about their children.

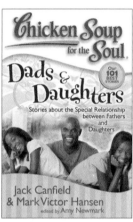

### Dads & Daughters

Whether she is ten years old or fifty – she will always be his little girl. And daughters take care of their dads too, whether it is a tea party for two at age five or loving care fifty years later. This wide-ranging exploration of the relationship between fathers and daughters provides an entirely new reading experience for Chicken Soup fans, with selections from forty past Chicken Soup books. Stories were written by fathers about their daughters and by daughters about their fathers, celebrating the special bond between fathers and daughters.

### On Being a Parent

Parenting is the hardest and most rewarding job in the world. This upbeat and compelling new book includes the best selections on parenting from Chicken Soup's rich history, with 101 stories carefully selected to appeal to both mothers and fathers. This is a great book for couples to share, whether they are just embarking on their new adventure as parents or reflecting on their lifetime experience.

*C*heck out our great books on

### Moms Know Best

"Mom will know where it is…what to say…how to fix it." This Chicken Soup book focuses on the pervasive wisdom of mothers everywhere, and includes the best 101 stories from Chicken Soup's library on our perceptive, understanding, and insightful mothers. These stories celebrate the special bond between mothers and children, our mothers' unerring wisdom about everything from the mundane to the life-changing, and the hard work that goes into being a mother every day.

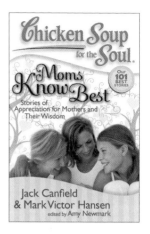

### Moms & Sons

There is a special bond between mothers and their sons that never goes away. This book contains the 101 best stories from Chicken Soup's library honoring the lifelong relationship between mothers and their male offspring. These heartfelt and loving stories written by mothers, grandmothers, and sons, about each other, span generations. Many of these stories will make readers laugh and some will make them cry, but they will all remind them of the eternal bond they share.

### Teens Talk Growing Up

Being a teenager is hard — school is challenging, college and career are looming on the horizon, family issues arise, friends and love come and go, bodies and emotions go through major changes, and many teens experience the loss of a loved one for the first time. This book reminds teenagers that they are not alone, as they read stories written by other teens about the problems and issues they all face every day.

Family

Our
101
BEST
STORIES

# FAVORITES!

### Christmas Cheer

Stories about the Love, Inspiration, and Joy of Christmas

978-1-935096-15-3

Everyone loves Christmas and the holiday season. We reunite scattered family members, watch the wonder in a child's eyes, and feel the joy of giving gifts. The rituals of the holiday season give a rhythm to the years and create a foundation for our lives, as we gather with family, with our communities at church, at school, and even at the mall, to share the special spirit of the season, brightening those long winter days.

### Happily Ever After

Fun and Heartwarming Stories about Finding and Enjoying Your Mate

978-1-935096-10-8

Dating and courtship, romance, love, and marriage are favorite Chicken Soup topics. Women, and even men, love to read true stories about how it happened for other people. This book includes the 101 best stories on love and marriage chosen from a wide variety of past Chicken Soup books. These heartwarming stories will inspire and amuse readers, whether they are just starting to date, are newly wed, or are veterans of a long marriage.

# Books for Pet Lovers

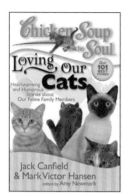

### Loving Our Cats

Heartwarming and Humorous Stories about Our Feline Family Members

978-1-935096-08-5

We are all crazy about our mysterious cats. Sometimes they are our best friends; sometimes they are aloof. They are fun to watch and often surprise us. These true stories, the best from Chicken Soup's library, will make readers appreciate their own cats and see them with a new eye. Readers will revel in the heartwarming, amusing, inspirational, and occasionally tearful stories about our best friends and faithful companions — our cats.

### Loving Our Dogs

Heartwarming and Humorous Stories about Our Companions and Best Friends

978-1-935096-05-4

We are all crazy about our dogs and can't read enough about them, whether they're misbehaving and giving us big, innocent looks, or loyally standing by us in times of need. This new book from Chicken Soup for the Soul contains the 101 best dog stories from the company's extensive library. Readers will revel in the heartwarming, amusing, inspirational, and occasionally tearful stories about our best friends and faithful companions — our dogs.

# About the Authors
# &
# Acknowledgments

# Chicken Soup for the Soul

# Who Is
# Jack Canfield?

Jack Canfield is the co-creator and editor of the *Chicken Soup for the Soul* series, which *Time* magazine has called "the publishing phenomenon of the decade." Jack is also the co-author of eight other bestselling books including *The Success Principles™: How to Get from Where You Are to Where You Want to Be, Dare to Win, The Aladdin Factor, You've Got to Read This Book,* and *The Power of Focus: How to Hit Your Business and Personal and Financial Targets with Absolute Certainty.*

Jack has recently developed a telephone coaching program and an online coaching program based on his most recent book *The Success Principles.* He also offers a seven-day *Breakthrough to Success* seminar every summer, which attracts 400 people from fifteen countries around the world.

Jack is the CEO of the Canfield Training Group in Santa Barbara, California, and founder of the Foundation for Self-Esteem in Culver City, California. He has conducted intensive personal and professional development seminars on the principles of success for over a million people in twenty-three countries. Jack is a dynamic keynote speaker and he has spoken to hundreds of thousands of others at more than 1,000 corporations, universities, professional conferences and conventions, and has been seen by millions more on national television shows such as *The Today Show, Fox and Friends, Inside Edition, Hard Copy, CNN's Talk*

*Back Live*, *20/20*, *Eye to Eye*, and the *NBC Nightly News* and the *CBS Evening News*.

Jack is the recipient of many awards and honors, including three honorary doctorates and a *Guinness World Records Certificate* for having seven books from the *Chicken Soup for the Soul* series appearing on the *New York Times* bestseller list on May 24, 1998.

To write to Jack or for inquiries about Jack as a speaker, his coaching programs, trainings or seminars, use the following contact information:

Jack Canfield
The Canfield Companies
P.O. Box 30880 • Santa Barbara, CA 93130
phone: 805-563-2935 • fax: 805-563-2945
E-mail: info@jackcanfield.com
www.jackcanfield.com

# Who Is
# Mark Victor Hansen?

**M**ark Victor Hansen is the co-founder of *Chicken Soup for the Soul*, along with Jack Canfield. He is also a sought-after keynote speaker, bestselling author, and marketing maven.

For more than thirty years, Mark has focused solely on helping people from all walks of life reshape their personal vision of what's possible. His powerful messages of possibility, opportunity, and action have created powerful change in thousands of organizations and millions of individuals worldwide.

Mark's credentials include a lifetime of entrepreneurial success. He is a prolific writer with many bestselling books, such as *The One Minute Millionaire*, *Cracking the Millionaire Code*, *How to Make the Rest of Your Life the Best of Your Life*, *The Power of Focus*, *The Aladdin Factor*, and *Dare to Win*, in addition to the *Chicken Soup for the Soul* series. Mark has had a profound influence in the field of human potential through his library of audios, videos, and articles in the areas of big thinking, sales achievement, wealth building, publishing success, and personal and professional development.

Mark is the founder of the *MEGA Seminar Series*. *MEGA Book Marketing University* and *Building Your MEGA Speaking Empire* are annual conferences where Mark coaches and teaches new and aspiring authors, speakers, and experts on building lucrative publishing and speaking careers.  Other

MEGA events include *MEGA Info-Marketing* and *My MEGA Life*.

He has appeared on *Oprah*, *CNN*, and *The Today Show*. He has been quoted in *Time*, *U.S. News & World Report*, *USA Today*, *New York Times*, and *Entrepreneur* and has had countless radio interviews, assuring our planet's people that "You can easily create the life you deserve."

As a philanthropist and humanitarian, Mark works tirelessly for organizations such as Habitat for Humanity, American Red Cross, March of Dimes, Childhelp USA, and many others. He is the recipient of numerous awards that honor his entrepreneurial spirit, philanthropic heart, and business acumen. He is a lifetime member of the Horatio Alger Association of Distinguished Americans, an organization that honored Mark with the prestigious Horatio Alger Award for his extraordinary life achievements.

Mark Victor Hansen is an enthusiastic crusader of what's possible and is driven to make the world a better place.

Mark Victor Hansen & Associates, Inc.
P.O. Box 7665 • Newport Beach, CA 92658
phone: 949-764-2640 • fax: 949-722-6912
www.markvictorhansen.com

# Who Is
# Amy Newmark?

my Newmark was recently named publisher of Chicken Soup for the Soul, after a thirty-year career as a writer, speaker, financial analyst, and business executive in the worlds of finance and telecommunications.

Amy is a graduate of Harvard College, where she majored in Portuguese, minored in French, and traveled extensively. She is also the mother of two children in college and has two grown stepchildren.

After a long career writing books on telecommunications, voluminous financial reports, business plans, and corporate press releases, Chicken Soup for the Soul is a breath of fresh air for Amy. She has fallen in love with Chicken Soup for the Soul and its life-changing books, and found it a true pleasure to conceptualize, compile, and edit the "101 Best Stories" books for our readers.

The best way to contact Chicken Soup for the Soul is through our web site, at www.chickensoup.com. This will always get the fastest attention.

If you do not have access to the Internet, please contact us by mail or by facsimile.

Chicken Soup for the Soul
P.O. Box 700
Cos Cob, CT 06807-0700
Fax 203-861-7194

Chicken Soup for the Soul

# Thank You!

Our first thanks go to our loyal readers who have inspired the entire Chicken Soup team for the past fifteen years. Your appreciative letters and e-mails have reminded us why we work so hard on these books.

We owe huge thanks to all of our contributors as well. We know that you pour your hearts and souls into the stories and poems that you share with us, and ultimately with each other. We appreciate your willingness to open up your lives to other Chicken Soup readers.

We can only publish a small percentage of the stories that are submitted, but we read every single one and even the ones that do not appear in a book have an influence on us and on the final manuscripts.

As always, we would like to thank the entire staff of Chicken Soup for the Soul for their help on this project and the 101 Best series in general.

Among our California staff, we would especially like to single out the following people:

- D'ette Corona, our Assistant Publisher, who is the heart and soul of the Chicken Soup publishing operation, and who put together the first draft of this manuscript

- Barbara LoMonaco our Webmaster and Chicken Soup for the Soul editor, for invaluable assistance in obtaining the fabulous quotations that add depth and meaning to this book

- Patty Hansen for her extra special help with the permissions for these fabulous stories and for her amazing knowledge of the Chicken Soup library

- and Patti Clement for her help with permissions and other organizational matters.

In our Connecticut office, we would like to thank our able editors, Valerie Howlett and Madeline Clapps, for their assistance in setting up our new offices, editing, and helping us put together the best possible books.

We would also like to thank our master of design, Creative Director and book producer Brian Taylor at Pneuma Books, LLC, for his brilliant vision for our covers and interiors.

Finally, none of this would be possible without the business and creative leadership of our CEO, Bill Rouhana, and our president, Bob Jacobs.

# Chicken Soup for the Soul

If you have enjoyed this book
or it has touched your life in some way,
we would love to hear from you.

Please send your comments to:
Hallmark Book Feedback
P.O. Box 419034
Mail Drop 100
Kansas City, MO 64141

Or e-mail us at:
booknotes@hallmark.com